JOURNAL FOR THE STUDY OF THE OLD TESTAMENT
SUPPLEMENT SERIES
5

Editors
David J A Clines
Philip R Davies
David M Gunn

Department of Biblical Studies
The University of Sheffield
Sheffield S10 2TN
England

Redating the Exodus and Conquest

John J. Bimson

Journal for the Study of the Old Testament
Supplement Series 5

Sheffield
1978

ISBN 0 905774 10 8 (hardback)
ISBN 0 905774 03 5 (paperback)
ISSN 0309-0787

Copyright © JSOT, 1978

Published by
JSOT
The University of Sheffield
Sheffield, S10 2TN

Printed in England by
Fengraphic, Cambridge

To my Parents

CONTENTS

CONTENTS

PART TWO

PALESTINIAN ARCHAEOLOGY AND THE EARLY DATE FOR THE EXODUS

10

PREFACE

The main arguments of this book were originally presented in a doctoral thesis written in the Department of Biblical Studies at the University of Sheffield. I take this opportunity to thank the members of that Department, especially Dr. D.M. Gunn, for encouragement and assistance in bringing the work to completion.

The original thesis was a good deal longer than the present book, since it contained chapters on the duration of the Hebrews' enslavement in Egypt, the historicity of the Joseph Story, and the dating of Joseph and of the patriarchal period. I hope to publish some of this material elsewhere. It is omitted here in order to concentrate attention on the archaeological aspect of the theory and its important implications.

Reference to works cited are incorporated in the text in parentheses. Normally only the author's surname, date of publication and page numbers are provided, thus: (Smith 1940: 20). The author's name may be omitted in cases where the context makes it unnecessary. The page number alone may be provided when several references to the same work are given in sequence, the other details being provided only in the first instance. Where an author has had more than one work published in the same year, these are distinguished by letters, thus: (Kitchen 1973a, 1973b,) etc. Where reference is made to a work in English translation which post-dates by several decades the publication of the original, I have provided the date of the original publication as well as that of the English translation, thus: (Alt 1925 ET 1966). Details of works referred to are to be found in the bibliography. Notes, indicated by numbers in the text, are reserved for the discussion of subsidiary points of interest where a digression would interrupt the flow of the main argument. They are to be found collected towards the end of the book.

INTRODUCTION

Introduction

0.1 *The Question of Historicity*

It is a fundamental assumption of this work that the biblical traditions of the bondage in Egypt and of the Exodus have a firm historical basis. In 1925 J.W. Jack wrote: "... It is far from likely that any nation would have placed in the forefront of its records an experience of hardship and slavery in a foreign country, unless this had been a real and vital part of its national life" (1925: 10). Similar statements affirming the basic historicity of the Exodus tradition have been made by many other writers since (cf. Noth 1960: 112; Yeivin 1971: 235-6; Bright 1972: 119, 120). It has been further pointed out: "... The national tradition of the enforced sojourn in Egypt, and the subsequent redemption from bondage, is so closely interwoven with all stages of the later development of Israel, that without it the whole process becomes incomprehensible". (Yeivin 1971: 235).

In view of the strength and centrality of the Exodus tradition, it seems difficult to doubt that an historical event lies at its root.

The present writer would express ths historical essence of the tradition as follows: A considerable body of people, who were in some way ancestral to the later tribes of Israel, were pressed into a state of servitude in Egypt. They eventually found their situation intolerable, but escape from it only became possible when Egypt's control over them was broken by events which the Bible depicts as miraculous. Then this body of people left Egypt and moved into the area south of Canaan under the leadership of

Moses. Subsequently the group entered Canaan itself and took possession of considerable areas of that land.

It seems legitimate to assume that this basic sequence of events is historical. The historicity of various other elements in the traditions will be suggested in the pages which follow, but the bare outline is all that need concern us for the present.

According to the biblical account, the descent into Egypt in the time of Jacob involved the settlement there of Jacob's twelve sons and their families, and the people who left Egypt under the leadership of Moses comprised twelve tribes descended from those families. In other words, the biblical tradition has the twelve tribes of Israel already existing before the Exodus. Martin Noth, on the other hand, offers a very different picture of Israel's origins. Noth does not begin his account of Israel's history until after the Exodus and the settlement in Canaan. This is because in his view the twelve tribes of Israel came into existence only in Canaan. Noth and several others believe that many elements found in the later twelve-tribe Israel were never in Egypt at all. I use the word "elements" rather than "tribes" here, because for Noth the word "tribe" is not a valid term for any constituent section of what was subsequently called Israel until after the settlement period. Hence Noth says it is meaningless to ask which tribes were in Egypt and which were not (1960: 119, 138).

While I believe that the historical facts must have been far more complex than the biblical account now implies, I do not think Noth's scepticism is justified by either biblical or extra-biblical evidence. The biblical traditions themselves certainly hint that the Israel which came into existence in Canaan contained elements which were not descended from its eponymous ancestor Jacob. Ex. 12: 38 refers to a "mixed multitude" leaving Egypt along with the children of Israel, and we subsequently find non-Israelite groups such as the Kenites, Kenizzites and Calebites involved in the occupation of Canaan (cf. conveniently de Vaux 1971: 487-510 on the role of these groups in the settlement). It is also plausible that various Canaanite groups were absorbed by the people who moved into Canaan after the Exodus, and that these also became constituent parts of Israel (cf. Jos. 9; Jdg. 1:29; etc.).

However, such hints in the biblical material do not give us reason to doubt that the major portion of the Israel which came

into being in Canaan after the Exodus was descended from the
group which took part in that Exodus. (Cf. Greenberg 1965: 38-40
for an interesting defence of the unity of "Israel" prior to the
occupation of Canaan). Nor is it improbable that the later Israel
had begun to take shape in Egypt before the Exodus occurred. We
can say this without insisting that the biblical picture of twelve
tribes in Egypt descended from twelve sons of Jacob is
historically correct. The view of the present writer is that
various groups of Semites in Egypt (whether closely related or
not is irrelevant here) came to feel a sense of unity during a
period of oppression by the Egyptians, so that by the time of
their escape they already felt something like national identity.

Israel as a true nation cannot, of course, be said to have
existed until after the settlement and the establishment of the
twelve-tribe system (which we may assume did not exist in Egypt
in its later form), and perhaps not even until the start of the
monarchic period. (Whether or not the twelve-tribe system was
amphictyonic is irrelevant to the present discussion; cf. Mayes
1974 for a recent examination of this question.) On the other
hand it does not seem inappropriate to use the term Israel to
describe the group which left Egypt at the time of Moses, but
the reader is asked to bear in mind the explanation just given
concerning my concept of the Exodus group.

This book will not concern itself with the numbers involved
in the movement from Egypt to Canaan, nor with the exact route
taken, nor with the events underlying the present accounts of the
plagues and the "Reed Sea" incident. Of the historicity of the
Sinai, wilderness and Conquest traditions, something will be said
on future pages.

0.2 The Importance of the Question of Date

At the beginning of his book From Joseph to Joshua, H.H.
Rowley (1950: 2) quotes with approval the following remark by
E.R. Thiele (1944: 137): "Chronology is the backbone of history.
Absolute chronology is the fixed central core around which the
events of nations must be correctly grouped before they may
assume their exact positions in history and before their mutual
relationships may be properly understood".

It is in the context of such a view of absolute chronology
that the date of the Exodus becomes a very important issue. Its

importance is increased when it is realised how much else depends
on it or is at least related to it. The date we adopt for the
Exodus affects our date for the entry into Egypt and hence our
view of the length and nature of the sojourn and the period of
bondage. This in turn affects our dating of the patriarchal
period. Our dating of the Exodus also affects our view of the
length and nature of the period of the Judges, which in turn may
affect our view of the origins of the monarchic system in Israel.

In fact this means that the dates we adopt for the Exodus
and the periods on either side of it decide the background
against which we view almost a third of the Old Testament. This
will influence our opinions of Israel's religious development to
a significant degree.

It is also important to notice that the dating adopted for
the Exodus will affect our handling of the biblical traditions,
not only concerning the Exodus itself but also concerning the
subsequent events of the wilderness wanderings and the Conquest.
This will be amply illustrated in the discussions which follow,
especially in that which deals with what I have called the
"two-phase" theories.

0.3 *A Brief History of the Popular Theories*

The oldest theory since the rise of modern Egyptology is
that which makes the XIXth Dynasty pharaoh Rameses II the pharaoh
of the Oppression and his successor Merneptah the pharaoh of the
Exodus. This theory was first put forward by C.R. Lepsius (1849).

. It is worth noting that when Lepsius offered his theory,
Egyptology was still very much in its infancy; indeed, Lepsius
himself was one of the men responsible, along with Chabas and
Brugsch, for establishing Egyptology as a moderately exact
science. Champollion had only succeeded in deciphering
hieroglyphics in the 1820's, and it was not until 1866 that the
discovery of the Canopus Decree provided confirmation that
Champollion had hit on the correct method.

At the time Lepsius put forward his theory, the dating of
the Egyptian dynasties was in a state of flux. Dates suggested
for the XIXth Dynasty then ranged between the 16th and 12th
centuries BC. Lepsius himself mistakenly supposed Merneptah to
be the Menophres mentioned by the Greek writer Theon in

connection with a Sothic Cycle which began in 1322 BC, and hence when he chose to date the Exodus near the end of Merneptah's reign, he dated it to 1314 BC, a full century earlier than would be required by a similar placing on the basis of the chronology employed for Egypt today.

Lepsius' theory was followed by other important Egyptologists (e.g. F.J. Chabas 1873), and by the turn of the century it was well established (cf. Naville 1893: 1024; Poole 1893: 591-2; Sayce 1897: 158; Curtis 1898: 398; McNeile 1908: xciv, 13).

In the 1890's the XIXth Dynasty was still being dated about a century earlier than in the presently accepted chronology, the accession of Rameses II being placed at c. 1400 BC, though Brugsch preferred an even earlier dating (cf. Poole 1893: 591). By 1901, however, Müller and others had lowered the date of that pharaoh's accession to 1340 BC. Today dates of 1290-1224 BC are usually cited for Rameses II (but cf. Bierbrier 1975: 109-113).

Naville's discoveries at Tell el-Maskhouta in the 1880's, to be discussed in detail later in this work, were seen as confirmation of Lepsius' theory of the Exodus (Poole 1893: 591-2; Curtis 1898: 398). The so-called *Israel Stele of Merneptah,* on the other hand, discovered by Petrie in 1895, caused some confusion. Müller saw this evidence that Israel was "evidently dwelling in Palestine" in Merneptah's reign as an indicator that he was unlikely to have been the pharaoh of the Exodus (Müller 1901: col. 1242). On the other hand, J. Rendel Harris and A.T. Chapman (1898: 802-6) preferred to keep to the view that the Exodus occurred in the reign of Merneptah and to take the Stele to show that Israel in part was "already in Palestine at the time of the Exodus, so that the migration must have been partial and not national".

Many writers have continued to place the Exodus in Merneptah's reign (Petrie 1911: 55ff; Mercer 1922-3: 96-107; Rowley 1950: 137ff; de Wit 1960: 9-10), and while most have viewed the relevant lines on the Stele as referring to an incident subsequent to the Exodus, some have viewed it as referring to the Exodus itself (Montet 1940: 149; North 1967a: 112-13).

The second oldest theory since the rise of modern Egyptology seems to have had its origin with E. Lefébure in 1896 (cf. de Wit 1960: 4). In this view, the pharaoh of the Oppression was the XVIIIth Dynasty pharaoh Thutmosis III, and the pharaoh of the Exodus was his successor Amenhotep II. By the turn of the century Egyptian chronology had been refined to the point where it was clear that this view was more in keeping than the older one with the Bible's own note on the date of the Exodus (I Kgs. 6:1), which places the event roughly in the middle of the 15th century BC. The theory was taken up by J. Orr (1909: 422ff), and was widely diffused among Roman Catholic scholars by Mallon (1921). It was favoured by Peet (1922), and was argued in detail by Jack (1925).

Jack noted in his book: "There are signs that the old idea of an Exodus in the reign of Merenptah [Merneptah] is losing its hold, and that the earlier date is being generally accepted by scholars" (ibid: 257). This change was probably the result of two things, one being that the apparent conformity of the newer view with the biblical chronology gave it, for many, an attraction which the older one lacked; the other being the uncertainty which the Israel Stele had introduced into the Merneptah dating.

Jack also expressed confidence "that further archaeological and documentary discoveries will only confirm the argument" (ibid). At that time, the only relevant excavations in Palestine were those of Sellin and Watzinger at Jericho, and their results appeared to indicate the Amarna period as the latest date for the destruction of the Canaanite city, a date which was well suited to the theory Jack was propounding, though he made only a brief and parenthetical reference to these results (ibid: 168, n.1). Further support for the early date seemed to come from the Amarna letters. Jack and others made extensive use of the references to the Ḥabiru in these letters, arguing that here was extra-biblical evidence for the arrival of the Hebrews in Canaan.

Garstang's excavations at Jericho in the 1930's appeared to confirm a date at the beginning of the 14th century BC for the Israelite destruction of the Canaanite city, and therefore a date in the middle of the previous century for the Exodus (Garstang 1931: 143-8). Garstang's findings therefore gave the early dating a new lease of life, and were used enthusiastically in support of it by Sir Charles Marston (1934 and 1937) and by Garstang himself (1940: 130-31).

However, excavations by W.F. Albright at various other sites, and Kenyon's subsequent excavations at Jericho, which showed

Garstang to have been in error on many points, have effectively
removed much of the support for the early date. In addition,
there has been a growing awareness that the theoretical link
between the Amarna Ḥabiru and the biblical Hebrews cannot bear
the weight which was once placed on it. As a result, the early
date for the Exodus has now been abandoned by the majority of
scholars. A few conservative writers, interested in supporting
the accuracy of the Bible's own chronological references, have,
however, maintained the position (Rea 1960: 58-69; 1961: 5-13;
Hoehner 1969: 306-16; Wood 1970: 67-86; Waltke 1972: 33-47).

The theory which seems to be most widely favoured at the time
of writing was first formulated by W.F. Albright. Albright
appears to have always held that there were two Exoduses, and
that the Joseph tribes returned from Egypt to Canaan much earlier
than the group led by Moses (Albright 1918: 138ff; 1921: 66;
1935b: 15). In Albright's view, the Joseph tribes, which he
identified with the Ḥabiru of the Amarna letters, arrived in
Palestine at about 1400 BC. But his archaeological discoveries
later caused this initial Hebrew penetration to lose its
significance in his overall view. In 1934, while excavating
Bethel (Beitin), Albright found a massive destruction layer which
he felt "compelled" to identify with an Israelite capture of
the city, and which he dated to the 13th century BC. He wrote:
"In reaching this obvious and inescapable conclusion, the writer
abandons a position he has held for eleven years, and adopts the
low date for the Israelite conquest of central Palestine"
(1934: 10). Subsequently his date for the Exodus of the Leah
tribes under the leadership of Moses, c. 1290 BC (cf. 1935b: 16),
came to the fore in Albright's theory, with the main wave of the
Conquest, supposedly attested by finds not only at Bethel but
also at Lachish (cf. 1939: 22-3), dated to the second half of the
13th century BC. (Though Albright never officially repudiated
his original two Exodus theory, the hypothetical earlier Exodus of
the Joseph tribes dropped out of his later writings, so that in
them Albright always means the 13th century event which occurred
under the leadership of Moses when he refers to the Exodus.) In
1939 Albright wrote: "... The burden of proof is now entirely on
those scholars who still wish to place the main phase of the
Israelite conquest of Palestine before the thirteenth century
B.C." (1939:23).

Albright's dating of the Exodus places the event early in
the reign of Rameses II, and the Oppression is held to have begun

during the reign of his predecessor, Seti I. This placing of the
Exodus was offered earlier, though on completely different
grounds and in the framework of a different Egyptian chronology,
by E. Mahler (1901: 33-67), and was objected to by Naville
(1893: 1023) on the grounds that it "raises a considerable
historical difficulty, for it is hardly possible to admit that
the Hebrews should have left Egypt at the beginning of the reign
of Rameses II, when the king was at the pinnacle of his might and
power". This objection has been revived in connection with
Albright's theory by Rowton (1953: 49).

Notwithstanding this difficulty, Albright's placing of the
Exodus has been followed broadly, with some variations in the
precise date adopted, by a great many scholars (Burrows 1941: 79;
Wright 1945: 39; 1962a: 60; 1962b: 190-91; Finegan 1946: 105-8;
Aharoni 1957: 139-40; 1967: 178; Freedman 1961: 207; Kitchen and
Mitchell 1962: 214-15; Kitchen 1966: 57-75; Anderson 1966: 28;
Harrison 1970: 325; de Vaux 1971: 368; Bright 1972: 121-2).

Some scholars maintain reservations concerning the precise
placing of the Exodus, but still date it confidently to the 13th
century BC. Thus Bruce (1963: 12) and Hyatt (1971: 42-4) both
hold that the Exodus could have occurred under either Rameses II
or Merneptah; Eissfeldt (1965a: 17-18) and Herrmann (1975: 62)
both place the Exodus in the latter part of the 13th century
without naming the pharaoh concerned, and Noth, while affirming
that the Oppression included building tasks carried out under
Rameses II, dates the Exodus simply to the 13th century without
attempting a more precise placement (1960: 120). The recent
theory which rejects Albright's evidence for the Conquest and
shifts that event to the beginning of the 12th century, still
leaves Moses and the Exodus in the latter part of the 13th
(cf. Campbell 1975: 153).

Thus we may say that the 13th century BC is presently the
most widely preferred time for the Exodus. The following
remark by D.N. Freedman (1961: 207), though written some years
ago, is still an accurate expression of the prevailing view:
"The thirteenth century is now all but unanimously agreed upon
as the date of the Exodus; both earlier and later centuries have
been discarded, and it alone remains both plausible and inevitable".

It will be shown subsequently, however, that the reasons
generally given for preferring a date in the 13th century BC are
in fact invalid.

0.4   A Critique of Some Two-Phase Theories

Alongside the theories outlined above, a number of theories
.have been formulated which involve a two-phase Exodus and/or a
two-phase Conquest.

We have already noted that Albright's view involved two
Exoduses and two movements into Canaan, though his theory
concerning the earlier movement was never clearly worked out.
In 1918 he wrote: "The circumstances and date of the first
Exodus are obscure; I do not know of any passages in the
Heptateuch which may have any bearing on the problem" (1918: 138),
and, as we have seen, this hypothetical movement lost
significance in the light of Albright's later archaeological
discoveries.

Most of the two-phase theories have been formulated in an
effort to incorporate both the Ḫabiru disturbances of the Amarna
period and various supposed links with 13th century events into
a scheme in which the history of the biblical Hebrews can be
traced in extra-biblical events. Albright's scheme was no
exception, since he saw the Joseph tribes as the Amarna Ḫabiru.

The theory of C.F. Burney is a further example of this
tendency. In this rather complex scheme the SAGAZ-Ḫabiru are seen
as moving into Syria and Canaan from the north-east at the end of
the 15th century BC. These are viewed as including the Hebrews
of the Old Testament. At a date of c. 1435 BC the Joseph tribes
are supposed to have broken off from the rest and moved into
Egypt, to be joined at a later date by Simeonite and Levite
elements. These tribes suffer oppression in Egypt during the
reign of Rameses II, for whom Burney gives dates of 1292-1225 BC.
He places the Exodus of these groups either during the reign of
Merneptah or immediately after. At Kadesh Barnea the main body
of Levi, along with Simeon, is supposed to have merged with
proto-Judahite clans which had not been in Egypt, and to have
moved northwards with them into the Negeb and the hill-country
beyond. Meanwhile the Joseph tribes and some Levites are
supposed to have split off and travelled (carrying the ark and
led by Joshua) round Edom to enter Canaan from east of the
Jordan (Burney 1919a).

In the theory of T.J. Meek, the Ḫabiru are identified with
the Joseph tribes led by Joshua. These tribes are assumed to

have never been in Egypt. Their attack on the central highlands
is dated to the first half of the 14th century BC. The Exodus
from Egypt led by Moses is supposed to have occurred at the end
of the 13th century. In other words, Meek makes Joshua antedate
Moses by a century and a half (Meek 1936).

Rowley argued that a northward movement from Kadesh of
Hebrew groups which had not been in Egypt occurred about 1400 BC
and that these groups were the Ḥabiru of the Amarna letters. The
SAGAZ of the letters, he theorized, were kindred groups pressing
into Palestine from the north. Rowley placed Joseph and the
descent into Egypt in the reign of Akhenaten, the Oppression
during the reign of Rameses II, and the Exodus at the beginning
of Merneptah's reign. By extracting the tradition of the forty
years in the wilderness from the history of the Exodus group,
Rowley placed the entry into Palestine only two years after the
Exodus, thus allowing the Israel Stele to refer to a clash with
this group later in the pharaoh's reign (Rowley 1950).

All these views have one feature in common, and that is an
attempt to identify some section of the biblical Hebrews with the
Ḥabiru of the Amarna letters. It is the view of the present
writer that the Ḥabiru were nothing to do with the movement of
any Hebrew group; nor should the ᶜApiru of Egyptian records be
linked with the biblical Hebrews. If this is correct, and it is
a view expressed by several writers at the present time, then one
of the main reasons for the existence of these two-phase theories
disappears.

In addition to this, other more specific criticisms can be
laid against the individual theories. In connection with
Burney's view, Rowley (1950: 9) has pointed out that no evidence
can be adduced for the assumed migration of Simeon and Levi to
Egypt at a later date than the entry of the Joseph tribes; he also
remarks that the idea that after the Exodus Simeon and Levi should
have left the Joseph tribes to rejoin Judah, from which group they
had been separated for the duration of the sojourn in Egypt,
"seems improbable".

Rowley has argued (ibid: 141-144) at greater length against
the view of Meek. It will suffice to mention one telling point
here. The biblical tradition makes Joshua Moses' successor; the
association of the ark with both these figures is so strong in
the traditions, that there is no plausibility in placing Joshua

over a century before Moses as Meek does. Of Joshua Rowley says:
"His association with the Ark is not something extraneous to the
tradition, but intimately belonging to it .... Yet it is equally
impossible to dissociate the Ark from Moses, or to suppose that
the story of its making is either free invention or a transfer
to Moses of something that Joshua did" (ibid: 142). Moreover,
Rowton has pointed out, in reply to Meek's theory that the Joseph
tribes were never in Egypt, that this is contradicted by "the fact
that alone among all the eponym ancestors of the Israelite tribes,
Ephraim and Manasseh are explicitly stated to have been born in
Egypt". (1953: 50).

One of the major problems for Rowley's theory is that it
makes necessary the omission of the generation spent in the
wilderness. As Rowton observes, "This datum is one of the
essential features of the O.T. account of the Exodus, and it is
very difficult to see why it should have been included at all
unless it be substantially true" (ibid). Rowley does in fact
suggest that the tradition originated with a Hebrew group which
spent thirty-eight years at Kadesh before the entry into Egypt
(cf. conveniently Rowley 1950: 164). But it seems unlikely that
the tradition would ever have achieved its present form and
position if it originated in this way. In its present form it
relates to an act of gross disobedience and failure on the part
of the Israelites, and it is difficult to conceive of such an
uncomplimentary tradition arising except from a sequence of
events roughly the same as is described (cf. Freedman 1961: 226,
n.14).

Rowton has offered a two-phase theory which does not involve
any hypothetical links between the Ḫabiru and the Hebrews and
therefore belongs in a different category from those considered
above.

In Rowton's view the first Exodus involved the Josephites, who
left Egypt and entered Canaan early in the 13th century. This
movement took place with the full consent of the Egyptians. The
second involved the Levites, who left Egypt c. 1170 BC and entered
Palestine about a generation later, c. 1125 BC. They had been
taken into Egypt during the previous century as the captives of
Merneptah, following the incident referred to on the Israel Stele.
Moses and Joshua belong to this second Exodus.

Concerning Rowton's earlier Exodus, two comments need to be made. One is that Rowton supported the entry of the Josephites into Canaan early in the 13th century partly with archaeological evidence from Jericho which is now obsolete. The second concerns his view that this movement occurred with Egyptian consent. Rowton believes that the Exodus story as it now stands contains a blend of two traditions relating to different Exoduses; one in which there was bitter hostility between Egyptians and Israelites, and "the rival tradition according to which the Israelites left Egypt loaded with presents" (Rowton 1953: 52; for similar but not identical views on two Exoduses, cf. Hooke 1957: 83; de Vaux 1971: 496). This latter tradition is supposedly to be found in Ex 12: 35-6, and it is this which is supposed to refer to an Exodus occurring with Egyptian consent. But these verses do not demand this conclusion; nor do they warrant de Vaux's distinction between an expulsion-Exodus and a flight-Exodus. The tradition as it now stands makes perfect sense viewed as a unity; there *is* hostility between the Egyptians and the enslaved Israelites, and though the Egyptians are at first anxious to retain their labour force, in a moment of crisis and panic the Israelites are commanded to leave. The writer of Ex 12: 35-6 delights in the irony of this situation, and underlines it with this little story in which the Egyptians are so keen to see the Israelites leave that they gladly give them whatever they ask. Whether this particular incident is historical or not is not an important issue here; what matters is that it is quite possible to conceive of a situation in which a sudden change of attitude on the part of the Egyptian authorities resulted from some crisis which was interpreted as a consequence of their determination to detain the Israelites. Unless the tradition portrays an historically implausible sequence, it is hazardous to use this kind of distinction as a basis for a hypothetical reconstruction of the events. Furthermore, the taking of valuables by the Israelites is certainly not related in such a way as to imply friendliness with the Egyptians. Against de Vaux, we may add that the Exodus was still a flight from Egypt rather than an expulsion, because the panic felt by the Egyptians was only temporary (cf. Ex 14:5), and had to be taken advantage of immediately.

Another criticism of Rowton's argument is that it gives far too much weight to the absence of references to Egyptian campaigns in Palestine in the books of Joshua and Judges (Rowton 1953: 49-50), an issue which will be taken up in Chapter 2 of the present work (2.2). In particular, Rowton gives unwarranted importance to Egypt's clash with Israel referred to on Merneptah's Stele (cf.

Rowley 1950: 137-8). Furthermore, his dating of the entry into
Canaan of the second Exodus group relies partly on archaeological
evidence which is no longer valid.

Rowton's theory also relies on various data from the biblical
narratives which suggest to him that the account of the Exodus is
a compound of two similar but distinct episodes; the same applies
to the accounts of the journey from Egypt to Canaan and of the
Conquest. These data will be discussed under the next heading.

0.5 *Handling the Traditions*

Is there any justification within the text itself for
assuming a blend of traditions which originally belonged to
separate groups? In the opinion of the present writer, there is
nothing in the narratives to support the theory of a double
Exodus, a point which was conceded even by Albright (1918: 138).
But what of the events narrated subsequently? It is widely held
that the Sinai tradition and the Exodus tradition belonged
originally to two distinct groups. It has also long been
recognized that two separate routes of entry into Canaan seem to
be referred to in the book of Numbers, and that Joshua and Judges
1 preserve different accounts of the Conquest. Here the problems
are seemingly real.

Von Rad (1938 ET 1966) and Noth (1960: 110-138) have both
offered the view that the main traditions in the Pentateuch
originated with distinct groups and only became a unity as
those groups became merged into a single people. Von Rad's work
cited above deals particularly with the Sinai tradition and its
omission from what he believes is Israel's earliest "historical
Credo", to be found in the cultic prayer of Deut 26: 5-9.

Von Rad's handling of these traditions has already been
criticised by various writers, and their criticisms have recently
been brought together by Hyatt (1970) in an effective reply to the
views of both von Rad and Noth. E.W. Nicholson (1973) has recently
provided yet another critical examination of the views of these
two writers, in a work which substantiates the conclusions
reached by Hyatt.

An important point to note is that the "historical Credo" in
Deut 26: 5-9 does not appear to be very early, as von Rad's view
requires, but either exilic or immediately pre-exilic; this has

been argued by L. Rost (1965: 11-25) from the language of the
passage. A. Weiser (1961: 83-90) has plausibly suggested that the
Sinai revelation is omitted from such summaries as Deut 26: 5-9
simply because those summaries deal with God's acts of salvation,
and the Sinai event does not belong to that category.

Noth has isolated five separate "themes" in the Pentateuch,
and has argued that the Sinai tradition was the latest of these to
be developed, considering Moses to be an insertion into that
tradition and not an original part of it (cf. 1960: 133-8). But
Moses' role in the Sinai tradition is hardly to be explained away
in this fashion. As Hyatt says: "... Moses plays such an
outstanding role in the traditions of Sinai, as well as in those
of the Exodus and later events, and he is so well integrated into
all of them, that we should not under any circumstance consider
him as only a secondary insertion into those narratives. His
presence is required as a historical figure, not simply as a
literary figure to bind the various traditions together" (1970: 167).

Aharoni and Yeivin have both tackled the problem of the two
entry-route traditions and have approached it in a similar way.
In Num 21ff. we have traditions concerning the by-passing of the
territory of Edom and Moab by Israel, while in Num 33 we have an
itinerary which contradicts these traditions, giving a list of
stations which lead straight through Edom and Moab. Aharoni and
Yeivin both suppose that the Num 33 list refers to a movement
through Transjordan which occurred before there were settled
kingdoms there, while the traditions of Num 21ff. belong to a
later group which reached the area after settled kingdoms had been
established. But while Yeivin (1971: 76-7) identifies the first
group as the Leah tribes and the later group as the Rachel tribes,
Aharoni (1957: 142) adopts opposite identifications.

The belief of Aharoni and Yeivin that the two traditions are
to be explained in this way rests on the assumption that settled
kingdoms established themselves in Transjordan at the beginning
of the 13th century BC. As will be seen subsequently, this
assumption, though widespread, is very probably erroneous.

There have been attempts to harmonize the two itineraries
(Wright 1945: 39; Haran 1971: 113-43), but not in a way which has
proved convincing (cf. Rowton 1953: 51, n.24; Yeivin 1971: 270).

It has been noted by Bartlett (1972: 27; 1973: 232) that the
tradition concerning Edom (Num 21: 14-21) is vague in comparison

with the other narratives concerned with obstructions to Israel's
progress; the king is not named, and the references to Edom's
brotherhood with Israel and to Kadesh lying on the border of Edom
possibly reflect a fairly late period. In view of this, we may
perhaps suggest that the clash with Edom was not a part of the
original tradition concerning the passage through Transjordan.
(More will be said on this topic on a later page.) It is also
noteworthy that no refusal of passage by Balak of Moab is recorded,
only an effort on his part to remove the Israelites by curses
when they had already established their camp in "the plains of
Moab" opposite Jericho (Num 22: 1ff). It is therefore possible
that in Num 33 we have a simplified version of the real route
taken (omitting reference to the clash with the Amorites), dating
from before the diversion around Edom was introduced into the
full narrative. It is perhaps along these lines that we should
seek an explanation for the two entry-routes rather than in
theories which necessitate the positing of two separate migrations.

The problem of the overlapping but far from identical
Conquest accounts in Joshua and Judges 1 has already been
tackled a number of times in such a way as to explain their
relationship without assuming two waves of Conquest in different
periods.

For example, Jack (1925: 70-75; 147-151) has argued for a
two-pronged invasion of Canaan in which Judahite and Simeonite
groups, and possibly others, moved directly northwards into the
Negeb and the hill-country while another group, consisting
chiefly of the Joseph tribes led by Joshua, proceeded via
Transjordan to enter the land from the east at Jericho. Jack's
reconstruction of the movements of the former groups makes good
sense of the biblical material, and de Vaux's more recent
reconstruction (1971: 487-510) parallels it very closely. The
views of Jack and de Vaux differ from the biblical picture in
presenting the northward movement through the Negeb as ultimately
successful rather than abortive. It should be noted, however,
that the Old Testament preserves traditions of both unsuccessful
(Num 14: 45; 21: 1) and successful (Num 21: 3; Jdg 1: 17) attacks
in the region around Zephath/Hormah, and these may relate to
attempts made before and after the generation spent in the
wilderness respectively. In other words, there is no reason why
there should not eventually have been effective penetration from
the south as well as from the east, and it is easy to see why a
successful penetration from the south would have been almost

completely neglected in the main accounts: it had nothing to do with Moses or Joshua, with whom the main lines of tradition are chiefly concerned.

An important point to note is that Num 23:3 relates a successful attack on Hormah (and implies a defeat of the king of Arad) from the south. Here, in Jack's words, is a victory "at the very gates of the Promised Land"; Arad is sixty miles from Kadesh Barnea and only eighteen miles from Hebron; "... A way must have been opened up for an advance further north still" (Jack 1925: 148; cf. also de Vaux 1971: 490-91). Jack and de Vaux both argue that the movement into the Negeb related in Jdg 1: 16-17 took place from the south; the "city of palms" mentioned here as the place from which the movement began appears not to be Jericho as in certain other texts, but the Tamar (= "Palm Tree") of I Kgs 9: 18 and Ezek 47: 19, lying south-east of the Dead Sea (Jack 1925: 149; de Vaux 1971: 112). In other words, both Num 21: 3 and Jdg 1: 16-17 may refer to the same successful attack on Hormah, which opened up a route into the central hill-country from the south.

Concerning the contrast between the accounts in Jos 1-11 and Jdg 1, it is probably safe to assume that the latter preserves a truer picture of the settlement in the south and central regions by attributing the capture of various cities to separate groups rather than to all Israel under Joshua. But that is not to say that the account of the penetration from the east by Joshua and his followers is unimportant or unhistorical. Lack of suitable archaeological evidence from Jericho and Ai has led many to suppose a lack of historical basis for the stories of Joshua's exploits. The present work will offer an alternative viewpoint. The list of cities destroyed by Joshua in Jos 10:28-39 has been described as redactional, with the implication that its historical value is small (cf. de Vaux 1965: 27). It is true that some of the cities in this list are mentioned also in Jdg 1, where their capture has no connection with Joshua. Quite possibly these should not be included in the list of cities taken by Joshua (though the possibility still remains that in some cases a city needed to be defeated twice, once by Joshua's troops and again later by another group), but that does not mean that other cities mentioned only in Jos 10 were not taken by Joshua, and even less that they were not taken by Israel at all during the time of the Conquest.

Some scholars, in particular Alt (1925 ET 1966) and Noth (1960: 69), have been completely sceptical concerning the Conquest traditions, preferring to view the settlement in Canaan as a peaceful process and explaining the traditions concerning destroyed cities as chiefly aetiological (Noth 1960: 82, n 2). The present writer's response to this approach to the Conquest is in essence that of Albright (cf. especially 1939: 11-23): " - the ultimate historicity of a given datum is never conclusively established nor disproved by the literary framework in which it is embedded: there must always be external evidence" (ibid: 12). However, the external (i.e. archaeological) evidence to which appeal will be made in this work is completely different from that to which Albright referred.

More recently G.E. Mendenhall (1962: 66-87) has offered another view of the Conquest which differs markedly from the picture presented by the biblical traditions. Mendenhall affirms: "... There was no statistically important invasion of Palestine at the beginning of the twelve tribe system of Israel. There was no radical displacement of population .... In summary, there was no real conquest of Palestine at all; what happened instead may be termed ... a peasants' revolt against the network of interlocking Canaanite city states" (ibid: 73). Mendenhall does not deny that a group of people escaped from Egypt and reached Canaan, but he sees the role of this "small religious community of Israel" (ibid: 81) as merely having a polarizing effect on existing populations which were suffering the tensions of the city-state system. Men withdrew from the existing political regimes and effectively became part of the community of Israel; others, primarily the kings and their supporters, fought to maintain control: "Since the kings were defeated and forced out, this became the source of the tradition that all the Canaanites and Amorites were either driven out or slain en masse ..." (ibid).

The validity of Mendenhall's reconstruction stands or falls with this statement: "The fact is, and the present writer would regard it as a fact though not every detail can be 'proven', that both the Amarna materials and the biblical events represent politically the same process: namely the withdrawal, not physically and geographically, but politically and subjectively, of large population groups from any obligation to the existing political regimes..." (ibid: 73). I do not deny that this process of withdrawal from political affiliations probably

describes extremly well what was happening in Palestine during
the Amarna period (cf. Campbell 1960). But since Mendenhall does
not date the Israelite settlement to this period, there seems no
warrant for assuming that the same process underlies the biblical
traditions of the Conquest. He does not offer a single piece of
evidence for his assertion that the same process was occurring in
each case, and without this evidence Mendenhall's theory remains
extremely weak. No reasons have yet been brought forward for
preferring Mendenhall's hypothetical reconstruction of events to
the picture presented by the biblical narratives. Mendenhall
seems to have committed the opposite error to that of many
writers earlier this century; while they misinterpreted the
Amarna letters by assuming they described the same events as the
biblical Conquest narratives, Mendenhall has offered an
interpretation of the Conquest narratives which rests on an
unfounded assumption that they describe a situation similar to
that now known to be depicted in the letters. (For further
criticisms of Mendenhall's approach, see de Vaux 1965: 21-2, 25;
Weippert 1971: 55-126.

In summary, there seem to be no good reasons for separating
the major biblical traditions (Exodus-Sinai-Wilderness-Conquest)
and assigning them to originally distinct groups; nor has any solid
reason yet emerged for abandoning the basic biblical representation
of events from the Exodus to the Conquest in favour of some
radically different picture.

0.6 *The Approach to be Taken*

The approach which will be taken here will have become clear
already from the preceding discussions. It is here proposed that
the main traditions of the Hexateuch - the Exodus, the journey to
Sinai, the generation spent in the wilderness, and the Conquest -
originated with historical events which all befell the same body
of people. That body of people may well have been quite
heterogeneous, and may have split into two or more groups during
the initial stages of the Conquest, so that the whole group was
not involved in the conquest of every area; also, it is possible
that just prior to, during, and immediately after the Conquest,
this body of people was joined by others who had not been
involved in the Exodus event. The important point is that there
is no good reason to reject the implication of the overall
tradition in its present form; namely, that the same group which
came out of Egypt moved first to Sinai, subsequently spent about
a generation in the wilderness to the south of Canaan, and then

moved into Canaan itself (cf. Nicholson 1973: 84).

The view which one takes of the traditions clearly affects
the way in which one tackles the search for extra-biblical data
relevant to these events. A view which dissociates the main
elements of the tradition from each other and assigns them to
originally distinct groups of people is free to assume an order
of events quite different from that presented in the Old Testament.
It is proposed here that such a view should not be adopted unless
it remains the only possibility. In other words, I suggest that
the order of events in the overall tradition as it now stands
should be given another chance to speak for itself.

A feeling has been expressed that theories concerning the
time of the Exodus and Conquest have been explored to their
limits, leaving the discussion exhausted (cf. Pritchard 1965: 323).
Pritchard has remarked in addition that the problematical
discoveries at Jericho, Gibeon and Ai "suggest that we have
reached an impasse on the question of supporting the traditional
view of the conquest with archaeological undergirding" (ibid: 319).
The present work reopens these issues and offers new placements
for both the Exodus and Conquest events. The Conquest is viewed
afresh as a deliberate assault on the Canaanite cities, which met,
in its initial stages, with a considerable degree of success.
Moreover, as was explained above, Israel is seen as already
existing, at least in its formative stages, at the time of the
Exodus.

There will be no major discussion of the numbers involved in
the Exodus and subsequent events, but the present writer considers
the view of J.W. Wenham (1967: 27-32), arrived at from a
consideration of biblical data, to be quite plausible: this
suggests a total of about 72,000 for the whole migration
(compared with about two and a half million on the oldest
reckoning, and about 20,000 on Petrie's), and a fighting force of
about 18,000 men. That a large fighting force was available by
the beginning of the Conquest is in fact a major requirement in
the argument that there was a fairly concerted and successful
attempt to destroy the main Canaanite cities.

Part One of the work begins with an examination of the
arguments on which the firmly entrenched 13th century date is
based, in an effort to expose their weaknesses. The final chapter
of Part One offers an earlier date as an alternative. Part Two

34

considers afresh the question of archaeology and the Conquest, offering new evidence within the framework of a modified chronology for Palestine's archaeological strata.

PART ONE

A CRITICAL EXAMINATION
OF THE
THIRTEENTH CENTURY
DATING OF THE EXODUS

CHAPTER 1:
THE TWO MAIN PILLARS
OF THE
THIRTEENTH CENTURY DATE

Chapter 1: The Two Main Pillars of The Thirteenth Century Date

Early in the 1930's, T.H. Robinson wrote concerning Ex 1: 11: "The whole theory of a nineteenth dynasty date for the Exodus rests on the two names in that verse" (1932: 79). This is no longer true, for since then another main pillar for the 13th century date has been supplied by archaeological discoveries at many sites in Palestine, interpreted as evidence of an Israelite Conquest towards the end of the 13th century. Bright (1972: 121) has described this archaeological evidence as the chief reason for a 15th century date being "almost universally abandoned".

It therefore seems legitimate to speak of the 13th century dating as having two main pillars, one being the information contained in Ex 1: 11, the other being archaeological evidence for a Conquest in the decades around 1230 BC. These will be examined in turn.

1.1 Pithom and Raamses: the argument from Exodus 1: 11

The information contained in Ex 1: 11 has been used by various writers as support for a 13th century date for the Exodus. The precise import of the verse therefore needs to be discussed. However, before examining the views of those writers who have placed great emphasis on the verse, we shall make some general comments on it.

Ex. 1: 11 informs us that the Egyptians pressed the Hebrews into forced labour, using them to build for the pharaoh store-cities ($^{c}\bar{a}r\hat{e}$ $misk^{e}n\hat{o}\underline{t}$), Pithom and Raamses.

The precise meaning of $misk^{e}n\hat{o}\underline{t}$ is unknown. It is rendered "store-cities" in RSV, RV, JB and NEB. The KJV has "treasure

cities". The LXX renders the expression as *poleis ochuras*,
"strong" or "fortified cities"; *misk^enôt* occurs five times in
Chronicles (II Chr 8: 4, 6; 16: 4; 17: 12; 32: 28) and in one
other place, I Kgs 9: 19; only one version of the LXX (A) has the
section I Kgs 9: 14-25, and in that we find the expression replaced
by *poleis tōn skēnōmatōn*, "cities of abode". When E. Naville
located Pithom at the site of Tell el-Maskhouta, and discovered
what he believed to be store-chambers for grain there, the
evidence seemed to favour the term "store cities" (Naville 1888):
10). However, since the remains at Tell el-Maskhouta have been
reinterpreted as fortress foundations, the LXX rendering of
"fortified cities" has been favoured by some scholars (Helck 1965:
47). Whether Pithom should really be located at Tell-el-Maskhouta
will be discussed below.

Most scholars consider Ex 1: 11 to belong, along with the
surrounding verses (8-12), to the J source (cf. Redford 1963: 401
for references; also Hyatt 1971: 56; Childs 1974: 7), though quite
a number consider it not a part of 8-12 and assign it instead to
E (cf. Redford 1963: 401 for references). Recently Redford has
argued for considering 11b to be an insertion by the Priestly
redactor and not original to Ex 1 (ibid: 401-18). Much of
Redford's argumentation is unconvincing, and has been refuted by
Helck (1965: 35-48). However, two points do perhaps indicate a
Priestly origin for 11b in its present form. One is that the name
Raamses/Rameses only occurs elsewhere in passages assigned to P
(Gen 47: 11; Ex 12: 37; Num 33: 3, 5); the other is that the word
misk^enôt is probably a late word; the phrase containing it in
I Kgs 9: 19 may well be an insertion (Redford 1963: 413-14), which
would mean that all other datable instances of the word belong to
the Chronicler. Therefore, Ex 1: 11b in its present form may be
late.

Redford has drawn attention to the fact that if the name
Raamses refers to the royal residence of Rameses II, as is
normally supposed, the prefix Pi- (as in Pi-Thom) would be
expected. The absence of this prefix leads him to doubt whether
the name really does refer to Rameses II's Delta residence
(1963: 409-10). In view of the fact that Gen 47: 11 speaks of a
"land of Rameses", it has been suggested that Ex 1: 11 originally
spoke of the building of "Pithom in the land of Rameses" (cf. Jack
1925: 23). However, Helck, in his reply to Redford, says there is
no reason why the form found in Ex 1: 11 may not refer to the
Delta residence of Rameses II, which he believes is to be

identified with the city later called Tanis (1965: 42).

The locations of Raamses at Tanis and of Pithom at Tell
el-Maskhouta have both been claimed to prove a 13th century date
for the Exodus.

Naville's discoveries at Tell el-Maskhouta showed that the
city had been built by Rameses II. A.H. Sayce wrote of the
discovery as proof that Rameses II "must have been the Pharaoh
of the Oppression". He added: "Unless we deny the historical
character of Ex 1: 11, the date of the Exodus is definitely
fixed" (1900: 887; cf. also Curtis 1898: 398). Similarly
A.H. McNeile, commenting on Naville's identification of Pithom,
wrote: "The discovery is important; for if the statement in
Ex 1: 11 is accurate - which there is no evidence to lead us
to doubt - the Pharaoh of the Oppression is proved to be
Rameses II..." (1908: xciv).

Since the archaeologist Montet located the residence city
of Rameses II at Tanis, the mention of the city Raamses in
Ex 1: 11 has also been taken as proof that the Exodus occurred
in the 13th century. Thus G.E. Wright, after discussing the
possibility of dating the Exodus to about 1440 BC on the basis of
the figure given in I Kgs 6: 1, writes: "Now that the site of
Rameses has been located at Tanis, we are forced to conclude
that this figure must be explained in another way...". No
remains from Egypt's XVIIIth Dynasty have been found at Tanis,
therefore: "We now know that if there is any historical value at
all to the store-city tradition in Exodus (and there is no
reason to doubt its reliability), *then Israelites must have been
in Egypt at least during the early part of the reign of
Rameses II*" (1962a: 60, Wright's emphasis). Similarly K.A.
Kitchen (1966: 58-9, 59, n.11) states that the Exodus must be
placed during the XIXth Dynasty, because both Tanis and Qantir
(a possible alternative site for Raamses, on which see below)
"were original foundations by Sethos I and Rameses II, so that
the Exodus can hardly be dated in the preceding Eighteenth
Dynasty as was once thought by some scholars ...". M. Noth has
also attached great historical significance to Ex 1: 11,
describing it as "a strikingly concrete item of information"
which "takes us to the period of the Pharaoh Rameses II (1290-1223
B.C.)" (1960: 120). Other scholars could be cited as expressing
similar views (cf. Rowley 1950: 32-3; Albright 1957a: 194;
Nicholson 1973: 54).

It is therefore of great importance to examine the history of
the debate and the present state of the evidence to decide whether
Ex 1: 11 does indeed have this significance.

1.1.1. *Raamses*

E. Brugsch first suggested that the Egyptian city
Pi-Ra^cmesse, the Delta residence of Rameses II, was to be located
at Tanis (1872: 16-20). He further suggested that this was the
biblical Raamses (1875). Lepsius (1849: 348) suggested that the
biblical Raamses should be located at Tell el-Maskhouta, the place
which Naville later identified as the site of Pithom. Maspero,
who published some of the inscriptions from the place in 1877,
also concluded that this was the site of Raamses, because of the
number of inscriptions from the reign of Rameses II which were
found there (1877: 320). Naville distinguished between the
Pi-Ra^cmesse of Egyptian documents and the biblical Raamses,
locating the latter at Tell er-Retebah, while believing that
Pi-Ra^cmesse should be located at Kantara (1924: 20-21). In his
location of Raamses he was following Petrie, who excavated Tell
er-Retebah at the start of this century and believed he had
discovered remains of the biblical city (Petrie 1906: 28-34).

Gardiner argued that Pi-Ra^cmesse should be identified with
Pelusium (1918: 127ff). This view was adopted by Mallon
(1921: 106-19) and by Peet (1922: 83-91). Gardiner defended
this identification against Naville's criticisms in 1924 (1924:
88-94), but he retracted it less than ten years later (1933:
122-28), when Montet brought forward compelling arguments for
locating Pi-Ra^cmesse at Tanis (Montet 1930: 4-28; 1933). Montet
believed that Tanis was also the Raamses of Ex 1: 11. When
Gardiner abandoned Pelusium in favour of Tanis, most other
scholars followed suit (cf. Van Seters 1966: 130, n.11).

However, in 1930, while Montet was excavating Tanis, M. Hamza
published the suggestion that Pi-Ra^cmesse should be located at
Qantir, some fifteen miles south of Tanis (Hamza 1930: 31-68).
This notion did not at first receive a great deal of attention
(though cf. Hayes 1937: 5-8; 1959: II, 332-9; also Lucas 1938:
25-8. Wright, 1942: 34, wrote of "an outside chance... that the
site may have been Qantir", but he opted for Tanis, though cf.
1962a: 57, n.2; 58, n.3), while Montet's identification was widely
accepted (Albright 1948: 15; 1957a: 169, 194; Rowley 1950: 28;
Wright 1962a: 60; Finegan 1963: 34-7; Bright 1972: 119-20). But

since the publication of new evidence by L. Habachi (1954), who
also came to the conclusion that Qantir was the site of
Pi-Raᶜmesse, the identification has been more widely favoured.
It has been strongly argued for by J. Van Seters (1966: 127-151)
and E.P. Uphill (1968: 291-316; 1969: 15-39), and Kitchen, who
earlier suggested that the term Pi-Raᶜmesse should be taken as
indicating an administrative district including both Tanis and
Qantir (1966: 59, n.9; cf. also the suggestion of North, 1967a:
119-22), has since accepted the identification more confidently
(1973a: 426, n.13).

Some writers have spoken of a lack of evidence for a city at
Qantir before the XIXth Dynasty, and have therefore seen this
identification as favouring a 13th century date for the Exodus
just as strongly as the view that Pi-Raᶜmesse was at Tanis. Thus
Rowley wrote: "So far as evidence at present goes, this
identification would be definitely in favour of the later date"
(1950: 28, n.4). We may compare this with the quotation from
Kitchen on both Tanis and Qantir given above.

However, the investigations of L. Habachi have brought to
light a great deal of fresh evidence on the history of the city.
There is some evidence that a town flourished in the area during
the Old Kingdom, and much more certain evidence that a sizeable
town existed during the Middle Kingdom. I intend to show
elsewhere that the time when the enslaved Hebrews were employed
on the building of Pithom and Raamses should be placed in the
Middle Kingdom /1/.   If Qantir is the correct site of
Pi-Raᶜmesse, then unless we deny that the name Raamses in Ex 1: 11
is intended to indicate this town, there is no need to limit the
work on the cities to the time of Rameses II.

In addition to Habachi's own lengthy article of 1954, we
have three more recent detailed discussions of the location of
Pi-Raᶜmesse which conclude that it should be identified with
Qantir. The first of these to appear, that of Van Seters
·(1966: 127-151) is really concerned with the location of the
Hyksos capital Avaris, which is commonly assumed to have been on
the same site as the later Pi-Raᶜmesse. But since evidence for
the location of the Hyksos capital is very scanty, Van Seters has
to rely on evidence for the location of Pi-Raᶜmesse.

Van Seters questions whether any of the architectural
features of Tanis can be assigned to the Ramesside period. He
points out that neither the Hyksos monuments found there, nor the

Ramesside monuments, were found *in situ* in any instance (ibid:
128-31). Also, Tanis has a "complete lack of any archaeological
strata before the Twenty-first Dynasty" (131). His conclusion is
that the town at Tanis "did not come into existence until the
Twenty-first Dynasty" (131). All the granite building blocks and
statuary from earlier periods were brought to the site from
elsewhere by rulers of the XXIst Dynasty "in order to construct
and adorn their new capital" (131; cf. Hayes 1959: II, 339, n.6).
The site from which the monuments and building blocks were
brought is conjectured to have been Qantir (Van Seters 1966:
136-7), which Van Seters concludes was the true Pi-Raᶜmesse. At
Qantir are many finds from Ramesside times, all of which are
in situ. Qantir had "a great palace of Ramesses II of exceptional
beauty", and also "palaces with extensive bureaucracy,
storehouses and workshops, military installations, and temples"
(ibid: 134, 135).

The second lengthy discussion of the location of Pi-Raᶜmesse,
contained in two articles by E.P. Uphill (1968; 1969), reaches
roughly the same conclusion concerning the archaeological
evidence at Tanis. Uphill writes: "One need not go so far as
Van Seters in suggesting that the Twenty-first Dynasty marked
the foundation of Tanis ... but it seems fairly certain ... that
it was not a place of outstanding importance in its own right,
nor the royal residence suggested by Montet" (1968: 315).

The most recent and most thorough discussion of the question
is by M. Bietak (1975a: 28-43). This writer traces the history
of occupation at the neighbouring sites of Tell el-Dabᶜa,
Khataᶜna, and Tell el-Qirqafa, which lie in the district of
Qantir, mentioning evidence of temple and palace areas, and of
graves and settlements dating from the Middle Kingdom and the
Second Intermediate Period (29-37). In contrast, Tanis has
yielded no indications of buildings or ceramics from before the
XXIst-XXIInd Dynasties; all statues and other stonework of
XIXth-XXth Dynasty dates were found to have been transported to
Tanis from elsewhere. A canal existed between Qantir and Tanis
during the XXIst and XXIInd Dynasties, and Bietak suggests that
via this, the monuments and blocks from the XIXth and XXth
Dynasties were moved from Qantir to Tanis during the XXIst
Dynasty. He suggests this was done because the rulers of that
dynasty did not have access to the quarries of Upper Egypt and
were therefore short of stone for their own monuments and
buildings (41). Hence at Tanis there are clay statue-bases for
statues whose real stone bases are still to be found at Qantir.

The evidence leads Bietak to affirm the Avaris and
Pi-Raᶜmesse are to be identified with Qantir, not with Tanis or
with any other place (ibid).

Van Seters, Uphill and Bietak all deal at length with
Egyptian literary evidence for the location of Pi-Raᶜmesse. This
seems to point decisively to Qantir as the correct site. The
description in *Papyrus Anastasi III, 9,* speaks of Pi-Raᶜmesse as
"the marshalling place of thy [i.e. pharaoh's] cavalry, the
rallying point of thy soldiers, the harbourage of thy ships'
troops". It was "between Palestine and Egypt", "the forefront
of every land". The description makes good sense when referred
to Qantir, while Tanis, from a military point of view, was very
badly placed and in Ramesside times the site would not have been
a good port either (cf. Van Seters 1966: 140; Uphill 1969: 19).
The description of the area surrounding Pi-Raᶜmesse, contained in
Anastasi III, 2 (given in full by Uphill, 1969: 15-16), fits very
well the area around Qantir, while being quite unsuitable as a
description of the environs of Tanis (Van Seters 1966: 140-41;
Bietak 1975a: 39-40). One telling point is the location of
Pi-Raᶜmesse on "the Waters of Re", which makes sense in terms of
Qantir, on a branch of the Nile which is now dry, "but it is
impossible to apply to Tanis" (Kitchen 1973a: 426, n.13).

Anastasi III, 9, describes the palaces of Pi-Raᶜmesse as
"beauteous of balconies, dazzling with halls of lapis and
turquoise". Many beautiful glazed tiles from Qantir show that
in the Ramesside period there were indeed palaces there with
"halls of lapis and turquoise" (Hayes 1937; also 1959: II, 334-8).
No palace has yet been found at Tanis (Van Seters 1966: 141).
Papyrus *Anastasi IV* speaks of the location of the gods Amun,
Setekh, Astarte and Ptah in different quarters of Pi-Raᶜmesse, a
statement which both Van Seters (1966: 142) and Uphill (1969: 31)
are able to explain in terms of the area around Qantir, while "it
is difficult to offer any explanation whatever for the vicinity of
Tanis" (Van Seters).

After accepting Montet's view that Pi-Raᶜmesse should be
identified with Tanis, Gardiner (1947: II, 173) argued against
locating the city at Qantir. He pointed out that the existence
of Qantir was not due to Rameses II but to rulers of much earlier
dynasties. As Uphill points out in reply, this is hardly a
problem, as a virtual rebuilding could have been carried out
under Rameses II.

A very serious problem for the identification of Pi-Raᶜmesse
with Tanis is the fact that *both* Pi-Raᶜmesse *and* Tanis (as Sekhet-
Djanet) appear separately in the Memphis geographical list of the
time of Rameses II, and also in the later *Onomasticon of Amenemope*
(cf. Kitchen 1973a: 426, n.13; Bietak 1975a; 33).

In short, both archaeological and literary evidence seems to
show that Tanis can not have been Pi-Raᶜmesse, while Qantir has
now emerged as the most likely site for the city among those
advanced so far. Since statements to this effect can be found
from Hayes (1959: II, 339), Van Seters (1966: 149), Uphill (1968:
316), Kitchen (1973a: 426) and Bietak (1975a: 41), we may say that
contemporary scholarship substantially favours Qantir as the site
of Pi-Raᶜmesse.

As was mentioned above, the site of Qantir has a long history,
and if Raamses is located here, there is no reason why the work
done at the city by the enslaved Hebrews must be dated to the time
of Rameses II. It is perfectly plausible to suggest that the
Hebrew slaves worked there at a much earlier time, and that
Ex 1: 11 simply gives to the city the name by which it was
commonly known in a later period when Ex 1 was either compiled
or revised.

Jack argued for this view in 1925. He suggested that we
find the name Raamses in Ex 1 because that was the name of the
city "when the earliest Jewish records were written (c 850 B.C.)"
(1925: 24-5). He pointed out that in Gen 14: 14 we have a mention
of Dan, though we know that the city did not bear that name in
Abraham's day, when it was called Laish or Leshem; it only
acquired the name Dan after the Danite conquest of the city
(Jdg 18: 29). Jack therefore advocated the view that the use of
the name Raamses in Ex 1: 11 is retrospective. He compared the
method of its author to that of a modern writer stating that the
Romans built York, while they actually built the city under the
name of Eboracum.

The only objection which has been made to this view is now
removed by the location of Pi-Raᶜmesse at Qantir. Accepting the
earlier identification of the city with Tanis, Albright and
others argued that the name Pi-Raᶜmesse would not have been used
after c. 1100 BC, when the city acquired its new name, i.e. Tanis
(cf. Albright 1957a: 194; Rowley 1950: 32-3, 32, n.5; Wright
1962a: 59; Harrison 1970: 115). At Qantir there are no monuments

of consequence later than the XXth Dynasty (Bietak 1975a: 29, 31);
but though the city of Pi-Raᶜmesse came to an end at that time,
there is no reason to suppose that it was not referred to
retrospectively by that name. Indeed, there is evidence for the
name continuing in use. Redford (1963: 409) draws attention to a
XXIst or XXIInd Dynasty manuscript of the *Onomasticon of Amenemope*
(Gardiner 1947: II, 171; I, 25), i.e. 10th-8th centuries BC, to a
XXXth Dynasty inscription from Bubastis (Naville 1891: pl. 46b),
and to Ptolemaic inscriptions from Tanis, in each of which the
name Pi-Raᶜmesse occurs. Similarly S. Yeivin, wishing to argue
that the name Raamses is anachronistic in Ex 1: 11 (1971: 36),
points to the *Onomasticon of Amenemope* and to a statue from the
4th century BC, bearing an inscription in which the name appears,
as evidence of its continued use long after the 12th century.
Since Egyptian writers could refer to the city retrospectively
by the name Pi-Raᶜmesse, there is no obvious reason why the
Hebrew writer of Ex 1: 11 should not have done the same in his
use of the name Raamses.

It should also be noted that we find the name Rameses used
retrospectively in Gen 47: 11, where the area of Egypt in which
the clan of Jacob settled is referred to as "the land of Rameses".
(This is clearly a retrospective usage, since the descent into
Egypt must have preceded the reign of the first Rameses; cf.
Rowley 1950: 31-2.) If we admit that the name is used in this
way here, why not also in Ex 1: 11?

The view offered here is that the Raamses of Ex 1: 11 is the
Egyptian Pi-Raᶜmesse, that it is to be located at Qantir, and
that the enslaved Hebrews worked on the city not in the reign of
Rameses II but as early as the Middle Kingdom.

The commonly held view that the work of Pithom and Raamses
was done during the reign of Rameses II requires a somewhat
unnatural interpretation of the account of the Oppression in
Ex 1: 7-14. This view requires that the Hebrew slaves built
Pithom and Raamses very shortly before the Exodus, while the
building of the cities is actually placed in the narrative as
the *first* task of the enslaved people. The biblical traditions,
in speaking of a bondage spanning a number of centuries, clearly
separate by a considerable period the first task of the people
and their eventual escape from Egypt (see note 1).

Yet Kitchen has expressed the view that because Ex 1: 11
uses the name Raamses it provides "an indication of date for the

end of the oppression"; he suggests that verses 7-14 describe the
Oppression "very briefly in general terms", not attempting to
present events in any chronological order (1966: 57 with n.3).
One may ask, however, why the building of Pithom and Raamses should
be placed at the start of a general summary when it was actually
the last of the events of the Oppression. Indeed, if verses 7-14
are only a general summary of the period of Oppression, why is the
work on Pithom and Raamses singled out for inclusion in it while
other specific events are recorded later? (Cf. Wood 1970: 83,
n.12.)

The implication of Ex 1: 7-14 is in fact that the Hebrews
were employed in the building of Pithom and Raamses at the
beginning of their time of enslavement. It is not difficult to
believe that the work was particularly remembered because it was
the first which they were forced to do.

1.1.2. *Pithom*

As early as 1864 Chabas suggested that the Pithom of
Ex 1: 11 was equivalent to an Egyptian Pi-Tum, and that Tell
el-Maskhouta, in the west of the Wadi Tumilat, may possibly have
been the site of this place (cf. Sayce 1900: 886). But he later
withdrew this suggestion in favour of locating Pi-Tum at Thmuis.
As was noted previously, Lepsius and Maspero both considered Tell
el-Maskhouta to be the site of Raamses, because of the number of
remains from the time of Rameses II. Naville, however, noticing
that many monuments were inscribed as dedicated by Rameses to the
god Tum, or Atum, suspected the place may have been the biblical
Pithom. His subsequent excavations at the site in 1883 uncovered
indications of a temple of Tum or Atum, and what Naville
considered to be the remains of storehouses. The toponym *Pr-Tm*
(= Pi-Tum, "Abode of Atum") occurred in a couple of inscriptions.
Naville also found Latin inscriptions bearing the name Ero, the
Latin form of Heroonpolis, generally considered to be a Greek
translation of Pi-Tum. Naville interpreted this evidence as
proof that here lay the biblical Pithom.

As noted above, since Rameses II appears to have built the
city which stood at the site of Tell el-Maskhouta, the location
of Pithom at this spot has been pointed to as evidence that the
Hebrews in Egypt worked on Pithom no earlier than his reign.

Naville's interpretation of the evidence was challenged,
however, by Gardiner (1918: 267-9: 1924: 95-6), who favoured

locating Pithom at Tell er-Retebah, the site which Petrie
(followed by Naville) had earlier claimed was Raamses. Gardiner's
articles point out that neither of the two inscriptions found by
Naville which mention Pi-Tum actually proves that Pi-Tum was at
Tell el-Maskhouta. Gardiner did not question that there was a
temple of Atum at Tell el-Maskhouta, but he queried the conclusion
that the city there had borne the name Pi-Tum. He preferred the
view that the name of the city at Tell el-Maskhouta had been
Tcheku, which also appeared on the inscriptions. Naville had
argued that *both* names should be applied to the site, Tcheku
having been the civil name of the city, and Pi-Tum its religious
title. Gardiner differentiated between the two, accepting that
Tell el-Maskhouta was Tcheku, but placing Pi-Tum at Tell er-Retebah,
some nine miles further west along the Wadi Tumilat.

The main piece of evidence in favour of this is a Roman
milestone mentioning Ero. This is the Latin form of the name
Heroonpolis, Heronpolis, or Heroopolis, which occurs in the
LXX of Gen 46: 28-9. This name meant originally "City of Heron"
(not "City of Heroes" as in the later forms of the name), "Heron"
being equivalent to Tum or Atum (Gardiner 1918: 267-9; Gardiner
later expressed a doubt whether the original form was Heropolis
or Heronpolis, 1924: 96, n.1; but the view that the name
originated from a translation of Pi-Tum has since been confidently
expressed by Redford 1963: 407, and Finegan 1963: 11-12). The
milestone was taken by Naville to indicate that Ero was to be
located at Tell el-Maskhouta itself. Gardiner argued, however,
that the milestone could only mean that Tell el-Maskhouta lay nine
Roman miles along the road from Ero to Clusma. This places Ero
(and hence Pi-Tum) exactly at Tell er-Retebah.

Naville subsequently replied to Gardiner's argument,
re-affirming his view that Pi-Tum lay at Tell el-Maskhouta (1924:
32-6). Much of Naville's reply was, however, misdirected. He
spent time re-arguing the case for a temple of Tum at Tell
el-Maskhouta, a fact which Gardiner had never denied (see
Gardiner's response to Naville's reply, 1924: 95-6). Naville
also argued against locating Pi-Tum at Tell er-Retebah by stating
that the site shows "no trace whatever of a temple of Tum" (1924:
35), an assertion which, as Gardiner subsequently pointed out
(1924: 96), is not correct. Furthermore, Naville offered no reply
at all to the most telling point in favour of Tell er-Retebah,
namely the interpretation of the Roman milestone.

T.E. Peet dealt a further blow to Naville's theory by
pointing out that the remains which Naville had taken to be those
of "store-chambers" were in fact "the foundation walls of a
fortress" (Peet 1922: 86).

Evidence of a fortress at Tell el-Maskhouta makes possible
an understanding of a passage in *Papyrus Anastasi VI* which
strengthens the view that Pithom is Tell er-Retebah.   This
passage refers to "pools of Pithom" in connection with Tcheku and
its fortress.   Naville located a hypothetical "fortress of Tcheku"
in the eastern end of the Wadi Tumilat, so that the "pools of
Pithom could be located near Tell el-Maskhouta (1924: 34).
Gardiner points out that we have no evidence of a fortress in
this area (1924: 96), but if we take the fortress of Tcheku to
have been at Tell el-Maskhouta, then the "pools of Pithom",
which lay some distance westward of the fortress, would have
been in the region of Tell er-Retebah.

An objection has been raised to Gardiner's view by H.M.
Weiner (1923: 75), who cites Petrie's statement that Tell
er-Retebah shows no signs of Roman occupation (Petrie 1906: 28).
This is clearly a problem for the view that the Ero on the Roman
milestone is Tell er-Retebah.   This objection has recently been
noted again by Redford (1963: 407-8), who cautiously adopts
Naville's view in preference to Gardiner's.   Gardiner himself
was aware of the objection, and wrote that "there seems to be a
conflict of evidence" (1924: 96); but he continued to prefer
Tell er-Retebah as the site of Pithom.

Most modern scholarship presently accepts Gardiner's view
(Albright 1948: 15; 1957a: 194; Wright 1962a: 58; Finegan 1963:
12; Harrison 1970: 322; Bright 1972: 119), though Uphill has
recently suggested that the name Pithom in Ex 1: 11 actually
refers to the city of Iunu or On, better known by its Greek
name of Heliopolis (1968: 296-9).

Uphill argues that to an Egyptian the name Pi-Tum "would
recall the great national shrine of this god at Heliopolis".
Heliopolis was perhaps Egypt's greatest religious centre, and
the name Pi-Tum frequently occurs in connection with this
massive complex of shrines.   One may question, however, Uphill's
assertion that to a Hebrew writer the term Pi-Tum "meant the
same thing as to an Egyptian" (299).   His explanation of why the
writer of Ex 1: 11 did not use the name On when speaking of

Heliopolis, as the writer of Gen 41: 45 and 50 did, is
unconvincing, and relies on the assumption that the Hebrews
worked to rebuild the temple area in the reign of Rameses II
(ibid).

It is interesting that the LXX of Ex 1: 11 adds to the
mention of Pithom and Raamses the words "and On, which is
Heliopolis". Unless we dismiss these words as a gloss without
historical significance, there are clearly two ways of
understanding their presence. Either the LXX version of the
verse is correct in stating that Hebrew slaves worked at
Heliopolis and in distinguishing between this place and Pithom,
or the mention of three cities arises from the conflation of two
earlier versions, in one of which the name Heliopolis replaced
the name Pithom. The latter suggestion is compatible with
Uphill's view that Pithom and Heliopolis are the same place; the
former obviously is not. But while we cannot use the verse to
determine the correctness or otherwise of Uphill's theory, we
must accept, as Uphill says, that "the editors of the text in
that period considered that this work at Heliopolis formed an
integral part of the great building program..." (1969: 38).

For the purposes of the present discussion, it does not
matter whether Pithom should be located at Tell er-Retebah or at
Heliopolis. Both Heliopolis (Uphill 1968: 299) and Tell
er-Retebah (Petrie 1906: 28) existed in Middle Kingdom times,
and therefore could have been places where the Hebrew slaves
were employed at the beginning of the Oppression. R.K. Harrison,
while accepting the identification of Pithom with Tell er-Retebah,
still affirms that the tradition of forced labour there must
refer to the time of Rameses II, because "no traces of Eighteenth
Dynasty construction or expansion were evident" (1970: 322).
This completely overlooks the possibility that the Hebrews worked
there in a period long *before* the XVIIIth Dynasty.

Rowley has written: "The suggestion that the names may be
interpolated or anachronistic in Ex 1: 11 still requires to be
supported by evidence that there was royal building activity and
residence in the cities referred to in the earlier age in which
the story is located" (1950: 33).

This condition is met by the location of Raamses at Qantir
and by the location of Pithom at either Tell er-Retebah or
Heliopolis. At Qantir, as mentioned above, there was "royal
building activity and residence" during the Middle Kingdom, and

evidence uncovered by Petrie points to activity at Tell er-Retebah during this same period (Petrie 1906: 28).

In conclusion it can be stated quite simply that the appearance of the names Pithom and Raamses in Ex 1: 11 does not confine the building activity of the enslaved Hebrews to the time of the XIXth Dynasty, and therefore does not constitute evidence for a 13th century date for the Exodus.

1.2 *Archaeological Evidence for a Conquest Towards the End of*
     the Thirteenth Century BC

As was stated earlier, archaeological discoveries made during and since the 1930's have been a major factor in resolving the Exodus debate in favour of a date in the 13th century. These discoveries supposedly attest a Conquest of Canaan by Israel from about 1230 BC onwards.

However, discoveries at Jericho have constituted a notable exception. Garstang's excavations led him to affirm in 1931 that the walls of what he called City D had fallen before 1400 BC (1931: 146), though he subsequently preferred a date slightly later, between 1400 and 1385 BC (1940: 125). Garstang's conclusions exerted a strong influence in favour of the early date for the Exodus.

Albright and others attempted to modify Garstang's conclusions. Albright at one point dated the fall of Canaanite Jericho to between 1360 and 1320 BC (1935b: 13), and later broadened the limits to between 1375 and 1300 BC (1939: 20). Vincent (1930: 403-33; 1932: 264-76 1935: 583-605; 1939: 580) and de Vaux (1938: 237) both opted for an even later date, between 1250 and 1200 BC, a date which Albright was subsequently prepared to accept (1949: 108; cf. Rowley 1950: 13). This brought the fall of Jericho into line with the dates being arrived at for the destruction of other Palestinian cities.

In the 1950's however, Jericho was excavated again by Kathleen Kenyon. Garstang's analysis of the strata of the site was found to be completely wrong, and his conclusions had to be abandoned. Kenyon concluded that there was no city at Jericho between c. 1550 BC and c. 1440 BC, and that the city which came into existence at the latter date ceased to be occupied c. 1325 BC. The site then remained unoccupied until the Iron Age (Kenyon 1957: 256-65). Kenyon's conclusions therefore fail to elucidate the

issue, since they fit with neither the early nor the late date for
the Exodus.

Since Kenyon's work at Jericho, much more emphasis has been
placed on the archaeological evidence from other sites. This is
due largely to the writings of Albright and Wright.

The finds at Bethel (Beitin) were particularly important in
shaping Albright's views. The evidence discovered here was what
first led Albright to accept the late date for the main wave of
the Conquest. Here was evidence of "a tremendous conflagration"
which marked a complete break between Late Bronze and Iron Age
strata. Albright wrote of this break as so great "that no
bridge can be thrown across it, and we are compelled to identify
it with the Israelite conquest" (1934: 9-10).

Albright hesitated a great deal over the precise date for
the Israelite conquest of Bethel. He referred on various
occasions simply to a time in the 13th century BC (1934: 9; 1939:
17; 1957a: 212), though at one point he clearly preferred a date
in the first half of that century (1935a: 30), and even stated
that a "slightly earlier" date was possible (1935b: 13).

At Lachish (Tell ed-Duweir) there was similarly a destruction
accompanied by a great conflagration, which has been dated towards
the end of the 13th century (Vincent 1939: 419; Tufnell 1940: 22).
Albright arrived at a very precise date for this destruction,
deriving his conclusion from a small bowl bearing an Egyptian
hieratic inscription found in the remains of the last Canaanite
city. The inscription contains a reference to the fourth year
of a certain pharaoh, whom Albright believed to be Merneptah.
Albright took this inscription to indicate roughly the time of
the city's destruction, and therefore dated the fall of Lachish
into Israelite hands at 1231 BC or shortly after (1937: 24; 1939:
21; 1957a: 111; 1963: 27 - as late as 1220 BC). He wrote: "This
new evidence is, therefore, of decisive value for the question
of the date of the main phase of the Israelite conquest" (1937:
24).

Albright identified Tell Beit Mirsim as the site of Debir,
and dated the destruction of this Canaanite town to roughly the
same time as the fall of Lachish (1935b: 10; 1938b: 78; 1939: 23).

As was noted in the Introduction, in 1918 Albright argued
the case for a two-phase entry into Canaan, suggesting that the

Joseph tribes returned from Egypt much earlier than the tribes
led by Moses. He still held this view in 1935, when he appears
to have inclined to the idea that Jericho and Bethel were destroyed
by this group of earlier settlers, since he placed the fall of
Jericho c. 1360-1320 BC, the fall of Bethel c. 1300-1250 BC, the
taking of Sihon's territory at shortly before 1250 BC, and the
campaigns of Joshua in Palestine at c. 1235-1220 BC (1935b: 16-17,
table on 18).

However, with the Jericho problem becoming more obscure
after Kenyon's excavations, Albright seems to have preferred to
associate the fall of Bethel with the fall of Lachish and Debir,
c. 1230-1220 BC.

In 1955 he stated on the basis of ceramic evidence that the
end of Bethel preceded the fall of Lachish "by a respectable
interval", without specifying the length of this interval (1955:
16). In subsequent editions of the same work, we find the date
for the end of Lachish brought as low as 1220 BC; there is no
mention of by how far the fall of Bethel preceded this, the end
of that city being dated simply "in the thirteenth century"
(1963: 27). In the 1960 revised edition of *The Archaeology of
Palestine,* while it is stated that the fall of Bethel preceded
the end of Debir and Lachish, it is implied that the interval
may have been small; Albright mentions the possibility that
sherds found in the stratum which was destroyed could reflect "a
time decades before the final destruction". He offers no specific
date for the destruction, however, referring simply to "a date in
the thirteenth century" (1960: 108-9). In the full report of the
excavations, published in 1968, the end of Bethel is dated
"somewhere between c. 1240 and 1235 B.C." (Albright 1968a: 48).

Thus the destruction of Bethel has been brought roughly into
line with the destructions at Debir and Lachish; we find Bright
referring all three destructions to the latter half of the 13th
century (1972: 128), and Aharoni using all three destructions to
date "the main stage of the Israelite conquest" to the second
half of the 13th century (1957: 139); Kitchen and Mitchell
(1962: 215) similarly group these three cities together as sites
which "show evidence of clear destruction in the second half of
the thirteenth century BC" (cf. Kitchen 1966: 65-6, 67).

A fourth major site which shows evidence of violent
destruction and burning at roughly the same time is the northerly

site of Hazor, excavated in the 1950's and 1960's by Yigael Yadin.
Hazor had earlier been briefly excavated by Garstang, who dated
the end of the Canaanite city to c. 1400 BC, seeing this date,
like that at which he arrived for the end of Jericho, as
confirmation of the correctness of the date indicated for the
Exodus by I Kgs 6: 1 (cf. Yadin 1972: 27-8). But Yadin's
excavations and the reports published by him have turned Hazor
into another site supplying strong evidence for a Conquest in the
latter part of the 13th century BC (conveniently, Yadin 1967:
260).

In addition to Hazor, Bethel, Lachish and Debir, Eglon has
also been mentioned as providing evidence of violent destruction
towards the end of the 13th century (Campbell 1960: 12; Bright
1972: 129).

We must also note that the appearance of new settlements at
the beginning of the Iron Age (c. 1200 BC) at Ai, Gibeah, Mizpeh
and in Galilee, has been cited as evidence for the arrival of
the Israelites (Aharoni 1957: 136, 146-9).

A great deal is made of this material by proponents of the
13th century date for the Exodus and Conquest. We have already
noted Albright's assertion that the 13th century destruction at
Bethel marks a break so great that "we are compelled to identify
it with the Israelite conquest" (a claim which he repeated in
1968a: 32). Bright describes the archaeological evidence as
"very impressive", and asserts that it gives us "every right to
suppose that these destructions are to be connected with Israel"
(1972: 129). The destructions are spoken of in popular works as
the achievement of the Israelites as if there is no doubt about
the matter (e.g. Wright 1962a: 81-4), and the settlements which
appear in various parts of Palestine at the end of the 13th
century and the beginning of the 12th are described as "Israelite
settlements" (Aharoni 1957: 136); the strata which follow the
destruction layers at Debir and Lachish are also described as
the result of "Israelite settlement" (ibid: 139, 140), and the
culture which appears at many sites after the time of the
destructions is often described as "Israelite" (Albright 1933:
101ff; Wright 1941: 30-33; 1962a: 81, 88-9; Kitchen 1966: 68;
Bright 1972: 129).

The impression gained from such works, therefore, is that
the question is now quite firmly settled, that early Israelite

culture has been identified with certainty, that the arrival of
the Israelites can therefore be pinpointed with considerable
accuracy, and that the destruction of various cities towards the
end of the 13th century can be confidently attributed to the
Israelite Conquest of Canaan.

Yet despite the confidence with which many writers interpret
the archaeological evidence, there are factors which cast serious
doubt upon the commonly held view. When these factors are
considered together, the case for an Israelite Conquest of
Palestine towards the end of the 13th century is seen to be very
weak.

These factors may be considered under three headings.

1.2.1. The anomaly of Jericho and other cities

The correct date for the destruction of Canaanite Jericho
will be discussed at length in a later chapter. Here I wish to
concentrate on the difficulty posed by Jericho for the theory of
a 13th century Conquest.

Kenyon's excavations at Jericho have revealed no evidence
of occupation during the 13th century. Thus Jericho constitutes
an anomaly for the late date for the Exodus. At the time when
the cities discussed above were supposedly destroyed by the
Israelites, there was no city at Jericho for the Israelites to
destroy. The suggestion that a 13th century city did exist at
Jericho but has since been completely eroded away (Kenyon 1957:
262; Kitchen 1966: 62-3 with n.21) has against it the fact that
no silt survives as evidence of this erosion. The view of Noth
and others that the story of the Israelite capture of Jericho
is an aetiological legend, arising from the presence of a city
already desolated when the Israelites entered Canaan (Noth 1953:
21; 1960: 74, 149, n.2; Gray 1962: 93), is very difficult to
accept in view of the importance which the destruction of the
city has in the narrative. The fall of Jericho is placed in the
book of Joshua as the first major event following the crossing
of the Jordan, and much more space is devoted to relating it than
is devoted to the capture of any other city except Ai. This is
indeed strange if the event never really happened.

Moreover, Jericho is not the only city which poses this
kind of problem. The sites of Gibeon, Hebron, Arad and Hormah
all lack evidence for cities during the Late Bronze Age, as will

be shown in the discussions in Part Two. We will see there that over half of the confidently identified cities mentioned in the Conquest narratives were either not occupied or only very scantily occupied during the Late Bronze Age. Ai is also notoriously problematical, though the issues surrounding Ai are somewhat different from those surrounding the other cities just mentioned, since Ai's identification with et-Tell may turn out to be mistaken. This problem will also be explored in Part Two.

The fact that so many cities provide no evidence of destruction or even occupation in the 13th century BC raises the question of whether the Conquest of Canaan really occurred at that time. If we were to find an alternative period for the Conquest in which Jericho and the other cities mentioned above *all* showed signs of violent destruction, there would surely be a strong case for preferring that alternative to the 13th century date. Part Two will show that an alternative does exist in which only Ai (et-Tell) need be excepted from the list of destroyed cities.

1.2.2. *Alternative explanations for the 13th century destructions*

There is no evidence to prove that the cities which fell in the 13th century were Canaanite cities destroyed by the Israelites. H.J. Franken has pointed out that in none of the cases of destruction is there any certainty that Israel was responsible, and that there are various other possible explanations for the fall of these cities.

Among the possible causes, Franken lists "accidental fire, earthquake, a local attack from a hostile neighbouring city state, a band of marauders or an Egyptian raid" (1968: 5). The destruction of Debir may have resulted from the campaigns of the pharaoh Merneptah, and Lachish could have been destroyed either by Merneptah or by the invading Sea-peoples. Franken also points out that not all the cities which fell in the Late Bronze Age are cities mentioned in the Old Testament as being taken by Israel. "Of the destruction of the Late Bronze Age cities of Megiddo, c. 1050, Beisan (Beth-shan), c. 1150, Tell Qedah (Hazor), only the last is attributed to the Israelites" (ibid: 6).

Wood makes a similar case, suggesting that the Sea-peoples' incursions, the campaigns of Merneptah, and inter-city warfare should be considered as the possible causes of the destructions

of that time, rather than attacks by Israelites (1970: 75; cf.
Noth 1960: 82).

M. Weippert has also pointed out that there are many possible
explanations for the fall of cities in the decades around 1200 BC.
In addition to earthquake and accidental fire he mentions the high
probability that there was a "general state of war between the
city-states and the territorial states" throughout this period, in
view of the unstable political situation which had begun with the
upheavals of the Amarna age and had never really settled since
then (1971: 130-31). While he admits the possibility that
Israelites were involved in this warfare, he is concerned to
point out that the conflagration levels "could have been caused
by very different people who cannot be immediately identified
from the written sources" (ibid: 131).

There is certainly no shortage of alternative agents of
destruction at the end of the 13th and the beginning of the 12th
centuries BC. Not only do we have extra-biblical evidence for
campaigns by Egypt, attacks by the Sea-peoples, and a Philistine
invasion, but also references in the Bible itself to the fall of
many towns in inter-tribal warfare. For if the Exodus is placed
earlier than the 13th century BC, then the frequent destructions
of towns in that century and at the beginning of the 12th fall
in the period of the Judges. And in the book of Judges we read
frequently of cities being destroyed, sometimes burned, in the
period beginning with the first signs of Philistine aggression.
Twenty Ammonite cities fell to Jephthah's troops according to
Jdg 11: 33. In the war between Israel and the Benjaminites, the
city of Gibeah was captured, its people killed, and the place
set on fire (Jdg 20: 40). In the battles which followed, the
men of Israel carried out a purge against the Benjaminites, and
it is related: "All the towns which they found they set on fire"
(Jdg 20: 48).

It should be noted that the many cities destroyed in the
13th and 12th centuries do not, when considered objectively,
provide evidence for a main wave of attack at any particular
time, in spite of the fact that writers have spoken of a "main
wave of destruction" (Albright 1938a: 23) and of "the main stage
of the Israelite conquest" (Aharoni 1957: 139).

Objectively considered, the ceramic evidence from Bethel
does seem to indicate a date for the destruction of this town

somewhat earlier than the date assigned to the destructions at
Debir and Lachish /2/. While the destructions at Debir and
Lachish have both been assigned to c. 1230-1220 BC by Albright,
this is by no means a fixed conclusion. Kenyon has suggested
that Debir may have fallen as late as 1200 BC during a raid by
the Sea-peoples (1970: 214). Tufnell argued in 1953 that Lachish
may have been destroyed by the Philistines in the 12th century.
She associated with the destruction level an Egyptian scarab
attributed to Rameses III, c. 1180-1149 BC (1953: 46, 51; cf.1958:
37). Albright has replied that the object may be a scarab of
Rameses II (cf. Wright 1962a: 83, n.10), but this is by no means
certain. It is worth remembering that the hieratic inscription
on the bowl which is commonly assumed to refer to the fourth year
of Merneptah, could equally well refer to the fourth year of at
least two of Merneptah's successors (Wright 1962a: 82). And
even if it was known for certain to refer to Merneptah, it would
only establish a *terminus post quem* for the end of Lachish.
Tufnell clearly does not accept the attribution of the reference
to the reign of Merneptah, since she states that the site has
yielded "nothing to commemorate ... Merneptah" (1967: 302). In
1967 Tufnell repeated her assertion that the scarab mentioned
above belongs to Rameses III, and dated the fall of Lachish to
"some time during the first decades of the twelfth century B.C.",
suggesting that the destruction was the work of either the
Philistines or the Egyptians (ibid; cf. Kenyon 1970: 214-5;
de Vaux 1970: 77).

Concerning Eglon, we should note that the destruction of
Late Bronze Age Tell el-Hesy, with which this city is commonly
identified, cannot be dated with any precision, and in any case
it may be that Eglon should really be identified with Tell
en-Negileh (Lilley 1962: 337). This site shows little trace of
occupation during the 13th century, so that if Eglon is really
to be located here, it falls into the same class as the various
other cities mentioned above, where Late Bronze Age occupation
is either negligible or totally lacking.

While some writers have referred to the destruction of Late
Bronze Age Hazor as providing unambiguous evidence for the
campaigns of Joshua (e.g. Yamauchi 1973: 50; cf. de Vaux 1965:
27), even here the picture is really by no means clear cut. For
though Yadin (1972: 132, n.1) insists that the Late Bronze Age
city fell in the second half of the 13th century, Aharoni (1970:
263) considers a date early in the 12th century possible.

V. Fritz has recently argued, on the basis of Woolley's chronology
for Mycenaean pottery, that Late Bronze Age Hazor was destroyed
c. 1200-1190 BC, and that the Sea-peoples, not the Israelites,
were its destroyers (Fritz 1973: 123-39).

It should be noted that various destructions did occur in
the 12th century, e.g. at Beth-shan, c. 1150 BC, and that there
is nothing to distinguish the second half of the 13th century
as the time of a "main wave of destruction"; throughout the 14th,
13th and 12th centuries there were periodic destructions of
cities in Palestine. Furthermore, no cultural change occurred
in the second half of the 13th century which could be said to
definitely attest the arrival of the Israelites at that time, as
we shall now see.

1.2.3. *The subjective identification of "Israelite" culture*

Bright, while admitting that we have "no absolute proof"
that Israel was the foe which destroyed the Palestinian cities
discussed above, adds:

> "But the fact that several of these destructions (Hazor,
> Bethel, Debir) were followed at no great interval by poor
> settlements of a sort typical of earliest Israel, as well
> as the fact that in the same period new settlements of
> essentially identical character were springing up in
> various parts of the central mountain range, gives us every
> right to suppose that these destructions are to be connected
> with Israel" (1972: 129).

This statement actually contains a piece of circular
reasoning, since the affirmation that certain settlements were
"of a sort typical of earliest Israel" is itself the product of
an assumption that the arrival of the Israelites should be dated
to this period.

The most striking difference between the culture which
precedes the destruction levels and that which follows them is
the comparative poverty of the latter. This poorer culture has
been taken as evidence for the arrival of the Israelites, since
it is assumed that, having lived a nomadic or semi-nomadic
existence since leaving Egypt, they would have possessed a low
standard of culture compared with that of the Canaanites
(Albright 1933: 101ff; Wright 1941: 30-33; 1962a: 81, 88-9;
Kitchen 1966: 68).

H.J. Franken has warned, however, against associating the
appearance of this poorer culture with the arrival of the
Israelites, or indeed with the arrival of any new ethnic group.
He writes: "... Shabby rebuilding of a flourishing Late Bronze
Age town cannot be taken as proof of the presence of Hebrews.
If the population of a town is practically decimated during a
destruction ... it may take more than one generation before
the survivors have even rebuilt their defences" (1968: 5).

Weippert has also urged caution in interpreting the cultural
decline which took place at the end of the Bronze Age. "One
cannot simply conclude from such a change in material culture,"
he writes, "that a change in population has taken place ...".
"The cause of the cultural decline here is not to be sought
primarily in population upheavals so that the anti-civilisation
nomadism of the 'Israelite' immigrants into Palestine is regarded
as responsible for the primitive wall and pottery techniques of
Iron I" (1971: 132). He points out that "the deterioration in
the material culture of Palestine, which led eventually to the
state of affairs in the First Iron Age, had already begun in the
Late Bronze Age ..." (ibid: 133). Kenyon also remarks that "the
biggest change" in culture occurred c. 1400 BC, with the
transition from LB I to LB II, when there was "a marked
deterioration". But "there is no complete break" within the
period 1400-1200 BC. Kenyon suggests that Israelite settlers
adopted the culture of the settled population, with the result
that their arrival is not reflected in the archaeological record
(Kenyon 1970: 209).

Weippert sees no need to look beyond a simultaneous
collapse of political and economic stability for an explanation
of the cultural decline which is apparent in the decades around
1200 BC. Weippert actually believes that a collapse of the
city-state system made possible "the infiltration of nomads who
later ... formed the confederacy of the twelve tribes of Israel..."
(1971: 133). He denies, however, that the arrival of nomads
caused the collapse. The present writer, on the other hand,
believes that the infiltration of the tribes which became Israel
occurred not after the period of collapse at the end of the
Bronze Age, but at least two centuries before. In the view
offered in the present work, this period of collapse is
included in the period on which the book of Judges is a
commentary. It is the period of Ammonite and Philistine
encroachments (Jdg 10: 7), and of internecine strife between

tribes and cities (Jdg 19-20), which began c. 1200 BC, resulting
in the chaotic situation in which, in the words of the editor of
the book of Judges, "every man did what was right in his own
eyes" (Jdg 21: 25).

Weippert proceeds to a criticism of the interpretation
placed on the appearance of new pottery types. Albright and
Aharoni both associate the appearance of what has become known
as Collared Rim Ware with the arrival of the Israelites, and
consequently describe it as "Israelite" pottery (Aharoni 1957:
136, 146, 149; Albright 1960: 118). But Weippert points to
instances in which the appearance of a new pottery type
definitely does not indicate the arrival of a new ethnic group
("No one will want to deduce from the extremely numerous
imitations of Mycenaean ring ware in Palestine that there had
been a 'Mycenaean invasion'"), and remarks that it appears to
him "very dubious" whether Collared Rim Ware is to be associated
with the Israelites, especially since "the same type is also
found in Megiddo, which remained Canaanite till as late as the
tenth century ...". He suggests therefore that "we are surely
dealing here with a particular fashion of the Early Iron Age"
(1971: 134 and references there; for biblical references to
Megiddo, see Jdg 1: 27, I Kgs 9: 15; cf. Yadin 1960a: 62-8
Kenyon 1964: 143-151).

Writing of the lack of real evidence for the arrival of the
Israelites at the end of the Bronze Age, Franken has remarked
that without the thesis which makes the 13th century the time
of the Conquest of Canaan by Israel,

"no archaeologist would have had any reason to suppose that
the thirteenth century B.C. in Palestine saw the birth of a
new nation which came to its fullest development about the
end of the eleventh century B.C. With one exception there
is no evidence, in the proper sense of the word, that a new
ethnic group was taking over power in the land at this time"
(1968: 4; cf. de Vaux 1970: 78).

The exception to which he refers is the chain of small
settlements found by Aharoni in the southern part of Upper
Galilee. These are dated to the start of the Iron Age and "seem
to be distinctive of a new group of settlers" (Franken 1968: 7).
Concerning the identity of these settlers, Franken remarks that
"there seems at least to be no alternative rival identification

to that of the Hebrew tribes", but at the same time admits that
"their identity cannot yet be fixed on internal evidence ..."
(ibid).

Weippert similarly refers to these settlements as "the only
archaeological fact which can, with a great degree of probability,
be connected with the settlement of the 'Israelite' tribes", but
he adds: "... Here too, one cannot decide definitely in individual
cases whether we are dealing with an 'Israelite' village or a
Canaanite one; but there is, nevertheless, a stronger probability
in favour of 'Israelites'" (1971: 135).

However, when one looks at the results of the excavations at
these Galilee settlements, one finds nothing whatever to justify
this claim of a "stronger probability in favour of the 'Israelites'".
Aharoni actually uses the results of the Galilee survey to
illustrate his thesis that "the Israelites did not bring a
consolidated tradition of material culture with them.   Instead,
they borrowed everything from the previous inhabitants" (1967:
219).   He asserts that when they first arrived in Canaan,
Israelite craftsmen imitated Canaanite products, and says: "This
phenomenon was quite apparent in the Galilee survey" (ibid: 220).
He compares vessels from these settlements, and similar vessels
from the so-called "earliest Israelite occupation at Hazor"
(Stratum XII), with the vessels of the Canaanite culture which
preceded them (from Strata XIV-XIII at Hazor), and shows that
although there are some differences between vessels from the two
phases, these are comparatively minor, and that *in form* the
so-called "Israelite" cooking pots and storage jars exactly
resemble their "Canaanite" predecessors (ibid).

It is interesting to note Franken's own recent comments on
Aharoni's view.   Franken points out that such reasoning is
circular, being based on two assumptions which have nothing to
do with the archaeological material in which the argument is
ostensibly grounded; these are: that the Israelites came with no
consolidated tradition of material culture, and that they came
in the second half of the 13th century BC.   He adds: "No invasion
can be 'proved' archaeologically if it does not leave traces in
the soil ....   A decline in the quality of the potter's product
does not necessarily point to invasions.   Archaeology is completely
silent about invasions in the second half of the thirteenth
century B.C." (1976: 7-8).

The pottery evidence from Hazor has also been discussed by
J.B. Pritchard, who compares the Iron Age forms with those of the
Late Bronze Age and concludes, like Aharoni, that no real
discontinuity can be detected. He then adds this point: "When
we compare the more specialized articles of cultic use - a
sensitive area where one would normally expect to find a definite
break in continuity - the picture is essentially the same"
(1965: 320). Pritchard's conclusion is therefore as follows:
"Thus at the one site where there is good evidence for a fairly
continuous occupation throughout Late Bronze and Iron I, there
seems to be a continuity in the assemblages of artifacts. Those
who built after the destruction of Stratum XIII may have been
poorer than their predecessors, but exhibited basically the same
ceramic technology and the same traditions in the making of
cultic articles" (ibid: 321).

Therefore we find in effect that so-called "Israelite"
vessels are nothing other than primitive versions of the previous
forms, and we may question whether this constitutes evidence for
a newly-arrived group of settlers at all, let alone for the
arrival of Israelites. It is surely quite conceivable that
after the destruction of a major city like Hazor (from whatever
cause), the survivors would found new settlements on the site and
in the neighbouring regions, and that these settlements would
display a culture which at first would be an impoverished
variation on the one possessed previously.

Finally we may note the view put forward by Mendenhall and
Callaway, that destructions commonly attributed to the
Israelites, and the culture commonly assumed to reflect the
Israelite arrival, should in fact be associated with other
peoples who arrived, according to the view of these writers,
before the Israelite settlement took place.

Mendenhall has suggested that some of the peoples which the
Israelites discovered to be in occupation of Canaan when they
arrived had, in fact, only entered the land themselves a short
while before. He relates the appearance of these groups to the
movement of Sea-peoples which, he points out, should be viewed
as a general movement of many different groups into Palestine
from regions further north, only a few actually moving south by
sea, the majority migrating over land (1973: ch.6). Mendenhall
considers it a probability that the biblical Hivites were one
of these groups, and that they came from Cilicia (biblical *Kue* or
Quwe, I Kgs 10: 28; cf. Callaway 1968: 318).

Callaway has suggested that these Hivites, and not Israelite settlers, were responsible for "the cluster of villages in the region that has been associated with Benjamin" (1968: 318). He also suggests that Iron Age I settlements at et-Tell, Tell en-Nasbeh and Gibeon were established by these people rather than by Israelites as was previously assumed by Aharoni (Aharoni 1957: 136, 146-9).

Callaway rejects the notion that the earliest Iron Age culture at et-Tell should be attributed to the Israelites, saying: "There seems to be increasing evidence pointing to an origin in the direction of Anatolia instead of Egypt, and it is not improbable that the settlers may be traced eventually to Luwian antecedents" (1970: 19). He adds that the archaeological material from the first Iron Age stratum at et-Tell "seems to complement" Mendenhall's theory concerning the Hivites, which was arrived at on linguistic grounds (ibid; cf. 1968: 317-19).

Callaway also rejects Albright's picture of the Late Bronze Age cities falling before the invading Israelites, suggesting that "Late Bronze Bethel, isolated from the centers of power, could very well have fallen before the onslaught of these pre-Israelite invaders, who resettled it with the same crude culture found at the other sites mentioned" - i.e. et-Tell, Tell en-Nasbeh and Gibeon (1968: 318). He also writes: "I think we can no longer take for granted that the conquest of Canaan by invading Israelites accounts for the Late Bronze destructions of Bethel, Lachish, Tell Beit Mirsim, or Hazor. The conquest was more complex than we have assumed, because there were other people moving into Palestine at the same time the Israelites found it expedient to infiltrate the land ..." (ibid: 320). (Callaway actually thinks that the Israelites may have been responsible for the *Phase II* Iron Age culture at et-Tell (ibid: 319).)

It is clear that Callaway also rejects the view of Aharoni, Franken, Weippert and Yadin/3/ that the Galilee settlements should be described as Israelite, since he writes of "the presence of an Iron Age I people in Upper Galilee who preceded the Israelites at Hazor" (1969: 9).

It is quite apparent from this disagreement among scholars and archaeologists that there is no way whatever in which "Israelite" culture can be distinguished in the decades around 1200 BC. It is doubtful whether the decline observable during that period should be interpreted in terms of the arrival of new

groups at all. But even if a new group is postulated to explain
the appearance of certain settlements, it is perfectly clear that
there is no evidence to link those settlements with the arrival
of "Israelites". Settlements which Aharoni confidently describes
as "Israelite", Callaway ascribes to the Hivites or other (on his
view) "pre-Israelite" groups. Destructions which Albright and
others confidently attribute to the Israelites, others attribute
to Egyptians, Sea-peoples, Philistines, inter-city warfare and
other causes.

Before concluding this discussion something must be said
of the view of Callaway, Mendenhall and Campbell concerning the
date and nature of the Conquest. These writers prefer to date
the Conquest in the 12th century rather than the 13th, in
keeping with the view that the Iron Age I cultures of the 13th
century are pre-Israelite. A precise date for the Conquest has
not yet been offered in connection with this view, but Campbell
has remarked that Mendenhall's interpretation of the
archaeological evidence will probably require a lowering of the
currently popular 13th century date "to the point where the
conquest/settlement is placed around 1200 B.C. or even a bit
later" (Campbell 1975: 153). Callaway simply says that the
Israelite attack on the Iron Age I settlement at et-Tell "probably
occurred in the twelfth century B.C." (Callaway 1969: 5).

It should be noted firstly that since it is not yet possible
to identify Israelite culture, there is no more evidence for
this view than there is for the currently popular one. Secondly,
this later dating runs into difficulties with the so-called Israel
Stele of Merneptah (to be discussed in the next chapter), which
shows the Israelites to have been in Palestine by c. 1220 BC at
the latest. Thirdly, the view of Mendenhall, Callaway and
Campbell cannot be supported at all from the biblical traditions.

This last point has already been made in the Introduction to
this work in connection with Mendenhall's general theory. A
further aspect of the problem can be noted here. We may recall
that Mendenhall's theory concerns a peasant revolt against the
city-state ruling establishment, rather than a conquest of the
country by a group of invaders. As Campbell has pointed out,
there is no reason why there should have been any destruction
of the cities freed from the ruling establishment, since many
who lived in those cities were now the victors wanting to
return to their homes (Campbell 1975: 152). The deliberate and

widespread destruction of cities therefore finds no place in
this view of the "Conquest". Yet this is precisely what
characterises the Conquest as it is related in the biblical
traditions. In the view of the present writer, this drastic
discrepancy between the Mendenhall-Campbell concept of the
"Conquest" and the picture offered by the biblical traditions
poses a major problem for the former, since it is difficult to
envisage how or why the traditions should have achieved their
present form if they really arose from events totally different
from the ones they relate.

In Callaway's view, however, Ai provides an exception to
the general rule concerning the non-destruction of cities.
Callaway notes that the first phase of the Iron Age village at
et-Tell was destroyed some time in the 12th century, and he
relates this destruction to the Israelite assault on Ai described
in Jos 8 (Callaway 1968: 317ff.; 1969: 5). At first sight this
may seem to be a point in favour of a 12th century date for the
Conquest, the evidence of Merneptah's Stele notwithstanding.
Placing the Conquest in the 12th century BC seems to provide
archaeological evidence for the capture of Ai, something which
every other theory has so far failed to do.

However, two points should be noted here. Firstly, it is
extremely subjective to assume the basic historicity of the
account of Ai's capture and destruction merely because
archaeological evidence happens to be available, when Mendenhall's
view of the "Conquest", which Callaway accepts, denies the basic
historicity of the Conquest traditions as a whole.

Further, Callaway's position is not merely subjective but
also rather illogical. Following Mendenhall, he views the
Israelite "Conquest" as in the main a process of "political
integration" with the Iron Age I inhabitants of Canaan, not an
attempt to destroy Canaanite strongholds (Callaway 1968: 319).
He thus prefers a later dating of the "Conquest" to the one
arrived at by linking it with the destructions of various Late
Bronze Age cities. The destruction of the Iron Age I village
at et-Tell is therefore the one fact which appears to support
Callaway's dating of the Conquest/settlement, but it is at the
same time a major anomaly for the theory from which he arrives
at that dating.

More importantly, Callaway's claim that the archaeological
evidence from Iron Age et-Tell supports "the essential

historicity" of the conquest of Ai (1968: 320), is open to serious
question. Just how strong is the evidence for identifying this
Iron Age I village as the Ai destroyed by Joshua?

In 1965 Callaway wrote that both phases of Iron Age
occupation at et-Tell "seem to have been terminated by abandonment
of the village. There is *no extensive evidence of burning or
violent destruction* of either phase" (1965: 27; emphasis mine).
He concluded at that time: "Nothing in the present evidence
warrants an identification of the *[Iron Age]* village with the city
of Ai captured by Joshua as described in Joshua 8: 1-29" (ibid:
27-8). But in his report of the 1966 excavations, Callaway wrote:
"My study of the problem ... leads to the conclusion that the
biblical conquest of Ai was a conquest of the small, unfortified
Iron Age I village on the acropolis at Et-Tell" (1969: 5). Yet in
this report he mentions no new evidence which has led him to this
conclusion. It is true that he refers his readers to his article
"New Evidence on the Conquest of Ai" which appeared in 1968, but
this article similarly gives no compelling reason for preferring
Callaway's later theory to his earlier negative statement. While
he refers in it to "some evidence of burning" in Area B XV on the
tell (1968: 320), this contrast with his previous statement
appears to be the result of a reinterpretation of the evidence
rather than of the discovery of new evidence. Callaway's 1965
statement that there was "no *extensive* evidence of burning or
violent destruction" (emphasis mine) implies that there was *some*
evidence of burning known at that time, and there is no reason to
believe that the evidence referred to in the 1968 article is
additional evidence. Indeed, it appears to be quite unextensive,
pertaining to a single building (ibid). In other words, Callaway's
earlier statement that there is "no extensive evidence of burning
or violent destruction" of either phase of et-Tell's Iron Age
village still appears to be true. Yet Jos 8: 28 records that Ai
was completely destroyed by burning.

The account in Jos 7-8 also requires that Ai was a fortified
city, while Callaway admits that the Iron Age village was
unfortified. In order to make his identification more plausible,
Callaway makes the strange assertion that "There is actually no
demand for fortifications in the conquest accounts" (1968: 320).
The only support he adduces for this claim is the fact that the
LXX substitutes the word "pit" for the MT's reference to the city
gate in Jos 8: 29. The LXX reading actually makes better sense
than the MT here, for at this point in the narrative we would not

expect a reference to the gate of the city; the previous verse has related the razing of the whole city. It should be noted, however, that in 7: 5 the LXX agrees with the MT in referring to the city gate. It is a clear implication of the account that the Ai attacked by Joshua was a walled stronghold rather than an open village.

I am forced to conclude, therefore, that there is no reason to date the Conquest in the 12th century BC. Evidence from et-Tell does not support such a date, since it is not clear that there was a deliberate destruction of the Iron Age village at that time.

1.2.4. Conclusion

In conclusion, we must say that the archaeology of Palestine for the 13th and 12th centuries provides no convincing evidence for a conquest or settlement of the land by incoming Israelites during that period. To interpret what evidence there is in terms of an Israelite settlement of the land involves a large subjective element and risks becoming a circular argument (i.e. dependent on a prior assumption that the Exodus and Conquest should be dated to the 13th-12th centuries BC).

The interpretation of the archaeological material which this section has been criticising could only be justified if there were other pieces of evidence for an Exodus in the 13th century. Yet we saw in the preceding section (1.1) that the information contained in Ex 1: 11 does not provide such evidence. We must now examine other factors which have been said to point towards a 13th century Exodus, to discover whether they in turn carry the weight which has been attached to them.

CHAPTER 2:
OTHER ARGUMENTS USED TO SUPPORT THE THIRTEENTH CENTURY DATE

Chapter 2: Other Arguments Used to Support The Thirteenth Century Date

2.1 *The Archaeology of Transjordan*

In the book of Numbers we find it related that prior to entering Canaan the tribes which had left Egypt attempted to pass through Edom. We read that Moses sent messengers from Kadesh to the king of Edom requesting permission to traverse his territory. The king was assured that the migrating tribes would keep strictly to the route known as the King's Highway (Num 20: 17), but he refused the Israelites access to his land.

Next we read how Balak, king of Moab, attempted to have the wandering tribes cursed by Balaam, in order that he might "defeat them and drive them from the land" (Num 22: 6).

These events transpired in regions east of the Jordan. But it has been alleged that these areas show a complete lack of sedentary occupation from *c.* 1900 BC until *c.* 1300 BC. Nelson Glueck's surface explorations led him to assert that if their passage through Transjordan had taken place before the 13th century, the migrating Israelites would have come across no people who could have withheld permission to traverse the land; his archaeological discoveries resulted in the conclusion that the region had had only nomadic or semi-nomadic occupation for the five or six centuries before Iron Age I (Glueck 1935: 138; 1939: 268; 1940: 114, 125-47; 1967: 434, 436). In terms of archaeological periods, the gap in occupation affirmed by Glueck extended from the end of Middle Bronze I, through Middle Bronze IIB-C, and through the whole of the Late Bronze Age.

Adherents of the 13th century date for the Exodus therefore argue that the detour made by the Israelites around the regions of

Edom and Moab must have taken place some time after 1300 BC
(Wright 1945: 40; Rowley 1950: 20-22; van Zyl 1960: 109, n.2,
112; Kitchen and Mitchell 1962: 215; Kitchen 1966: 61; Harrison
1970: 323- 4; Bright 1972: 121).

This argument for the 13th century date only holds if the
following three assumptions are correct: (a) that the accounts
in Num 20ff are historical, (b) that those accounts, if
historical, require the existence of a sedentary population
settled in permanent towns at the time of the Israelite
migration, and (c) that Glueck's interpretation of the
archaeological material is correct. A consideration of this
argument must undertake an examination of these assumptions.

The present writer does not doubt the basic historicity of
the Numbers accounts. The very existence of such traditions
seems to require that the migrating Israelites came into
conflict with other peoples who obstructed their progress
through the territory east of the Jordan. There are, however,
certain features in the accounts as they now stand which should
possibly be regarded as later accretions to the original
traditions.

J.R. Bartlett has remarked on the fact "the tradition of
Israel's contact with Edom appears vague in the extreme when
compared with the traditions of Israel's contact with the
Moabites and with such kings as Balak and Sihon" (1972: 27).
Bartlett (who considers that the Exodus "perhaps belongs to the
thirteenth century B.C.", ibid: 26) also notes elsewhere that
certain details of the narrative of Num 20: 14ff, "such as Edom's
brotherhood with Israel and Kadesh's situation on the border of
Edom, may reflect a later period than the thirteenth century B.C.,
and the king of Edom, who is unnamed, is a very shadowy figure
who has disappeared from the narrative by verse 18" (1973: 232).
Bartlett and others have also argued that the victory song of
Num 21: 27-30 applies to a victory over the Amorites in a
period later than the time of the migration from Egypt, and is
therefore not in its correct historical setting as it now stands
(cf. Bartlett 1969b: 94ff; also de Vaux 1971: 522-7). In view
of such arguments, the historicity of the narratives in Numbers
20ff should perhaps be held with certain reservations. Events
of periods subsequent to the Israelite migration *may* have
influenced the present form of the narratives, but the evidence
does not justify dogmatism /1/.

Secondly we must ask whether these narratives, given that
they have a basic historical core, require a permanent urban
population in Transjordan at the time of the events related.
De Vaux and J. Rea have both suggested that the answer is no.
De Vaux points out that the kings mentioned in Num 20ff. could
have been the chiefs of nomadic or semi-nomadic groups rather than
the rulers of fortified cities or permanently held territories.
He draws attention to the fact that the nomadic Midianites have
kings in Num 31: 8 and Jdg 8: 12, and that the Amalekites have a
king in I Sam 15: 8ff. He also points out that semi-nomadic
tent-dwelling kings are known from other historical texts from
the Near East (de Vàux 1971: 368, 481). It is therefore possible
that the kings we read of in Num 20ff were chieftains of
semi-nomadic groups who refused to let another nomadic group, the
Israelites, pass through their areas of pasturage.

It must not be assumed that the references to cities in these
narratives refer always to permanent fortified sites. References
to cities actually occur only in Num 21: 25-7 and 22: 36. The
former verses refer to "all the cities of the Amorites", and in
particular to Heshbon as "the city of Sihon", while the latter
speaks of a single "city of Moab". Rea has pointed out that the
word usually translated as "city", ʻîr, need not always indicate
a large fortified town (1961: 5-6). The same word is used to
describe the temporary Israelite settlement at Kadesh in Num 20:
16, and in Num 13: 19 Moses sends men to spy out the Negeb to see
whether its people are weak or strong, "whether the cities [ʻàrîm]
that they dwell in are camps or strongholds". It would appear that
in Num 21: 25 "all the cities of the Amorites" is synonymous with
"Heshbon and its villages". The distinction made in the latter
phrase does imply that Heshbon, "the city of Sihon" (verse 26),
was much more significant than its daughter settlements (benōṭeyhā).
As will be mentioned shortly, Heshbon is one site where current
discoveries are changing the picture of an occupational gap
between Middle Bronze I and the Iron Age.

There is no reason why the peoples who obstructed the passage
of the Israelites through Transjordan should not have been nomadic
or semi-nomadic groups. In Ex 17 we find an example of a nomadic
group, the Amalekites, opposing the progress of the Israelites,
and in Num 14: 25 the presence of Amalekites in the hill-country
is given as part of the reason why Yahweh commanded the
Israelites to change their direction of march from north to south
(cf. G.M. Landes 1962: 101)

Traditions preserved in Gen 36: 12, 16 and I Chr I: 36 trace back Amalekite origins to the early ancestry of the Edomites, implying that their original habitat lay in the land of Edom. In view of this, we may perhaps be correct to summarise Ex 17: 8-16, Num 14 and Num 20: 14ff. by saying that the Israelites found their progress barred, both west and east of the Dead Sea, by groups of semi-nomads which were somehow related to each other, and which were anxious to guard their joint monopoly of the pastureland of the area and also perhaps certain caravan routes.

In addition to Bartlett's reservations concerning Num 20:14ff. already mentioned, we may note that nothing in that narrative requires a settled status for the Edomites. The nomadic or semi-nomadic character of the Moabites at the time of the Israelite migration is attested in the narratives themselves. Thus we find Moabites in the area around Shittim in Num 25: 1, while according to Num 21: 24 the territory north of the Arnon was not Moabite but Amorite until the Israelite defeat of Sihon (cf. also Num 22: 36). In Jdg 3: 12-13 the Moabites may still be only semi-sedentary; they temporarily occupy the area of Jericho along with bands of Amalekites and Ammonites.

The narratives concerning the kingdoms of Sihon and Og contain no such hints of a semi-nomadic status for the peoples of those kings, and it is precisely as we move northward into their territory that archaeological evidence for sedentary occupation during the Middle and Late Bronze Ages begins to emerge.

Thus we arrive at an examination of Glueck's conclusions based on his own surface surveys of Transjordan.

Those conclusions now seem to require considerable modification. It is beginning to appear that the complete break in sedentary occupation which Glueck says persisted for several centuries until the start of the Iron Age may not have existed, at least not throughout southern Transjordan as a whole. Certain finds made since Glueck first arrived at this conclusion concerning the occupation gap have led a number of recent writers to reject it.

Several tombs from Middle Bronze II have been discovered near Amman,and, about two miles outside of Amman, a temple which has yielded a considerable amount of Late Bronze Age pottery. Other discoveries include Middle Bronze tomb groups at Mt Nebo and

Naur and a Late Bronze tomb at Madaba (cf. G.L. Harding 1958:
7-18; J.B. Hennessy 1966: 155-62; Campbell and Wright 1969:
104-16; J. Sapin 1974: 558-65).

G.L. Harding has commented that such finds suggest very
strongly

> "that this part of the country at least was not deserted
> and unoccupied during the Middle and Late Bronze Ages....
> There is no doubt that surface surveys [such as Glueck's]
> can be very deceptive; indeed, if we were to try and
> deduce the history of occupation of Amman from a
> collection of surface sherds, we should say without
> hesitation that it had not been occupied before the
> Iron Age, for there are no surface remains earlier than
> this to be seen.... So perhaps we should consider the
> case for non-occupation, at least of the kingdom of
> Ammon, during the eighteenth to thirteenth centuries
> B.C. as not proven" (1958: 12).

Elsewhere he says that as far as Ammon is concerned, "there
was a sedentary population during the Hyksos phase of the Middle
Bronze, for large family tombs well equipped with burial objects,
such as those found at Amman and Naur, are not the work of nomads"
(1959: 33). Harding also expressed a conviction that the Amman
temple could not have been the work of nomads (1958: 12).

Not all scholars agree with Harding's assessment, however.
Glueck himself asserted in 1967 that the Middle Bronze tombs
could have belonged to nomadic peoples (1967: 444), and Campbell
and Wright have suggested that the Amman temple was constructed
by "nomads or semi-nomads", possibly as the centre for a tribal
league structured by a covenant, "not unlike Israel of the
pre-monarchic period..." (Campbell and Wright 1969: 111, 116).
These two writers also comment: "Excavation in Amman proper and
at Heshbon will probably end by introducing one or two permanent
settlements into the picture, but the period still presents
itself as primarily one of semi-nomadic peoples without permanent
settlements" (ibid: 116).

We should note that Glueck himself modified his conclusions
shortly before his death. In the first edition of his *The Other
Side of the Jordan,* he affirmed that in Transjordan after about

1900 BC, "Permanent villages and fortresses were no longer to
rise upon the earth in this region till the beginning of the
Iron Age" (1940: 114). But sweeping statements like this are
absent from the second edition, where Glueck admits that his
original conclusion was too radical, and accepts a suggestion
offered by Albright in 1943. At that time Albright pointed out
that if the population of the area east of the Jordan was
concentrated in walled towns during the Middle Bronze II and
Late Bronze periods, "sherds belonging to the 17th-15th centuries
would be buried in the accumulating debris inside the walls and
would seldom appear on either surface or slopes of a site. The
relative paucity of sherds would then find a simple explanation
- the decrease of public security in the Hyksos age" (Albright
1943: 17, n.77a). Glueck's revised opinion was therefore that
between *c*. 1900 BC and *c*. 1300 BC the population of Transjordan
may have been concentrated in fortified towns instead of being
distributed also among unwalled settlements (Glueck 1970: 141;
for a criticism of Albright's suggestion, see Thompson 1974: 193).

D.M. Beagle, reviewing the second edition of Glueck's book,
has commented: "The 1968 excavations at Tell Hesban [Heshbon]
support this conclusion. In Area B, supervised by the reviewer,
some Late Bronze sherds (including a beautiful piece of
Mycenaean pottery) were found in layers of earthen fill. Although
these were laid down much later, they indicate, as future
campaigns will show, that the site was occupied by people of
some culture during the Late Bronze period" (Beagle 1971: 580;
cf. also Bartlett 1973: 231).

In view of the numerous discoveries which have now been made
in Transjordan pertaining to the Middle and Late Bronze Age
periods (for recent extensive listings see J. Sapin 1974: 558-65;
Thompson 1974: 194, n.37), it is hardly surprising that many
scholars are now rejecting Glueck's previous conclusions. Thus
Kenyon describes the occupational gap envisaged by Glueck as
"a most unlikely state of affairs" (Kenyon 1966b: 64), S. Mittmann
has said he is convinced that a careful re-examination of Glueck's
work would invalidate his conclusions (Mittmann 1970: 221, n.32),
and T.L. Thompson writes: "... That the population of Transjordan
during the Middle and Late Bronze Periods was nomadic is doubtful;
that Transjordan was totally without a settled population is
unquestionably false" (1974: 193).

On the other hand, others are more cautious. Thus we may
recall the comment of Campbell and Wright, that although "one or

two" permanent settlements may be coming to light, "the period
still presents itself as primarily one of semi-nomadic peoples..."
(Campbell and Wright 1969: 116). And Bartlett, after describing
some recent Late Bronze finds, comments that "it is as yet an
open question how far these finds modify Glueck's views..."
(1973: 231).

At the very least we can say that the situation was by no
means as clear-cut as Glueck maintained, and that the evidence
now makes the occupational gap theory very questionable. A
detailed re-examination of the whole problem is clearly very
necessary, as Glueck's work apparently resulted in misleading
conclusions. In one area where a systematic survey has
recently been carried out (Northern Transjordan), S. Mittmann
found plenty of evidence which alters the picture presented by
Glueck. From Middle Bronze II, Mittmann's survey found eight
sites in the basin south of the Yarmuk, six on the west flank
of Mt Ajlun, and four on the south and south-east flanks of the
mountain, as well as further traces of occupation in this
period from just above the Jordan valley; and the same area
yielded almost as many Late Bronze I-II sites, except in the
region west of Ajlun (Mittmann 1970; cf. Sapin 1974: 564-5;
Thompson 1974: 193-4). All these sites were missed in Glueck's
survey. Many of the sites visited by Glueck were investigated
only briefly, and Thompson has pointed out the striking fact
that at certain sites where Glueck's investigation was more
intensive than usual, the search often turned up sherds from the
Middle Bronze II and Late Bronze periods (cf. Thompson 1974: 193,
n.36; also 194, n.37 for a list of references to sites from the
Middle and Late Bronze periods mentioned by Glueck himself).

H.J. Franken and W.J.A. Power have recently shown from
another point of view that Glueck's pottery study and the
conclusions drawn from it "are in many ways both defective and
misleading" (Franken and Power 1971: 119). They point out that
Glueck published only those pottery shapes that were familiar
to him,

> "even in cases where he picked up unknown shapes in the
> areas immediately adjacent to Palestine, i.e. in the
> eastern Ghor and in Ammon. Those shapes that he did not
> recognize he omitted from publication, which is a curious
> procedure, for a survey of a largely unknown area ought to
> reveal and indeed to stress the new and the unknown rather
> than to emphasize the known" (ibid).

It appears that Glueck did not anticipate developments in
Transjordanian pottery forms which would differ from the
Palestinian ones. Franken and Power subsequently quote two
lengthy passages by Glueck concerning the gap in occupation;
they then comment: "From these statements it is clear that
Glueck assumed that he would have recognised Transjordanian
Middle Bronze IIB, IIC and Late Bronze shapes had he found them.
From what has already been said it is no longer clear that this
assumption can be accepted without question" (ibid: 122).

In view of all that has been said above, we may conclude
that there is no compelling reason to place the events of Num
20 ff. after 1300 BC. It is by no means certain that the
narratives refer to permanent kingdoms; it is especially doubtful
that they do in the cases of Edom and Moab. And a great deal of
evidence is available which suggests that north of the areas
occupied by the Edomites (if 20: 14ff. be historical) and
Moabites, the gap in occupation posited by Glueck never occurred.

2.2 *The Military Campaigns of Seti I and Rameses II*

Another argument used by advocates of the 13th century date
for the Exodus is that if the Israelites were in Palestine
before the start of the 13th century, we would find some
reference in the book of Judges to the campaigns made into
Palestine by the pharaohs Seti I and Rameses II. That there are
no such references has been taken to indicate that the Israelites
did not enter Palestine until after these campaigns, and therefore
not until the second half of the 13th century (e.g. Burney 1919a:
93-4; cf. Rowley 1950: 28-31).

The lengthy reply to this argument given by Jack (1925:
59-80) is now largely obsolete. Jack argued that the campaigns
of Seti I and Rameses II were limited in aims and scope; that
they were directed against territory north of Palestine, not at
Palestine itself (cf. Wood 1970: 77-8, where similar arguments
are offered), and that the Egyptian armies travelled to their
goal along the coastal plain, never through permanently settled
Israelite territory (Jack 1925: 70-79). Jack also suggested
that in some cases the records left by these pharaohs were simply
boastful concoctions, with little relation to the ruler's actual
achievements (ibid: 61-65).

Several items of archaeological and literary evidence now
make such a view quite untenable. Archaeological finds in

Palestine now make Jack's scepticism of the Egyptian records
impossible to maintain. Excavations at Beth-shan have uncovered
stelae of Seti I and Rameses II, and a statue of Rameses III,
showing that the town was probably in Egyptian hands from *c.* 1310
to 1150 BC (cf. Fisher 1923: 236). Since Beth-shan lies between
Jezreel and the Jordan, this one site is sufficient to disprove
Jack's view that the pharaonic expeditions never strayed from the
coastal road.

New inscriptional evidence has also discredited Jack's
attempts to limit the extent of Rameses II's campaigns. There is
now no doubt that Rameses II campaigned in Syria, Phoenicia,
Western Palestine, Edom and Moab (cf. Kitchen 1964: 47-70, esp.
68).

In view of this, it is clear that a 15th century dating of
the Exodus requires an explanation other than the one offered by
Jack for the absence of biblical references to campaigns by Seti I
and Rameses II.

As a starting point, we may note that Merneptah, Rameses II's
successor, and Rameses III, also led campaigns into Palestine.
On the prevalent 13th century dating of the Exodus, the Israelites
were in Palestine before the reign of Merneptah. The fact that no
mentions of clashes with Egyptian armies appear in the records of
the Judges period therefore still demands an explanation in terms
of the 13th century date. The important point is that whatever
explanation is offered for the absence of any biblical reference
to the campaigns of Merneptah and Rameses III can also be applied
to the activities of Seti I and Rameses II.

The Stele of Merneptah actually records a clash with Israel,
and hence provides a *terminus ad quem* for the entry into Palestine
by the Israelites. It has been used again and again as proof that
the Israelites were in Palestine by the time of Merneptah, *c.* 1220
BC (cf. Jack 1925: 224-36; Rowley 1950: 30-31; Kitchen and
Mitchell 1962: 214-15; Wright 1962a: 70-71; Kitchen 1966: 59-60;
Harrison 1970: 322-3; Yeivin 1971: 27-31, 85; Bright 1972: 121).

There have been attempts to suggest that the *Ysrᵓr* mentioned
on the Stele should not be equated with Israel, but none has found
general acceptance (cf. Kitchen 1966: 59-60; Yeivin 1971: 28).
Some scholars have wished to see the Stele as referring to the
Exodus itself, and therefore date that event to the early years
of Merneptah's reign (Montet 1940: 149; Drioton 1955: 43-6;

de Wit 1960: 10; North 1967a: 112-13). In reply to this view,
Rowley has pointed out: "The chastisement which the pharaoh
claims to have meted out ranged from the districts inhabited by
Hittites to the far south of Palestine. It is therefore unlikely
that Merneptah is here distorting his unsuccessful pursuit of
Israel at the time of their leaving Egypt" (1950: 30-31). Yeivin
points out that the Stele mentions defeated units in order from
south to north: Ashkelon, Gezer, Yenoam, then Israel, indicating
that Israel was defeated in the north; "It is impossible within
this historical frame to place Israel in Sinai immediately after
the Exodus" (1971: 30). The notion that Merneptah never really
campaigned in Palestine (Drioton) is disproved by other
inscriptional evidence (Kitchen and Mitchell 1962: 215; Kitchen
1966: 60)/2/.

The main point is this: Israel encountered Egyptian forces
during the reign of Merneptah, yet no mention of the incident
appears in the book of Judges, in spite of the fact that the
compiler of the book includes accounts of various other defeats
suffered by Israel. We should note that Rameses III also made
inroads into Palestine at the beginning of the 12th century BC,
and no mention of his campaigns appears in the book of Judges
either. While this pharaoh makes claims which caused his
records to be treated sceptically by earlier Egyptologists
(e.g. Breasted 1924: 177), the Beth-shan finds make it clear
that we can no longer dismiss them, as Jack (1925: 68) was
inclined to do.

Various reasons have been offered for the absence of
references to Egypt in the book of Judges. Rowley remarks
concerning the event recorded on the Israel Stele, that this
finds no place in the biblical record because it "was of trivial
significance for Israel's history compared with the event of the
Exodus" (1950: 31). This argument, however, derives its force
from Rowley's own reconstruction of events, according to which
the Exodus occurred only a short time before the clash to which
the Stele refers.

Garstang (1931: 258ff.) suggested that the book of Judges
does contain references to Egyptian activity, but that these are
veiled. He suggested that the various periods of peace recorded
there were in fact times of effective Egyptian control. The
reason for the suppression of this fact was religious, the aim
of the writer being to stress God's control of events and, in

this instance, to give God alone the credit for the removal of
Israel's oppressors. Rowley comments: "It is doubtful, however,
if the Israelites would recognize Egyptian rule to be beneficient,
especially since Egypt was the symbol of oppression to her, and
it is much more probable that such periods would have been
reckoned with the foreign oppressions" (1950: 29-30).

The possibility remains that Israel did not actually *suffer*
during these periods of Egyptian control, as she did during the
periods of oppression by the Moabites, Midianites, and others.
This would perhaps result in the periods of Egyptian control
being viewed differently from the times of oppression.

However, a simpler and more likely answer to the problem lies
in Rowley's comment that "there is no pretence to record every
detail of history in the book of Judges..." (1950: 31)/3/.

Wood has argued effectively that the reason for the lack of
references to Egyptian campaigns in the account of the Judges
period lies in the nature of that account. He points out,
reasonably, that the book of Judges is not intended as a full
history of the period, but as "an accounting of Israel's deviant
behaviour and corresponding punishments. Accordingly those
military encounters which served as means of punishment or
correction are mentioned, and those which did not are omitted";
hence encounters with Egypt are omitted because they "did not lead
to servitude and punishment on Israel's part" (Wood 1970: 78).

Peet has offered a slightly different argument which results
in a similar conclusion. Peet's argument constitutes a reply to
Burney, who saw the absence of biblical references to Egyptian
campaigns as an indication that the Hebrews were not in Canaan
when the campaigns took place (Burney 1919a: 93-4).

Burney's argument, says Peet, "loses its force when we read
the same scholar's own account of the extremely artificial
composition of the Book of Judges" (Peet 1922: 121). In Burney's
view, Judges consists mainly of a collection of incidents
arranged by an editor in such a fashion as to show that defection
from the worship of Yahweh invariably led to the deliverance of
Israel into the hands of foreign enemies, and that the ensuing
repentance was followed by the raising up of a deliverer. The
illustrations of this principle "are, at any rate in most cases,
merely *local,* some particular tribe or group of tribes falling
temporarily under the dominion of a foreign oppressor, but Israel

as a whole being unaffected" (Burney 1919b: xxxvi). "Surely in such a narrative as this", says Peet, "compiled long after the events, we can argue nothing from the absence of any reference to Egyptian invasions. These invasions, rapid and far-reaching, probably in many cases had but little effect on any part of Israel, and the fact that they have left no record in an account which by admission makes no claim to completeness hardly amounts to evidence" (1922: 122).

In conclusion we may say this: Israel was certainly in Palestine at the time of the campaigns of Merneptah and Rameses III, and since those campaigns are not referred to in the book of Judges, the fact that no reference is made to a campaign by either Seti I or Rameses II can not be taken to indicate that Israel was not in Palestine when they occurred. Furthermore, a plausible explanation for the omission of references to Egyptian activity is provided by the nature of the account.

The silence of the book of Judges concerning Egypt during the period with which it deals does not therefore constitute an argument for the 13th century date for the Exodus. This appears to have been recognized by recent major proponents of this date, who make no reference to this silence in order to support their views.

Before closing this chapter, however, we must note Kitchen's argument that the lack of a reference to Israel in certain records of Rameses II tells against placing the Hebrew invasion earlier than the second half of the 13th century BC.

Some time in the first half of the 13th century, Rameses II (or forces of his) raided Edom and Moab. This is recorded on the exterior of the east wall of Rameses II's forecourt in the Temple of Luxor, though it is not clear whether the territories were invaded in two separate campaigns or in one (cf. Kitchen 1964: 47-70, esp. 62ff. for discussion). This evidence shows "that the forces of Ramesses II penetrated the debatable territory north of the Arnon (taking Dibon) and probably the heartland of Moab between the Arnon and Zered (i.e. Wadis Mojib and Hesa)" (ibid: 65).

Kitchen remarks: "Now it would be highly unrealistic to have Ramesses' forces invading the region of Dibon north of the Arnon once the Hebrews under Moses and Joshua had taken over this area..." (ibid: 70), the reason being: "Otherwise, one might

expect a mention of 'Israel' in the same class of records of
Ramesses II that mention 'Se'ir' and 'Moab', before its known
occurrence on Merenptah's famous Israel stela" (ibid: 70, n.7).

However, although Num 23: 21-26 (cf. Jdg 11: 17-26) records
that Hebrews settled in the territory north of the Arnon after
the defeat of the Amorite king Sihon, there is reason to believe
that Hebrew settlement of this area remained politically
insignificant/4/. According to Num 21: 26-30, the region north
of the Arnon had been Moabite territory until it was taken from
Moab by Sihon the Amorite. In Num 25: 1-5, we read of Moabites
as far north as Shittim, east of the Jordan roughly opposite
Jericho. This suggests that after the Israelite defeat of
Sihon, Moabite groups began to drift back into their old
territory. There is no hint in Num 25 that the Israelites made
any attempt to oppose this Moabite presence north of the Arnon.
Moabites still appear to be occupying this area at the time
referred to in Jdg 3: 12-14; here we find them having crossed
the Jordan under the leadership of Eglon to occupy the Jericho
area. We are told that Yahweh had "strengthened Eglon the king
of Moab against Israel" (3: 12). Although subsequently the
Moabite groups which penetrated west of the river were severely
routed, according to Jdg 3: 28-30, the account makes no mention
of any attempt to carry the Israelite victory east of the
Jordan, nor are Israelite groups settled on that side of the
Jordan mentioned as giving any assistance against Eglon. In the
scheme to be presented below, the Eglon incident probably
belongs either at the end of the 14th century BC or at the
start of the 13th, i.e. not long before the probable date of
Rameses II's Moab campaign.

It is therefore not inconsistent with the implications of
the biblical material to suggest that Rameses II's records do not
mention Israelites north of the Arnon for the simple reason that,
at the time of the campaign(s) in question, the Israelite
presence in this region was quite negligible compared with the
renewed Moabite presence which seems to have followed the defeat
of Sihon. The lack of a reference to Israel here certainly need
not mean that the Hebrew invasion occurred later than Rameses II's
campaign into Moab /5/.

CHAPTER 3:
THE IMPLICATION OF THE OLD TESTAMENT'S CHRONOLOGICAL MATERIAL

Chapter 3: The Implication of the Old Testament's Chronological Material

The aim here will be to show that chronological notes and other material within the Old Testament point to a date for the Exodus in the 15th century BC, and that the ways in which this material is handled by proponents of the later date for the Exodus are unsatisfactory, since they neglect certain significant issues.

3.1 The Statement Contained in I Kings 6: 1

The Old Testament contains only one reference which bears directly on the date of the Exodus. This is the statement in I Kgs 6: 1 that the building of the first temple began in the fourth year of Solomon's reign, which was "the four hundred and eightieth year after the people of Israel came out of the land of Egypt". If we take this as a historically accurate piece of information, it provides a date of c. 1446 BC for the Exodus, if we adopt the chronology for Solomon's reign worked out by E.R. Thiele, which is now quite widely used, as this makes the fourth year of Solomon's reign 966 BC (Thiele 1965: 39-52;). On the basis of the dates worked out for Solomon by Albright (1945: 16-22), which are still adhered to by Bright (1972: 225, n.1), the Exodus would be c. 1440 BC (cf. Jack 1925: 200ff.; for other datings of Solomon's reign, and hence for the founding of the temple, see Rowley 1950: 10, n.4; Harrison 1970: 184-5; Gray 1970: 161).

The historicity of this information is, however, frequently rejected. Before discussing the reliability or otherwise of the information, we should note that the LXX^BA gives a figure of 440 years in place of the 480 of the MT. Wellhausen held that the LXX represents the original text (1885: 230; 1889: 264), but

Jack and Rowley have both offered compelling reasons for
accepting the MT as original. Jack asserts that in view of the
history of the copy of I and II Kgs in Codex Alexandrinus, this
verse "cannot be regarded as an original Septuagintal text", and
says: "Where the Authorised Version has 480 and the Septuagint
440, the former has every chance of being the correct figure"
(1925: 202; cf. Burney 1903: 58ff; Montgomery and Gehman 1951:
143). Further, the MT is supported against the LXX by Aquila
and Symachus, as well as by the Peshitta (Jack 1925: 202-3;
Rowley 1950: 89; G. Sauer 1968: 3, n.12).

Reasons given for rejecting the historicity of I Kgs 6: 1
are as follows: the figure resolves into twelve units of forty
years, the latter figure being commonly used in the Old Testament
to represent a generation; further, the succession of High
Priests from Aaron to the return from the Exile can be divided
into two sections, one bridging the time between the Exodus and
the first temple, and the other extending from the building of
the first temple to the Exile, each section consisting of
twelve generations; and the sum of the lengths of the reigns of
Judah's kings from the fourth year of Solomon to the destruction
of Jerusalem by Nebuchadnezzar, as given in the books of Kings,
with the addition of fifty years for the Exile, yields another
period of 480 years between the building of the first temple and
the founding of the second, which exactly balances the 480 years
between the Exodus and the building of the first temple. For
these reasons the figure is held to be artificial and unreliable.
These three reasons will be examined here in reverse order.

The argument that a further period of 480 years spans the
time between the building of the first temple and the founding
of the second, and that this cannot be merely coincidence, has
been offered as a reason for believing that the figure of 480
in I Kgs 6: 1 was inserted by a post-Exilic editor who wished to
balance the two periods in this way (cf. Burney 1903: 59ff.;
Gray 1970: 159).

This can be queried on two grounds. First, as Rowley has
pointed out, "attention is not drawn to the second period of
480 years, as it might have been expected to be in a marginal
gloss which was afterwards incorporated into the text, if that
gloss were made specifically to equate an earlier period with it"
(1950: 90). Secondly, it is unlikely that the writer of the
verse would have viewed the subsequent period, to the founding of

the second temple, as a period of 480 years. It is extremely improbable that he would have assessed the Exile as a period of fifty years, for although Josephus refers to the temple being left desolate for fifty years (*Against Apion* I, 21), which is about correct for the period between the fall of Jerusalem in 587 BC and the edict of Cyrus in 538 BC, the biblical tradition for the length of the Exile was that it lasted seventy years (Jer 25: 11; Zech 1: 12). The whole idea that the writer of I Kgs 6: 1 created the figure of 480 years because he had another 480 years in mind demands a peculiar inconsistency in the writer's thinking. The true length of time between the fourth year of Solomon and the fall of Jerusalem is 380 years. The above theory requires that the writer either ignored or was unaware of this, and produced a figure of 430 years by adding all the reigns of the kings of Judah recorded in the books of Kings, but then ignored the biblical traditions altogether and added to this the *true* length of time for the Exile. This is very unlikely.

In short, it does not seem probable that a post-Exilic editor of the books of Kings would have thought of the period between the foundings of the first and second temples as one of 480 years, and it is therefore out of the question that he would have created a figure of 480 years for the earlier period in order to balance it.

The idea that the genealogy of High Priests lies behind the figure 480 is expressed by Harrison in this manner:

"... By placing the Exodus some four hundred and eighty years prior to the building of the Temple in Jerusalem, there emerges a pattern of twelve generations of High Priests between the erecting of the wilderness Tabernacle, which prefigured the Temple, and the actual construction of the Temple by Solomon. Again, another period of 480 years, or twelve generations of forty years each, extends between the building of the First Temple and its restoration under Zerubbabel" (1970: 317).

The first thing to notice is that the period of 480 years in I Kgs 6: 1 is referred to as beginning when the people came out of Egypt; if the aim was to draw attention to the time between the erection of the tabernacle as prefiguring the temple, and the building of the temple itself, surely the erection of the tabernacle and not the Exodus would have been referred to as the starting-point of the 480 years.

Secondly, we should note that in the High Priestly genealogy
there is no clear indication that twelve generations spanned the
period between Solomon and the founding of the second temple. In
I Chr 6: 10-15, only nine names are given between the time of
Solomon and the Exile. Joshua, who was High Priest at the time
of the Restoration, is not included in the list, and a sequence
of twelve names is only arrived at by adding his name and by
transferring the reference to Solomon's temple in verse 10 to
verse 9, so that it applies to the first Azariah instead of to
the second (cf. Jack 1925: 206, n.2; Rowley 1950: 94 with n.4).

More important, since it directly concerns the first part
of the list in I Chr 6: 1-15, is the fact that this list is
itself quite clearly artificial. As Jack has pointed out, it is
apparent from other genealogies that there were more than twelve
generations between the Exodus and the time of Solomon. In I Chr
6: 33-37, we have eighteen generations between Korah, who was
head of a family at the time of the Exodus (Ex 6: 21), and Heman,
who was head of a family in the early years of David (I Chr 15: 17).
This implies about twenty generations between the Exodus and
Solomon's building of the temple. Jack remarks that the list of
High Priests "cannot be historically correct, but must on the
whole be artificial. It is not even in harmony with the
statements made elsewhere in the historical books. The order of
the priests appears incorrect, and there is no mention of the
priestly line through Eli (I Sam. 14: 3; 22: 10), nor of other
priests such as Jehoiada, Zechariah, and Urijah, who are known
to have existed" (1925: 206). We may also note that Josephus
apparently knew an independent tradition in which there was a
succession of thirty-one priests between the Exodus and the
Exile, not twenty-two as in the list of I Chr 6 (Josephus *Ant* XX,
x, 1).

It is therefore very probable that the genealogy of High
Priests in I Chr 6: 1-15 is an artificial construction with little
relation to historical fact. The High Priestly succession would
not therefore have guided the writer of I Kgs 6: 1 to mention a
period of 480 years unless he had before him the artificial
account of that succession produced by the Chronicler. And as
Rowley points out, "There is not the slightest reason to suppose
that the author of I Kgs vi.1 had access to the books of
Chronicles..." (1950: 95).

Rowley described himself as "unconvinced that the succession of High Priests had anything to do with the verse" - i.e. I Kgs 6: 1. This is also the position of the present writer. Is it not possible, however, that the influence was the reverse of that which is normally assumed? Since the list in I Chr 6: 1-10 appears to be artificial, is it not possible that the aim of its author was to produce a sequence of twelve generations between the Exodus and the building of Solomon's temple, in accordance with what he may well have taken to be the implication of the figure 480 in I Kgs 6: 1? By placing the reference to Solomon's temple against the name of the second Azariah instead of against that of the first (where many scholars have argued that it more correctly belongs; cf. Jack 1925: 206, n.2; Rowley 1950: 94 with n.4), the author of the list has artificially produced a sequence of twelve names between Aaron and the building of the first temple. If there is any relation between the genealogy of High Priests and the figure in I Kgs 6: 1, it is more likely that the former is derived from the latter than *vice versa*.

Further arguments concerning the derivation of the figure 480 from other biblical material will be discussed in the following section, which deals with the information contained in the book of Judges.

There is in fact only one reason to be suspicious of the figure 480, and that is the simple fact that it is a multiple of the two significant biblical numbers 12 and 40. For this reason, the figure should probably not be accepted as historically accurate. But that is not to say that it is to be dismissed as valueless.

Nor is there any reason, apart from a desire to force it to comply with a late date for the Exodus arrived at on other grounds, for handling the number in the way advocated by Bright and others. Having suggested that 480 is "a round number for twelve generations", Bright (1972: 121) says: "Actually, a generation (from birth of father to birth of son) is likely to be nearer twenty-five years [than forty], which would give us some three hundred years rather than four hundred and eighty, and a date for the exodus in the mid-thirteenth century". "This figure", he concludes, "would seem to be approximately correct". (See also Wright 1962a: 84; Harrison 1970: 317; cf. the earlier view of Petrie, who reduced the period of 480 years to one of 210 on the basis of a similar assumption, placing the Exodus in the reign of Merneptah, *c.* 1220 BC; 1911: 55ff.).

Bright's figure is, of course, only "approximately correct" for someone who has already decided on a 13th century date for the Exodus on other grounds. This treatment of the number 480 is quite inadmissable in the light of what has been said above. For even if the 480 years has been produced in order to represent 12 units of 40 years each, there is no reason to assume that each of these units represents a generation, and therefore no reason to reduce each of the units in the way Bright advocates. We must similarly reject Wright's suggestion that the 480 years "may easily have been computed by multiplying the twelve generations known to exist between the Exodus and Solomon by the forty years usually reckoned as the length of a generation" (1962b: 191; cf. also McKenzie 1967: 31; Cundall 1968: 30). As far as the writer of I Kgs 6: 1 was concerned, twelve generations were *not* "known to exist" between the Exodus and Solomon. There is no evidence whatever that the writer of this verse was thinking in terms of twelve generations when he produced the number 480.

The view offered here is that the period of 480 years in I Kgs 6: 1 should be treated with caution, but that it does nevertheless provide a rough guide to the time of the Exodus. It is doubtless a "round number", chosen because it embodies the numbers 12 and 40, both obviously significant to the writers of the Old Testament, but it need not be drastically different from the correct figure. It may be slightly higher than the correct figure, in the same way that a period of seventy years is used to represent the Exile in Jer 25: 11 and Zech 1: 12: or it may be two or three decades lower than the correct figure. It is perhaps more probable that the figure 480 derives from an original estimate somewhat higher than itself rather than from one somewhat lower. A figure lower than 480 would probably have given rise to a "round number" of 440 years, or even 400 years, which would have balanced the length of the sojourn in Egypt in Gen 15: 13. That the true length of time between the Exodus and the fourth year of Solomon was somewhat more than 480 years is actually implied by material to be discussed in the following section.

In conclusion we may say that no evidence exists to justify the reduction of the 480 years in I Kgs 6: 1 in order to date the Exodus in the 13th century BC, nor is there any reason to dismiss the figure as a total fabrication. Therefore, while the figure should not be taken at face value as historically accurate, it can be treated as an approximate guide to the time of the Exodus, and it places the Exodus firmly within the 15th century BC.

3.2 *Material in the Book of Judges*

The book of Judges contains several items of information
concerning the lengths of various judgeships and periods of
oppression. The question of whether this information can be
used as a guide to the date of the Exodus is a complex one. It
will be discussed under five headings.

3.2.1 *The result of totalling the periods*

It is quite clear that one cannot simply add together all
the periods of time whose lengths are given and treat the total
thus produced as the correct length of time between the Exodus
and the beginning of the Monarchy. The period produced by
totalling all the figures is far too long to be plausible.

The chronological information for the period of the Judges
is as follows:

Cushan-rishathaim oppresses Israel	8 yrs	Jdg	3: 8
Othniel; period of peace	40		3:11
Eglon oppresses Israel	18		3:14
Ehud; period of peace	80		3:30
Jabin oppresses Israel	20		4:3
Deborah and Barak; period of peace	40		5:31
Midian oppresses Israel	7		6:1
Gideon; period of peace	40		8:28
Abimelech's reign	3		9:22
Tola	23		10:2
Jair	22		10:3
Ammonites oppress Israel	18		10:8
Jephthah	6		12:7
Ibzan	7		12:9
Elon	10		12:11
Abdon	8		12:14
Philistines oppress Israel	40		13:1
Samson	20		15:20; 16:31

Adding these figures produces a total of 410 years. In order
to tie this period to our earliest fixed date, the beginning of
David's reign, c. 1010 BC (see below), we must add the judgeship
of Eli, which is given as 40 years (I Sam 4: 18), the judgeship
of Samuel, which was something in excess of 20 years (I Sam 7: 2),
and the reign of Saul, which was of unknown duration. To fill the
gap between the oppression by Cushan-rishathaim and the Exodus, we

must add the period spent in the wilderness, which is given as
40 years (Num 32: 13), and the time spanned by the war of
conquest and the rule of Joshua and the elders, a period of
unknown length (Jdg 2: 7). For the whole period between the
Exodus and the beginning of David's reign we have a total of 510
years, plus three periods of unknown length. This information,
when taken to indicate consecutive periods, yields a date for the
Exodus well before 1520 BC.

Thus the chronological notes in the book of Judges, taken
along with those in I Samuel, give a period greatly in excess
of 480 years for the period between the Exodus and Solomon.
Adding to the total of 510 mentioned above the following 44 years
between the start of David's reign and the fourth year of Solomon,
we have a period of 554 years, plus the three periods of unknown
length. Estimating 35 years for the period of the Conquest and
the rule of Joshua and the elders, and including 20 years for
the reign of Saul, but adding no extra time to the 20 years
included within Samuel's judgeship, Jack obtains a total of 609
years between the Exodus and the building of the temple (1925:
211-12) /1/. How is this chronological information to be
regarded?

3.2.2   *The material in the book of Judges and the 480 years of*
I Kgs 6: 1

It is quite clear that the compiler of the book of Judges
had no intention of producing a total of 480 years when he
included the figures which we find there. As Rowley (1950: 88,
n.4) has said (expressing agreement with J.S. Griffiths 1923: 63),
there is "not a particle of evidence that the author of the book
of Judges supposed that 480 years separated the Exodus from the
founding of the Temple".

Some writers have, however, tried to demonstrate the
reverse: an origin for I Kgs 6: 1 in the information contained
in the book of Judges. But their arguments are, without
exception, totally unconvincing.

Rowley has reviewed several of these attempts and pointed
out their weaknesses (1950: 90-98). All depend on the arbitrary
omission of some of the periods listed, coupled with the inclusion
of arbitrary estimates for some or all of the periods whose
lengths are not given. I do not propose to reproduce or
summarize Rowley's treatment of these schemes, but some obvious

weaknesses should be noted.

The omission of the periods of oppression, as proposed by Moore (1895: xli) and others, is quite illogical, and by itself does not reduce the total to 480 years. The inclusion of Abimelech as an oppressor by both Moore and Nöldeke (1869: 192) is not a move which is likely to have occurred to an Old Testament chronographer, and the inclusion of Saul in the same way, as suggested by Moore, seems even more unlikely.

Gampert's scheme ignores all three periods of unknown length, all the minor judges, and the reign of Abimelech (Gampert 1917: 241-7). The exclusion of the periods of unknown length assumes a very mechanical use of material by the author of I Kgs 6: 1, and the exclusion of Abimelech is quite without reason. As Rowley notes, the suggestion sometimes offered concerning the minor judges, that the verses concerning them were not originally part of the narrative and were added later than the writing of 1 Kgs 6: 1, cannot be applied to the story of Abimelech (1950: 93).

Garstang's scheme retains the reign of Abimelech, while excluding the minor judges. But it contains various unlikely assumptions which make it in no way preferable to that of Gampert. Garstang arbitrarily reduces the Ammonite oppression from 18 years to 1 year, estimates 40 years for the period of Joshua and the elders, 15 years for the reign of Saul, and adds nothing to the 20 years for Samuel, in spite of clear indications that Samuel's period as a judge was much longer (Garstang 1931: 55ff.). He also adopts the LXX reading of I Sam 4: 18, which gives Eli's judgeship as 20 years instead of 40 as in the MT, a move which, as Rowley points out, Garstang would probably not have made "unless it had been convenient for his calculation" (1950: 95).

Rowley's own suggestion however, is no more compelling than those which he himself rejects. He suggests that twelve great national leaders "might be expected to be recalled", namely: Moses, Joshua, Othniel, Ehud, Deborah and Barak (counted "for this purpose" as one), Gideon, Jephthah, Samson, Eli, Samuel, Saul and David. "Here we have twelve leaders to whom an average of forty years each might be attributed to yield the 480 years, without the expenditure of midnight oil and improbable ingenuity" (ibid: 98). This is somewhat unconvincing. Apart from the fact that it is difficult to imagine why the writer of I Kgs 6: 1

should have thought in this way at all, it is not very likely that
he would have attributed 40 years to Jephthah when Jdg 12: 7 gives
that leader a period of only 6 years; and Samson is said to have
judged Israel for only 20 years.

The view offered by Kitchen (1966: 72-4; cf. Kitchen and
Mitchell 1962: 216) is no more convincing. It is basically the
same as those mentioned above, that the 480 years are to be
explained as "a total of selected figures (details now unknown)
taken from the larger total". He believes that the figures added
together relate to periods which were really concurrent. He does
not, however, attempt to reconstruct the details behind the final
selection. He simply asserts that the practice of producing one
total length of time by adding various periods which were actually
concurrent is perfectly in accord with "Ancient Oriental
principles" (1966: 73).

To justify this assertion, Kitchen cites the example of the
Egyptian Turin Papyrus. This lists 170 kings whose reigns total
at least 520 years, but who all reigned within a period reckoned
by modern Egyptologists as only about 240 years (XIIIth-XVIIth
Dynasties, the Second Intermediate Period). It is questionable
whether this has any parallel with the 480 years of I Kgs 6: 1;
there we are not presented with a list of events or kings, but
simply told that the fourth year of Solomon was the 480th after
the Exodus. There is no reason to assume that the figure was
arrived at by totalling several periods of shorter duration. But
even if there were a clearer parallel here, the citing of an
example of the situation for which one is presenting a case by no
means proves the case.

The appeal to "Ancient Oriental principles" therefore does
not make Kitchen's case any stronger than the others we have
mentioned. The statement that "in the Ancient Orient, chroniclers
and other writers often used excerpts from fuller records, and
this might explain the 480 years" (ibid) is a weak argument,
unless it can be plausibly demonstrated that the 480 years in
fact resulted from a logical selection of details extracted from
the book of Judges and elsewhere. No demonstration of this sort
appears to have been made.

Boling has recently described as "the most plausible"
solution "one which simply adds together the first four years of
Solomon's rule, the 42 regnal years of Saul and David, the 136
years from Tola to Eli, the 200 years of peace under the saviours,

the 53 years of oppression, and the 45 years implied in Josh. 14:1. The total is 480" (Boling 1975: 23; cf. Richter 1964: 132-40). As we shall see below, the total regnal years of Saul and David cannot have been as little as 42 years and would not have been treated as such by a biblical writer/redactor. The total years from Tola to Eli are not 136 (though a total of 134 can be produced by adding the periods from Tola to the end of the Philistine oppression), the total for all the periods of oppression is 111, not 53, and the reference to Jos 14: 1 appears to be a mistake for 14: 10, though this latter verse is not related in any clear way to any of the chronological notices in the book of Judges.

The two schemes for the Judges material discussed by G. Sauer (1968: 10-13) fare no better. The first produces a total of 480 years by omitting not only the minor judges but also Abimelech and Jephthah, and by adding nothing to the 20 years of I Sam 7: 2. Only 5 years are allowed for the Conquest and the settlement of the land. The subjective selection of figures here is quite obvious. The second scheme is even more improbable. It involves 15 years for the loss of the ark in place of the 20 in I Sam 7: 2, and in addition to this 40 years for Samuel's judgeship. By overlapping the judgeship of Eli, the oppression by the Philistines, and the judgeship of Samson, 60 years are removed, and 25 years are obtained for the time of Joshua in a way which is quite inadmissable; Sauer argues that in Jos 14: 10 Joshua is 85 years old, and dies, according to Jos 24: 29 and Jdg 2: 8, at the age of 110. By subtracting 85 from 110, Sauer produces 25 years between the completion of the Conquest and Joshua's death. But in Jos 14: 10 it is *Caleb*, not Joshua, who is said to be 85 years old, and there is no hint in the Old Testament that Joshua and Caleb were exact contemporaries!

We must conclude, therefore, that no cogent demonstration has yet been made of how the writer of I Kgs 6: 1 obtained a period of 480 years between the Exodus and Solomon's fourth year from the information contained in the book of Judges. The book of Judges, along with the information given in I Sam, indicates a period well in excess of 480 years for this era, and there is no obvious way in which certain items would have presented themselves for selection in order to result in a total of 480 years.

3.2.3 *The extent to which the Judges period may be compressed*

We now turn to the problem of how the material in the book of Judges should be treated. Adherents of the late date for the

Exodus have argued for compressing the period of the judges by
overlapping the events so that the periods given are viewed in
many cases as concurrent rather than consecutive (Petrie 1911:
54ff; Kitchen and Mitchell 1962: 216; Kitchen 1966: 72-4;
Cundall 1968: 30; Harrison 1970: 177-80, 330-31; Boling 1975: 23).
As will be seen subsequently, there are indications in the book
of Judges itself that some of the judgeships need to be allowed
to overlap in order to be seen in their correct relationship.
The question to be tackled here is *to what degree* the various
periods should be overlapped and compressed.

Adherents of the 13th century date for the Exodus have to
reduce the period of the judges from over 400 years to about
170 years (c. 1200-1030 BC). There are three reasons for
suggesting that this degree of compression is incorrect.

(a) *The statement in Judges 11: 26*

In Jdg 11: 26 we are given the information that by the time
of Jephthah's battles with the Ammonites, Israel had "dwelt in
Heshbon and its villages, and in Aroer and its villages, and in
all the cities that are on the banks of the Arnon, three hundred
years...". Clearly, if this mention of 300 years between the
conquest of Sihon's kingdom and the time of Jephthah is correct,
even as a round number, there can be no question of reducing the
entire period of the judges to only 170 years.

However, the figure has been rejected, even as a round number
by several writers. Thus Wright suggests it is a late insertion.
"... The addition of the years ruled by the successive judges and
the intervening oppressions up to Jephthah's time gives a figure
of some 319 years. The coincidence is felt to be so close as to
suggest that the 300-year figure was artificially derived from
the chronology of the Book of Judges..." (Wright 1962a: 84-5;
for earlier writers who rejected the figure, see Rowley 1950:
98, n.4) /2/.

This view, however, presupposes that the editor who deduced
and inserted the 300-year figure was very mechanical in his
handling of the material before him. The Israelite occupation
of the territory around Heshbon, recorded in Num 21, occurred
before the end of the 40 years of wandering. To the 319 years
taken up by the period of the judges before Jephthah must be
added the time between the defeat of Sihon and the crossing of
the Jordan, the period of the Conquest, and the time of Joshua

and the elders. The implication of Jdg 2: 7 and 10 is that a
considerable time, long enough for the passing of a generation,
elapsed between the end of the war of conquest and the oppression
by Cushan-rishathaim.   The time of the Conquest may itself have
been quite lengthy.   (Rabbinical sources preserve a tradition
that the war of conquest lasted fourteen years [Seder Olam 12],
a figure which we should probably consider conservative /3/.)

        If an editor had attempted to create his own figure for
insertion into the story of Jephthah, then unless he arbitrarily
ignored some of the material before him, which seems unlikely,
he would have produced a figure well in excess of 300 years, and
probably one nearer to 400.

        Some scholars have attempted to derive the 300-year figure
from the other chronological material in the book of Judges by
postulating the same kind of selective approach on the part of
an editor which we have already seen suggested in connection with
the 480 years of I Kgs 6: 1 (cf. Rowley 1950: 96, 98; Kitchen
1966: 74).   These suggestions are open to the same criticisms
as were offered in the discussion of those selection theories.

        It would appear to be a safe assumption that the 300-year
figure of Jdg 11: 26 is not the result of an editor working with
other chronological notes in the book before him, but rather part
of an independent tradition, and probably a fairly reliable
guide to the length of time between the defeat of Sihon and the
battles of Jephthah.

        It is here submitted, therefore, that this figure constitutes
an obstacle to the view that the period of the judges as a whole
should be compressed to some 170 years.   Further, if Jephthah's
battles could be dated with some degree of confidence, the 300-
year figure could be used as a guide to the date of the Exodus.

        Before discussing the date of Jephthah's battles, however, we
must note   further objections to the compression of the period of
the judges advocated by adherents of the late date for the Exodus.

        (b)   The late appearance of Philistines in the book of
              Judges

        The date presently held for the incursion of Philistines into
Canaan, deduced from Egyptian records and archaeology, weighs

heavily against the degree of compression of the Judges period
which a 13th century Exodus makes necessary.

From Egyptian records, the main movement of Philistines into
Canaan has been dated to immediately after their defeat, along
with other groups of Sea-peoples, by Rameses III in the eighth
year of that pharaoh's reign /4/.

Egyptologists early this century placed the beginning of
Rameses III's reign at c. 1200 BC or just before (cf. Macalister
1913: 21 with n.3; Jack 1925: 20). Albright subsequently argued
for dating Rameses III at c. 1180-1150 BC (Albright 1932: 53-8),
a proposal which has been adopted by some scholars (e.g. Dothan
1957: 151; Wright 1966: 70; Bright 1972: 167), but rejected by
others who still hold to the higher dates (Yeivin 1971: 104;
Kitchen 1973b: 60).

If the early dates for Rameses III are indeed correct, and
the main wave of Philistines entered Canaan around 1200 BC or
shortly after, then the Philistines entered the land only a
short time after the Israelites if the late dates for the Exodus
and Conquest are adopted. The fact that Israel does not clash
with the Philistines until towards the end of the book of
Judges becomes a strange circumstance in this scheme of things.

Working with the currently popular date for the settlement
of the Israelite tribes in Palestine, we would expect to find that
the entire period of the judges was one of continual clashes with
the Philistines. Yet the fact is that apart from one curious
laconic reference in Jdg 3: 31, Philistines are not mentioned in
the book of Judges until just before the time of Jephthah (Jdg 10:
7), and do not play a major role as oppressors of Israel until the
last story in the main series, that of Samson /5/.

It has been suggested that the reference in Jdg 3: 31, which
records how Shamgar "delivered Israel" by killing 600 Philistines,
is out of place at that point in the text. C.F. Craft has remarked
(1962: 306) that the mention of Shamgar "not only omits the
customary statements about his judging and giving the land peace
for so many years, but also it is apparently awkwardly inserted
into the narrative at this point, for the beginning of the
Deborah account (4: 1) clearly implies that there was no deliverer
between Ehud and Deborah". Macalister makes the same point, and
also draws attention to the fact that in some manuscripts of the
LXX, the verse mentioning Shamgar is repeated, with minor

variations, after Jdg 16: 31, immediately after the story of
Samson. This, as Macalister remarks, "seems a better place for
it" (Macalister 1913: 41). The verse as repeated is quite explicit
in placing the Shamgar incident after the time of Samson. It
reads: "Semegar [Emegar] son of Anan [or Ainan, Enan] arose after
Samson, and slew of the Foreigners 600 men without the cattle, and
he also saved Israel" (cf. Macalister 1913: 41, n.4).

There is also a near-parallel to the Shamgar incident in II
Sam 23: 11-12 (see also I Chr 11: 12-14), where a certain Shammah,
son of Agee, kills a band of Philistine marauders. The name of
this character sounds tantalizingly similar to that of Shamgar, son
of Anath.

It certainly seems plausible to suggest that the Shamgar
incident is out of place in Jdg 3: 31. The placing of this verse
before the battle of Deborah and Barak could have arisen because
of the mention of a Shamgar, son of Anath, in the Song of Deborah
(Jdg 5: 6). The names in Jdg 3: 31 and 5: 6 may not originally
have been the same, however. The LXX has "Samegar son of Anath"
in 5: 6, but "Samegar son of Dinach" in 3: 31. But even if the
incident is held to be correctly placed (it could conceivably be
linked with earlier attacks by the Sea-peoples which occurred under
Merneptah), the fact remains that serious Philistine encroachments
into Israelite territory are not mentioned until much later in the
book of Judges (10: 7; 13: 1; 14: 4).

This implies that the greater part of the period of the judges
should be placed before the time of the Philistine expansion. Yet
on the basis of the 13th century date for the Exodus, the entire
period of the judges falls between c. 1200 BC and 1030 BC, and
the absence of Philistines from the account of the major part of
the period is without a satisfactory explanation/6/. On the
basis of a date for the Exodus in the 15th century, however, the
greater part of the period would be placed before 1200 BC.

Though not conclusive in itself, this argument, when taken
alongside the 300 years of Jdg 11: 26, suggests that the period
of the judges should not be compressed into the 170 years between
1200 BC and 1030 BC. Rather, the events of the first nine
chapters of the book of Judges should be placed before 1200 BC.
The feasibility of this will be demonstrated later in this chapter.
First, we may note a third piece of information which indicates a
much longer period for the judges than is currently allowed.

(c)   *The generations in I Chronicles 6: 33-37.*

I Chr 6: 33-37 gives the genealogy of "Heman the singer", who
is said to have served before the tabernacle in the time of David
(cf. also I Chr 16: 16-17). As we have already noted in a
different context (p.84), this genealogy puts Heman in the
eighteenth generation after Korah, who was head of a family at the
time of the Exodus (Ex 6: 21-24; Num 16: 1ff). It is not possible
to accommodate this number of generations in the period allowed
between the Exodus and David when the Exodus is placed at *c.* 1270
BC or later.

Indeed, this genealogy strongly suggests the approximate
accuracy of the 480 years of I Kgs 6: 1, since it implies nineteen
or twenty generations between the Exodus and Solomon. Following
Bright's suggestion of allowing twenty-five years for each
generation, reckoning with nineteen generations produces a date
for the Exodus roughly in line with that arrived at from I Kgs 6:
1, while reckoning with twenty naturally gives a slightly earlier
date /7/. It will be suggested below that the slightly earlier
date is correct.

What I wish to stress here is this: if the genealogy of
I Chr 6: 33-37 preserves the correct number of generations between
Korah and Heman, it precludes the drastic shortening of the
period of the judges required by the late date for the Exodus. It
also supports the 480 years of I Kgs 6: 1 against the view that
this figure is an historically worthless total derived from
non-consecutive periods.

We will now attempt to construct a chronology for the period
of the judges which takes all the above data into account.

3.2.4   *The chronology from Jephthah to David's accession*

Discussing the dates for Solomon's reign, Gray notes that
the 40 years attributed to it in I Kgs 11: 42 "may be the familiar
approximation of Semitic folklore and tradition", but adds that
"in the case of Solomon, who acceded when quite young, it is
probably not far from the truth" (Gray 1970: 298). Synchronisms

between Solomon and Hiram of Tyre suggest that Solomon's
accession occurred within a decade after 970 BC, and his death
must be placed near the beginning of the reign of Egypt's ·
Shishak I, who reigned 935-914 BC (cf. ibid: 55). "Actually
this agrees with the evidence of Kings, which suggests 931 as
the date of Solomon's death" (ibid). A number of writers have
arrived at a date of 931/930 BC for the end of Solomon's reign,
working closely with the biblical data, and have consequently
dated his accession at 971/970 BC (Thiele 1965: 39-52; Kitchen
and Mitchell 1962: 216-17; Harrison 1970: 184, 189). His reign
may have begun with a co-regency with his father David, but
this was probably for only a brief period (cf. I Kgs 1: 37-2: 11;
I Chr 28: 5; 29: 20-23, 26-28).

According to I Kgs 2: 11, David also reigned for 40 years,
7 in Hebron and 33 in Jerusalem. Again, there is no reason to
doubt that the figure is roughly correct, since David appears
to have been quite young at his accession. A strict handling
of the biblical material would place David's accession at
1011/1010 BC (cf. Kitchen and Mitchell 1962: 217). We will
assume here that it fell somewhere in the last decade of the 11th
century BC.

The length of Saul's reign is unknown, because the Hebrew
text of I Sam 13: 1 is defective. As it stands, this verse now
gives Saul's reign as only 2 years, but this is clearly not the
figure intended. Hertzberg (1964: 103) has actually suggested
that a larger figure, such as the 40 years of Acts 13: 21, was
deliberately "replaced by the figure two on dogmatic-historical
grounds". By this he means that a redactor may have changed
the figure in order to reduce Saul's reign from its actual length
to the period for which he ruled with the approval of Yahweh.
"The number is given because it was the later view that Saul was
actually 'king' for only quite a short time" (ibid). Mauchline
expresses a similar view. He suggests that the deuteronomist
would only have reckoned Saul's reign from his acclamation by
the people (I Sam 10: 24 or 11: 15) to "when he lost the
charisma.... It may be that the anointing of David took place
after Saul had reigned only two years; if that was so, the
deuteronomist would regard Saul's reign as then finished. But,
historically, Saul continued to reign as king" (Mauchline 1971:
111).

This view is obviously conjectural. There is no evidence
that the anointing of David took place 2 years after Saul's

accession, and no evidence that the deuteronomist viewed Saul's
reign as ending and David's beginning with David's anointing
by Samuel. More important, as Driver points out, the expression
now found in the Hebrew of I Sam 13: 1 "is not said in Hebrew
for 'two years'..." (Driver 1913a: 97). A more probable view
than that of Hertzberg and Mauchline is that something has
dropped out of the text (Rowley 1950: 87, n.23). Alternatively
we may have here "a misunderstood abbreviation for the numeral"
(Ackroyd 1971: 104), or it could be (since the figure for
Saul's age at the time of his accession is also missing) that
Smith is correct (1899: 92) when he suggests that "a scribe,
wishing to make his chronology complete, inserted the verse
without the numbers, hoping to be able to supply these at a
later date, which however he was unable to do".

Various reconstructions of the original length of reign
have been suggested. Some older commentators proposed reading
22 years for Saul's reign, and this is the figure adopted in
the New English Bible, on the grounds that it is "an easy
correction of the Hebrew 'two'" (Ackroyd 1971: 104).

A reign of 20 years is attributed to Saul by Josephus in
Ant X, viii, 4, a figure which Jack accepts as correct (1925: 211)
But in *Ant* VI, xiv, 9, Josephus gives a figure of 40 years, as
is also found in Acts 13: 21. Hertzberg has suggested that this
was in fact the number which originally stood in I Sam 13: 1
(1964: 103), and attempts have been made to support the accuracy
of this figure (Kitchen and Mitchell 1962: 217; Harrison 1970:
713). However, the arguments adduced depend to a great extent
on the assumption that Saul was between 20 and 30 years old at
his accession, and this is unlikely to be correct /8/. Mauchline
remarks on the fact that Jonathan, Saul's son, is already of
military age when he first appears in the narrative, shortly
after Saul's anointing (I Sam 13: 3), saying this "might
suggest for Saul at this time a minimum age of 40 years" (1971:
111; see also Driver 1913a: 97; Blenkinsopp 1972: 54-5).

A combination of the present state of the text and the
general tenor of the biblical narrative makes the figure of 22
years perhaps the most likely suggestion. We may therefore
suppose a date between 1030 and 1020 BC for Saul's accession.

Working back from Saul we come to Samuel and Eli.
Unfortunately the data here are not much clearer. It is implied

in I Sam 7: 2 that Samuel's judgeship included a period of 20
years. It is clear, however, that the length of Samuel's
judgeship was much more than 20 years, as will be shown below.
It is also fairly certain that the ark of the covenant was
lodged at Kiriath-jearim for considerably more than 20 years,
since the period for which the ark was kept there includes a
period of unknown length between the events of I Sam 7: 1 and
the anointing of Saul (during which Samuel became an old man,
7: 15-8: 1), the entire reign of Saul, the seven and a half
years for which David ruled in Hebron, and the first part of
David's rule from Jerusalem. The figure in I Sam 7: 2 is
therefore either incorrect or else indicates a period of 20 years
between the arrival of the ark at Kiriath-jearim and the
recommitment of the people in 7: 3ff. Smith (1899: 51) actually
remarks that the main verb in 7: 2 is probably corrupt, and
says: "We should probably read: 'From the day the Ark dwelt at
Kirjath Jearim all the house of Israel turned after Yahweh';
the inserted clause: 'the days were many and became twenty
years' is probably secondary". (See also Blenkinsopp 1972: 53-4.)

   Against those who accept 20 years as the total for Samuel
(Jack 1925: 211; Garstang 1931: 55ff; Wood 1970: 82, n.6), there
is the following information pertaining to Samuel himself: I
Sam 7: 15 says that Samuel "judged Israel all the days of his
life"; I Sam 8: 1-5 and 12: 2 state that Samuel was old and grey
when he provided Israel with a king; Eli the priest, who judged
Israel before him, died at the age of 98, according to I Sam 4: 15,
and it is also stated that Eli was "very old" when Samuel was
still young (I Sam 2: 18-22; 3: 1-2). It is clear, therefore,
that Samuel was only a young man when he began to judge Israel
after the death of Eli (see also I Sam 12: 2). Since in the
period before the anointing of Saul he himself had become old
and grey, we must assume that that period was well over 20 years
in duration, and perhaps we should allow a total of 50 years
between the death of Eli and the accession of Saul.

   According to I Sam 4: 18, Eli "had judged Israel forty years"
when he died. Since Eli died at the advanced age of 98, there is
no reason why this round number should npt be approximately
correct. We should therefore probably allow about 90 years as a
total for the combined periods of Eli and Samuel, placing the
beginning of Eli's judgeship at about 1120 BC /9/.

   The twenty years attributed to Samson's exploits against
the Philistines (Jdg 15: 20; 16: 31) appear to belong somewhere

within the period of Eli and Samuel. The Philistine oppression
is said to have lasted 40 years in Jdg 13: 1. The fact that this
is another round number need not trouble us. The point is that
the oppression ended during the judgeship of Samuel (I Sam 7:
13-14), and Samson clearly lived during the time of the
oppression (cf. Jdg 13: 1). It therefore follows that the 20
years attributed to Samson should not be added to our date for
the start of Eli's judgeship in order to continue our reverse
calculations from the reign of Solomon.

Moving back to the judges mentioned prior to the story of
Samson, we come to Jephthah, Ibzan, Elon and Abdon, who are
specifically stated to have succeeded one another (Jdg 12: 8, 11,
13). The periods allotted to these men are strikingly different
from those of 80, 40, and 20 years which occur elsewhere in the
book of Judges: Jephthah is assigned 6 years (Jdg 12: 7), Ibzan
7 years (12: 9), Elon 10 years (12: 11), and Abdon 8 years
(12: 4). The three minor judges are not said to have delivered
Israel from any oppressors. Jephthah's battles, however, ended
an Ammonite oppression of certain tribes which is said to have
lasted 18 years (10: 8-9), another figure which contrasts
strikingly with the round numbers found so often elsewhere.

We may be fairly certain that the Ammonite oppression had
ended before the judgeship of Eli, since Ammonites are not
mentioned at all in the narratives dealing with the time of Eli.
(They first reappear, under the leadership of Nahash, in I Sam 11,
at the beginning of Saul's reign). If we assume that Jephthah,
Ibzan, Elon and Abdon really succeeded each other as the extant
narrative implies, the next question is whether Jephthah should
be placed immediately before the judgeship of Eli, or whether the
period of the three minor judges, and perhaps even more time,
should be allowed between Jephthah's judgeship and Eli's.

The statements in Jdg 12: 8, 11, and 13 that the three minor
judges "judged Israel" cannot be taken at face value as
indicating that the whole of Israel was under the headship of
each of these men. The same statement is made concerning Samson
in 15: 20 and 16: 31, yet we have already seen that Samson's
exploits must be placed within the period when either Eli or
Samuel (or both) was judging "Israel". The question of the
degree of unity of the various Israelite tribes during the
period of the judges is a problem which need not be gone into
here. But it is logical to assume that many of the judges were

local heroes whose exploits did not involve the majority of the
tribes (cf. Moore 1895: xxxix; Burney 1919b: xxxvi; Fohrer 1970:
208). There is therefore nothing against placing the three
minor judges within the judgeship of Eli. On the other hand,
there is equally no evidence to support such a move.

There is however, in the narrative concerning Jephthah, an
indication that his battles should not be placed very much
before the time of Eli. For the account of Jephthah's activities
contains the first mention of trouble from the Philistines in
Judges (apart from the dubious Shamgar incident discussed above).
It is clear from Jdg 10: 7 that Philistine pressure began to
become troublesome for Israel at the same time that the
Ammonites began to oppress the tribes living in Transjordan and
to penetrate the territories of Judah, Benjamin and Ephraim.
That the Philistine threat did not equal the Ammonite one at
this stage may be fairly deduced from the fact that the
Philistines do not feature in the subsequent Jephthah narrative,
nor are any clashes with the Philistines recorded for the three
minor judges. · The Philistine oppression is under way by the
end of Eli's judgeship, however, since I Sam 4: 9 refers to the
Hebrews having been slaves of the Philistines for an undefined
period by the time of the battle in which the Philistines capture
the ark. Therefore, if Jdg 10: 7 refers to the beginning of
Philistine pressure, it is quite likely that the time of
Jephthah did not precede by many decades the Philistine
oppression which we find underway during Eli's judgeship.

If we place Jephthah's judgeship in the decade before Eli,
i.e. the decade 1130-1120 BC according to the dates worked out
above, then the beginning of the Ammonite oppression and the
first trouble from Philistine pressure would fall, according to
the figure given in Jdg 10: 8, roughly two decades previously,
i.e. in the decade 1150-1140 BC. This date accords extremely
well with the dating of the Philistine incursions arrived at
from extra-biblical material. As was noted previously, the
incursions into Canaan of Philistines and related groups may
have begun around 1200 BC, and the making of a major inroad into
Canaan is usually assumed to have followed the defeat of these
people by Rameses III, *c.* 1190 BC, or, according to Albright's
dating, *c.* 1170 BC.

The dating proposed here is certainly more probable than
the suggestion that Jephthah belongs in the 11th century BC
(cf. Wright 1962a: 84; 1962b: 191; Harrison 1970: 179). Such

a date seems far too late for the first Philistine pressure on
Israel in view of the date usually given to the initial appearance
and spread of the Philistines. The same objection can be levelled
against L.T. Wood's date of *c.* 1100 BC for Jephthah (Wood 1970:
67 and 82, n.6). Wood arrives at this date by a rather subjective
process of reckoning, in which he seems guided by a desire to
arrive at a date for the Exodus which accords exactly with a
face-value interpretation of I Kgs 6: 1. This requires that the
300 years of Jdg 11: 26 date from *c.* 1400 BC, and hence in Wood's
scheme the date for Jephthah is necessarily *c.* 1100 BC.

Here, however, we are assuming that I Kgs 6: 1 provides only
a rough guide to the time of the Exodus, not a precise indication.
If we work from a date of *c.* 1130 BC for Jephthah, the 300 years
of Jdg 11: 26 imply a date of *c.* 1430 BC for the Israelites'
clash with Sihon, and hence a date approximately 40 years earlier
for the Exodus, *c.* 1470 BC. This accords with the suggestion
made earlier, that the actual period represented by the 480 years
of I Kgs 6: 1 was probably longer than 480 years rather than
shorter.

Much of the above is admittedly speculative, and involves a
dependence on the chronological notices in the books of Judges
and I Samuel which many would question. However, it is submitted
here that the reliability or otherwise of this material, and of
the conclusions here drawn from it, should not be prejudged, but
rather tested through the consideration of other relevant data.

3.2.5 *The chronology of the earlier part of the Judges period*

While chronological notices are very regular for the early
part of the period of the judges, they do not provide sufficient
information to permit overlappings to be reconstructed as in the
latter part. In addition, the early part contains four lengthy
periods of "rest" where the duration is given in three cases as
40 years and in one case as 80 years (Jdg 3: 11; 3: 30; 5: 31;
8: 28). Since none of these periods is tied to the ages of
individuals, there is no way to assess their reliability, and they
may be completely artificial. A few conclusions can be drawn,
however, and in particular we shall see that there is nothing
amiss if all the events recorded here are placed between *c.* 1400 BC
and *c.* 1150 BC, whereas on the basis of the 13th century date for
the Exodus most of these events are placed *c.* 1150-1100 BC (cf.
Boling 1975: xx-xxi).

The first period of oppression, recorded as lasting 8 years, was under Cushan-rishathaim, described as king of Aram Naharaim (Jdg 3: 8). The deliverer in this instance is Othniel, the son of Kenaz, Caleb's younger brother (verse 9). The phrase "Caleb's younger brother" in this verse could apply to either Othniel or Kenaz. In Jos 15: 16-19 and Jdg 1: 12-15, Othniel son of Kenaz figures as the conqueror of Kiriath-sepher/Debir, after which victory he marries Achsah, Caleb's daughter. While the exact relationship between Othniel and Caleb (apart from that of son-in-law) is not clear, tradition does obviously make them part-contemporaries, and since Caleb himself features in the traditions as part-contemporary with Joshua (he is described as 40 years old just after the Exodus and 85 during the war of conquest, Jos 4: 6-11; cf. Num 14-15), the period of oppression by Cushan-rishathaim must be placed very early in the post-Conquest period. If the Exodus occurred in the first half of the 15th century, and the Conquest in the second half, as indicated by the dates arrived at above, the time of this oppression and the deliverance accomplished by Othniel would best fit at about 1400 BC or shortly after. It is impossible to be more precise, not simply because we cannot obtain a precise date for the Exodus, but also because we have no indication of the length of time occupied by the war of conquest and the period of Joshua and the elders.

Malamat has developed a theory in which Cushan-rishathaim is identified with an Asiatic usurper, whose name he reads as Irsu (but cf. Yeivin 1971: 94), who ruled Egypt for 8 years, c. 1205-1197 BC (Malamat 1954: 231-42). If this identification could be proved, it would create serious obstacles to the chronology of the period of the judges proposed here. However, the identification has not been widely accepted, and Yeivin has raised several objections to it (1971: 93-5). He denies Malamat's claim that Amurru could have been confused with Aram Naharaim, and describes the equation of the usurper's name with that of (Cushan-) Rishathaim as "extremely doubtful not only etymologically but also phonetically". Yeivin also argues that the name Kushan-Rom, which appears in a list of Rameses II (cf. Unger 1957: 135), indicates an area not in northern Syria, as is required in Malamat's argument, but in the southwest Shephelah (Yeivin 1971: 95; also 24 with n.38). Perhaps most significant is Yeivin's argument that at the end of the 13th century, no North-Mesopotamian or Syrian state was in a position to make even a raiding campaign southward. The Hittite dominions were only just surviving the attacks of marauding neighbours, and were in

no condition to invade Egyptian territory, "let alone Egypt
itself".

It is actually quite likely that Irsu (or Arsu) was not an
invader at all, but a member of the foreign community within
Egypt; it has been suggested that he is to be identified with the
Chancellor Bay (cf. Gardiner 1958: 21).

The name Cushan-rishathaim is clearly manufactured, since it
means "Cushan of Double Wickedness", and Unger is probably right
to say that attempts to reconstruct the original are futile
(1957: 134). The name Cushan does not help to locate the origin
of the oppressor, since it can be linked with an area in southern
Canaan and an area in north Syria with equal probability (Unger
1957: 134-5; Yeivin 1971: 95; Bright 1972: 171-2). The precise
limits of the area designated by the term Aram Naharaim are
uncertain (cf. Unger 1957: 41, 135), and in any case it is
possible that Aram is here a mistake for Edom (ibid: 40, 134-5;
cf. Albright 1941: 34; Bright 1972: 171). In short,
Cushan-rishathaim is, as Unger says, "historically very obscure"
(1957: 40).

Yeivin remarks that since the chronological argument of
Malamat is effectively annulled by the arguments which he raises
against it, one may in consequence "date the episode a good deal
earlier" (1971: 95). Yeivin himself places the episode in the
first half, or the middle, of the 13th century (ibid: 124),
witout seeking to link it with any extra-biblical material. In
view of the obscurity of Cushan-rishathaim and his place of
origin, there is certainly nothing against placing him at the
end of the 15th century or the beginning of the 14th.

Another episode in the book of Judges which many have
considered to be firmly dated to the 12th century BC is the
battle between the Israelite forces of Deborah and Barak, and
the Canaanite troops led by Sisera, recounted in Jdg 4-5. Many
complex issues surround this episode, the main topic of debate
being the relationship between the events described in these
chapters and the conquest of Hazor recounted in Jos 11: 1-15.
Jabin, king of Hazor, features in both accounts, and on the
basis of a 13th century date for the Exodus there is a difficulty
in placing the events of Jdg 4-5 after the destruction of Hazor
in the 13th century, because there is no archaeological evidence
for a recovery of "Canaanite" Hazor after that destruction.

These issues will be discussed in detail in Part Two of this
work. Here we will simply examine the reason why some scholars
(Wright 1962a: 95; Bruce 1962: 303; Bright 1972: 172) have
confidently dated the battle in Jdg 4-5 at *c*.1125 BC.

This date was first argued by Albright (1936: 26-31; 1937:
22-26) on the basis of his date for the appearance of what he
considered to be Israelite culture at Megiddo. Albright assumed
that Israelite culture appeared at Megiddo in Stratum VI, and
that the events of Jdg 4-5 must be placed in the interval
between this stratum and the preceding one, Stratum VII, which
he considered Canaanite. The date of 1125 BC was chosen as
falling within this interval.

R.M. Engberg subsequently argued that Megiddo Stratum VI
in fact remained Canaanite, and that Stratum V was the first
stratum which could be described as Israelite. He consequently
dated the events of Jdg 4-5 between Stratum VI and Stratum V,
c. 1050 BC (1940: 4-7), a view which Albright at first accepted
(Albright 1940b: 7-9), but later rejected in favour of his
original view. After studying pottery from the Megiddo
excavations, Albright concluded that "the break between VII and VI
was much more complete and more protracted than that between VI
and V, while the change in character of masonry and pottery also
was much greater". For this reason Albright withdrew his
acceptance of Engberg's view and returned to his own position
(1951: 13; also 1963: 102, n.82).

Albright's original arguments for dating the events of
Jdg 4-5 to *c*. 1125 BC therefore reappear in his writings at the
end of the 1940's. In *The Archaeology of Palestine* (1st edn)
we find it expressed as follows. Discussing the Song of Deborah
(Jdg 5), he says that the "total omission of any reference to
Megiddo itself, while Taanach becomes the capital of the
district, makes it practically certain that Megiddo was then in
ruins". Since Megiddo lay in ruins between the destruction of
Stratum VII and the "Israelite" reoccupation of Stratum VI, the
events of the Song "may be dated archaeologically about 1125 B.C."
(1949: 117-18; also 1963: 39-40; cf. G.W. van Beek 1962: 339).

This view has been repeated in various commentaries and
popular works. Cundall, for example, refers to the archaeological
discoveries at Megiddo as "of major importance", because they
"make it possible to pin-point Deborah's crushing victory over
the Canaanites" at "about 1125 B.C." (Cundall 1968: 34).

Albright's reasoning is, however, open to question. A.D.H.
Mayes has rightly pointed out that Jdg 5: 19, which refers to the
battle occurring "at Taanach, by the waters of Megiddo", "does
not imply what the exponents of this view propose.... There is
nothing in these words either to imply or preclude Megiddo's
having been unoccupied at that time" (Mayes 1974: 93). Mayes
also points out that the reasoning which makes Megiddo's Stratum
VI an Israelite settlement is also weak, since examples of the
so-called Israelite pottery found in this stratum also occur in
the preceding Stratum VII (ibid: 136, n. 32). Elsewhere Mayes
(1969: 353, n.3) cites the view of J.J. Simons (1942: 17-54),
that from a ceramic point of view, Stratum VI is a direct and
immediate continuation of VII, while VI seems to have been
followed by an occupation gap, after which Stratum V marks the
settlement of the site by people whom Simons conjectures were
Philistines. Simons takes Stratum IV to be the first Israelite
settlement at Megiddo.

This view of the archaeological evidence is in some respects
similar to the view of Engberg mentioned above, though Engberg
believed that Stratum V was Israelite. In spite of its rejection
by Albright, Engberg's view, or one very like it, has been
followed by Schofield (1967: 320-21), and recent excavations
have brought several writers to an opinion which is closer to
Engberg's view than to Albright's; it now seems probable that
either Stratum VB, or Strata VA and IVB, represent Solomon's
Megiddo, and that prior to Solomon's rebuilding of the city there
was no Israelite settlement but a period of abandonment, or at
most some scanty occupation during David's time (Yadin 1960a: 62-8;
1975: 207-31; Kenyon 1964: 151-2; 1970: 232, 235; Schofield 1967:
321).

Furthermore, Albright's deduction from the Song of Deborah
that the events recorded there occurred while Megiddo was in
ruins and Taanach was the capital of the district, has been
proven faulty by excavations at Taanach by P.W. Lapp in the 1960's.
These, together with Yadin's new excavations at Megiddo, require
a complete revision of the picture on which Albright's view was
based. It is now believed that both Megiddo *and* Taanach suffered
"a major destruction about 1125 B.C. followed by an occupational
gap" (Lapp 1967: 9; see also 1969: 5). The fact that both sites
suffered simultaneous destruction and remained unoccupied at the
same time "opposes Albright's interpretation of 'Taanach by the
waters of Megiddo' as making it 'practically certain that Megiddo

was then in ruins'. It also undermines the traditional argument
for assigning the Song of Deborah to the period between about 1125
and 1075 B.C. when Megiddo was probably not occupied" (ibid).

However, Lapp has attempted to produce a new argument for
assigning the events of the Song to c. 1125 BC. He writes: "The
most attractive hypothesis would seem to associate the victory
of Deborah and Barak with the destruction of these sites [Megiddo
and Taanach] about 1125 B.C. - a victory worthy of this epic
song" (ibid). Boling (1975: 116) has recently followed Lapp in
associating the destruction of Taanach and Megiddo with the
battle commemorated in the Song of Deborah.

Such a view is hardly tenable. The destruction of these two
cities would have been so noteworthy that it would certainly have
found a place in the Song if it had really been achieved during
Barak's battles. This is especially so when we recall that in
Jdg 1: 27 we read that the Israelites failed to take Taanach and
Megiddo during the Conquest. A reversal of this failure would
hardly have passed without mention in an epic poem like the Song
of Deborah.

We must conclude that no archaeological reason has been
produced for placing the events of Jdg 4-5 in the 12th century BC.
In Chapter 6 it will be shown that these events are best located
in the 13th century BC.

We should perhaps also consider here another link which
Albright has produced between Jdg 4-5 and the period after
1200 BC. He notes that the name of Sisera, the commander of
the Canaanite troops, is not Canaanite, but "may well have
belonged to one of the Sea Peoples", and asserts that the battle
involving him "was not fought until after the Philistine
invasion" (1963: 39).

Albright's argument depends partly on the assumption that
the Shamgar incident of Jdg 3: 31 is correctly placed (ibid: 102,
n.80/10/), an assumption which we have already seen to be rather
dubious. Concerning the name Sisera, two observations need to be
made. Firstly, it is by no means certain that Sisera's name
identifies him as one of the Sea-peoples. The name is not Semitic,
but various other suggestions have been made concerning its
origin. A Hittite origin has been suggested for it (cf. Macalister
1913: 43; Jack 1925: 83), also a Babylonian origin, and a

derivation from a north Arabian ethnic name (cf. Jack 1925: 83), and Jack has even suggested that the name is Egyptian (ibid: 83-4). Secondly, however, even if it is insisted that the name be linked with the Sea-peoples, there is no reason to confine Sisera to the period after 1200 BC. The evidence of skulls from Megiddo and Ugarit shows that groups from the Aegean had arrived in Syria and Palestine at the start of the Late Bronze Age, before 1400 BC (Guy and Engberg 1938: 192; Van Seters 1966: 47-8).

Mayes has argued that the clash with Sisera "should be seen in close connection with Israel's defeat by the Philistines at Aphek sometime in the course of the second half of the eleventh century BC" (1974: 94). "The battle at Aphek must be seen as swift retaliation by the Philistines for the defeat of Sisera..." (ibid: 95). Mayes therefore dates the Israelite victory over Sisera just before the battle of Aphek, and consequently "in the latter half of the eleventh century BC..." (ibid: 96; Bright 1972: 181 similarly dates the battle of Aphek "some time after 1050 B.C."; on the chronology worked out above for the time of Eli and Samuel, the Aphek battle would fall much nearer the beginning of the 11th century, perhaps c. 1080 BC). But this argument for dating Sisera is also invalid if Sisera was nothing to do with the Philistines.

The mention of the use of iron in the period of the judges has been held to date certain events after the introduction of iron by the Philistines. Sisera's forces are said in Jdg 4: 3 to have possessed nine hundred chariots of iron, which must clearly be taken to mean chariots with iron fittings (cf. also Jos 17: 16-18). There is also a reference to iron vessels at Jericho in Jos 6: 19, and in Deut 3: 11 we have a curious reference to Og, king of Bashan (encountered in Num 21: 33-35), having a "bedstead of iron" (RSV; Heb ʿereś barzel).

It should be noted first that some of these references to iron may be anachronistic. In Gen 4: 22 there is a clear anachronistic use of the term, and in Ps 105: 18 there is a reference to Joseph wearing a collar of iron (barzel) while imprisoned in Egypt, which is certainly anachronistic and may point to the use of "iron" in some of the Hebrew literature as a type for any impenetrable or unyielding metal. The "bedstead" of Og of Bashan may not necessarily indicate an iron object at all; the text may refer to a black basalt or ironstone sarcophagus (cf. Driver 1902: 53-4).

It should also be noted, however, that the use of iron was by no means confined to the period commonly referred to as the Iron Age. Iron objects have been found in Palestine in Late Bronze II archaeological contexts, and references in Egyptian texts indicate the use of iron in the 13th century (cf. Guy and Engberg 1938: 162). References to iron articles in the Amarna letters "indicate that iron was slowly working its way southward in the early part of the fourteenth century B.C." (ibid; also Rowley 1950: 99; for a full discussion of the spread of iron, cf. G.A. Wainwright 1936: 5-24). If the vessels of *bia*, mentioned in a list of tribute from one of Thutmosis III's campaigns into Syria, are vessels of iron, then here is an indication of the use of iron objects in Syria as early as the 15th century BC (cf. Breasted 1906a: II, 217).

It is clear that references to the use of iron should not all be lumped together in the period after 1200 BC, and they cannot be taken as evidence that certain events should be dated later than that time.

Another event in the early part of the Judges period which has been dated archaeologically is the destruction of Shechem's stronghold by Abimelech (Jdg 9: 46-49). Wright has dated this destruction to the second half of the 12th century, which is somewhat later than is required on the chronology proposed here.

However, the evidence for this destruction is very scanty, and more than one interpretation can be placed upon it. The evidence consists only of the contents of numerous pits dug through the last floor of the cella of Shechem's temple. These pits were "all filled with dark earth, a great deal of charcoal, and Iron IA (early twelfth century) pottery"; this debris in the pits "may very well represent Abimelech's destruction of Migdal-Shechem". There is, however, "no clear destruction level from the Iron I period inside the cella of the temple" (Campbell and Ross 1963: 17 /11/). In one place, Wright expresses his opinion as follows: "The logical conclusion is that the charcoal and quantities of twelfth century pottery found in these pits must have come from a twelfth century destruction of the city" (1965: 102).

Points to be noted are: the pottery from these pits cannot be dated precisely; in an article by Toombs and Wright, the difficulties in dating the pottery are discussed, and the

conclusion is that "we can safely date our Iron IA at Shechem no
more precisely than *ca* twelfth century B.C.". A date "no later
than the twelfth century" is suggested for the Abimelech episode
(Toombs and Wright 1961: 34). Further, while Wright appears to
view the pottery as actually belonging to the time of the
destruction, R.J. Bull appears to treat it only as an indicator
of the time when the pits were in use, a time which would have
post-dated the actual destruction (Bull 1960: 119). And since
Bull dates the pottery as "early twelfth century" (ibid: 116),
the evidence could be taken to indicate a destruction at the
beginning of that century, shortly after 1200 BC. This date
would be perfectly in keeping with the date for Abimelech
required by the chronology proposed above. Jdg 10: 1-5 states
specifically that after Abimelech's death, Tola was judge for
23 years, and that after him Jair was judge for 22 years. This
brings us to the start of the Ammonite oppression and the first
clash with the Philistines. The start of the Ammonite oppression
was dated above to the decade 1150-1140 BC. Adding to this date
the judgeships of Tola and Jair, we have a date of *c*. 1190 BC for
the burning of Shechem by Abimelech, which, as we have just seen,
is perfectly possible on the basis of the archaeological evidence.

While it is not possible to work back in any detail beyond
the time of Gideon, because there are no references which make
clear the extent to which events overlapped, we may logically
propose placing the Midianite oppression and the oppression by
Jabin in the 13th century, the oppression by Eglon in the
14th-13th centuries, and the oppression by Cushan-rishathaim
either at the start of the 14th century or the end of the 15th.
This general scheme will be substantiated further in the
chapter which deals with the archaeology of Hazor.

3.2.6 *Conclusion*

The material in the book of Judges is in keeping with a
date for the Exodus in the 15th century BC. The chronological
notice in Jdg 11: 26 and the absence of references to
Philistines in the early part of the book preclude the
possibility of placing the entire period between 1200 and 1030 BC.
None of the events in the first nine chapters of the book have
been located satisfactorily within this period; a chronology
which places those events before the time of Philistine expansion
is desirable.

A chronology reconstructed on this basis indicates a date for the Exodus in the first half of the 15th century BC, and a Conquest in the second half of that century. This is in keeping with the implications of I Kgs 6: 1. Taken literally, that verse places the Exodus in the middle of the 15th century, but we have seen reasons for treating the 480 years as a round number, and for assuming that the true period may have been slightly greater than this.

In Part Two, a date for the Exodus in the first half of the 15th century BC will be adopted as a working hypothesis.

PART TWO

PALESTINIAN ARCHAEOLOGY
AND THE EARLY DATE
FOR THE EXODUS

CHAPTER 4:
JERICHO

Chapter 4:   Jericho

4.1 *Introduction*

It has been demonstrated in Part One that no convincing archaeological evidence exists for a conquest of Canaan by the Israelites in the 13th century BC. If the early date for the Exodus proposed in the present work is correct, then we may reasonably expect evidence for the arrival of the Israelite tribes in Palestine in the second half of the 15th century BC. This part of the work will undertake a search for such evidence.

In view of the complexity of the problems involved and the novel nature of the solution here proposed, the issues will be set out in considerable detail. This part of the work will begin with a brief outline of the current interpretation of archaeological data from Middle Bronze Age Palestine, followed by an outline of the alternative interpretation proposed here. This will form the preface to a detailed discussion of the main sites mentioned in the biblical narratives of the war of conquest.

The Middle Bronze Age in Palestine has been subdivided in two different ways by Albright and Kenyon. The following table shows the correspondence between the two schemes and the dates commonly assigned to the various periods.

Date	Albright's terminology	Kenyon's terminology
c. 2100-1900 BC	MB I	Intermediate EB-MB
c. 1900-1750 BC	MB II A	MB I
c. 1750-1550 BC	MB II B-C	MB II i-iv

The abbreviations used here and throughout this part of the work (EB[A] = Early Bronze [Age]; MB [A] = Middle Bronze [Age]; LB [A] = Late Bronze [Age]) are the ones most commonly employed for the periods to be discussed. The move made by some scholars to substitute the term "Canaanite" for "Bronze" is rejected here for a reason which will become obvious as the discussion progresses. Here the terminology originated by Albright will be adopted, since it is the one commonly used in works which will be subsequently quoted /1/.

As will be seen in the following pages, there is some disagreement over the precise dates to be assigned to these periods, but the dates given above will serve as a guide for the present introductory discussion.

On the chronology of MB II B-C presently in vogue, that period is roughly synchronous with the era of Hyksos domination in Egypt. As a consequence of this (the reason will be explained fully later), the pottery, fortifications, and scarabs from Palestine in this period have often been described as "Hyksos". The fortified cities of MB II B-C Palestine are generally assumed to have been Hyksos strongholds, and are described as such by many leading authorities.

The end of the MBA in Palestine is marked by the fall of these cities and by the appearance of a pottery known as bichrome ware. The date for the appearance of this pottery in Palestine is dependent on the date given to the fall of the MB II cities. Archaeology has shown clearly that at the end of MB II C all the "Hyksos" cities were violently destroyed. It is commonly assumed that the cities were destroyed by Egyptian armies carrying out a war of retaliation against the Hyksos subsequent to the expulsion of the Hyksos from Egypt. The date of their destruction therefore depends on the date given to the expulsion of the Hyksos and the establishment of Egypt's XVIIIth Dynasty. There is no firm agreement over the exact time of this event; dates traditionally given to it range between 1580 BC and 1550 BC, though slightly later dates have recently been proposed. Some of the cities remained unoccupied for about a century after their destruction. Others were more quickly rebuilt.

The bichrome pottery which appeared in Palestine roughly at the time when the cities were destroyed, is generally considered a chief characteristic of the opening phase of the LBA. The LBA is viewed as extending through various phases to *c*. 1200 BC, when the transition to the Iron Age occurred.

In the following pages the current view of the latter part of the MBA will be challenged and an alternative proposed. The main points made will be as follows:

1. The MB II B-C cities of Palestine were not strongholds of the Hyksos, and their fortification-systems should not be described as Hyksos.

2. The destruction of these cities was nothing to do with an Egyptian war of retaliation against the Hyksos; Egyptian action against the Hyksos probably never extended beyond Sharuhen, in the south of Palestine.

3. The destruction of the MB II cities has been incorrectly dated, because of its association with a hypothetical Egyptian offensive against the Hyksos throughout Palestine. Their destruction should be dated not to the 16th century BC but to the 15th. Consequently the appearance of bichrome ware and the beginning of the LBA must also be redated.

4. The destruction of the MB II cities was the work of the Israelite tribes which left Egypt during the first half of the 15th century BC.

Each of these points will be argued in detail in the following pages. We will begin with a discussion of Jericho, in which the scheme outlined above will be applied to the problem. This will be followed by an Excursus on the chief methodological problem in Palestinian archaeology - that of formulating a reliable ceramic chronology. Then the new scheme will be discussed in relation to Hazor and the other cities mentioned in the Conquest narratives. The discussion of Jericho will bring out several points which are also valid for many of the other cities to be discussed, and will therefore serve to clear the ground for subsequent chapters.

4.2   The Problem of Jericho

4.2.1   Kenyon's revisions of the views of Garstang

We will begin with an outline of Kenyon's revision of the conclusions reached in the 1930's by Garstang. Parts of what is said here will repeat material from Part One. Since it is not only convenient but necessary for a clear presentation of the problem, to have all the relevant material together in one chapter, this repetition is preferable to simply referring the reader to what has gone before.

In the 1930's, Professor John Garstang's excavations at Old Testament Jericho (Tell es-Sultan) unearthed what Garstang believed were remains of the city which fell to Joshua's attack. Ruins of a double defensive wall, apparently broken down by an earthquake, were discovered in association with traces of extensive fire (cf. Garstang 1940: 133ff). This catastrophe marked the end of what Garstang called the Fourth City, or City D, and he dated the destruction to the beginning of the 14th century BC, "After 1400 and before 1385 B.C." (ibid: 125).

This date, as Garstang himself pointed out (ibid), fitted well with the date indicated for the Exodus by I Kgs 6:1, 480 years before the building of the temple; entering Palestine at the end of 40 years in the wilderness, the Israelites would reach Jericho around 1400 BC.

However, analysing Garstang's published material in 1951, Kathleen Kenyon suggested several alterations to Garstang's conclusions. She suggested that Jericho was not occupied at all for the 150 years before 1400 BC, that it only began to be re-occupied at that time after a period of abandonment (Kenyon 1951: 101-38). Her own subsequent excavations strengthened this conclusion. They also revealed that Garstang's double wall had nothing to do with what he termed the Fourth City. This was revealed to be two walls dating from different times, but both belonging to the EBA (third millennium BC) and therefore not possibly related to Joshua's attack (cf. Kenyon 1957: 170-71, 181).

Kenyon supposes that the Jericho destroyed by Joshua was a LBA town whose period of occupation she originally gave as c. 1400-1325 BC, though these dates have since been extended

slightly (cf. Kenyon 1971: 21-22). In other words, far from
being destroyed around 1400 BC, Jericho was only just being
rebuilt then.

Of this LBA town virtually nothing remains. Apart from
certain items of pottery from the tell and in tombs, all Kenyon
found of LBA date was "a row of stones", identified as the
foundations of the wall of a room, "a small irregular area of
contemporary floor", and on this "a small mud oven" and "a
single dipper juglet" (Kenyon 1957: 261). It is concluded that
erosion has removed all major traces of this town. Kenyon
writes: "It is a sad fact that of the town walls of the Late
Bronze Age, within which period the attack by the Israelites
must fall by any dating, not a trace remains" (ibid: 261-2).
Of the date of its downfall, Kenyon wrote in 1957: "As concerns
the date of the destruction of Jericho by the Israelites, all
that can be said is that the latest Bronze Age occupation
should, in my view, be dated to the third quarter of the
fourteenth century B.C." (ibid: 262; cf. also Kenyon 1970: 211).
We should note, however, that Kenyon has more recently offered
a slightly later date of "soon after 1300 B.C." (1971: 22).
Since there is no notable trace of the town itself, there is,
of course, no trace of any actual destruction.

4.2.2 _Kenyon's conclusions and the Exodus_

How do these conclusions fit with the usual theories
concerning the Exodus? The simple answer is that they do not
fit at all. Kenyon's conclusions dispose completely of an early
date for the Exodus, unless the historicity of the Jericho
tradition is denied altogether. According to Kenyon, there was
no town on the site at all for the 150 years before 1400 BC, and
no break in occupation for at least the next three-quarters of
a century. On the other hand, her conclusions do not fit with
the late date for the Exodus either. Kenyon herself points out
that her date for the Israelite destruction suits neither the
early nor the late date scheme, but offers no feasible solution
to the problem thus created /2/. At one point she writes: "It
must be admitted that it is not impossible that a yet later Late
Bronze Age town may have been even more completely washed away
than that which so meagerly survives. All that can be said is
that there is no evidence at all of it in stray finds or in
tombs" (1957: 262-3). But it is clearly not an idea which

Kenyon favours. "The evidence seems to me", she writes, "to be
that the small fragment of a building which we have found is
part of the kitchen of a Canaanite woman, who may have dropped
the juglet beside the oven and fled at the sound of the trumpets
of Joshua's men" (ibid: 263).

Kenneth Kitchen, however, wishing to place the Exodus and
the Conquest in the 13th century BC, adopts the suggestion that
Joshua attacked a later town of which there is now no trace at
all. Thus he writes: "It is possible that in Joshua's day
(13th century BC) there was a small town on the east part of the
mound, later wholly eroded away" (1962: 612). Elsewhere he cites
Mycenaean pottery from the tombs as evidence for a settlement
at Jericho in the 13th century (1966: 63, n.22). Here he is
following Albright (1963: 100, n.59), who claimed that the
pottery from Tomb 13 at Jericho was definitely of 13th century
date, but is contradicting Kenyon's assessment and her assertion
that no evidence for a later LBA town exists either in stray
finds "or in tombs" (1957: 262-3) /3/.

In addition to the problem posed by Kenyon's date for the
fall of LBA Jericho, the fact that remains from this period are
so scanty is itself a problem. The present writer is extremely
suspicious of the fact that so little remains of what is supposed
to have been the city attacked by Joshua. In order to increase
the credibility of her view that this city has been almost
completely eroded away, Kenyon points out that the major part of
the populous MBA city has also vanished, being eroded during the
period of abandonment (ibid: 261). However, many traces of the
eroded MBA town, and especially of its destruction, were
discovered by the excavators in the form of a layer of wash
extending down the sides of the tell. In some places this wash
of ash and silt was "about a metre thick" (ibid: 259-60; cf.
1970: 198). In other words, while large areas of the town were
themselves removed by erosion, the products of this erosion are
still preserved. But not even this much survives in the case
of the LBA town.

This point is brought out strongly by the puzzlement
expressed while Kenyon's excavations were being carried out.
Thus A.D. Tushingham wrote in a preliminary excavation report:
"But while the [LBA] walls themselves may have disappeared,
the detritus of those walls would have washed down the slope

and been discovered lower down the hill. But no trace of Late
Bronze Age pottery has been found in this area throughout the
whole extent of the trench [Trench I] .... There is no evidence
in Trench I for walls or strata of the Late Bronze Age" (1953:
64). The following year, after two further trenches had been
dug, the same writer reported: "The two new trenches at the north
and south ends, like Trench I on the west, have provided no
evidence of Late Bronze Age city walls *or debris from
once-existent city walls*. The mystery of the Canaanite city of
Jericho which fell to Joshua is therefore as great as ever"
(Tushingham 1954: 103, my emphasis). G.E. Wright also remarked
at that time: "The radical denudation of the site and the
failure to find expected materials washed down the slopes of
the mound are very puzzling facts indeed" (1953: 67).

It seems particularly strange that there are no traces of
any fortifications for the LBA town. Kenyon has suggested that
perhaps the LBA occupants re-used the MBA rampart, of which
sections were still extant in their day (1957: 262). Wright takes
up this idea, but with little enthusiasm: "If the settlement of
Joshua's time had a fortification wall at all, it would probably
have been a re-use of the 16th-century bastion, though of such
re-use there is no evidence" (1962a: 80; also earlier in 1953:
64; cf. also Soggin 1972: 85-6).

Wright's own feeling is that "The Jericho of Joshua's day
may have been little more than a fort" (1962a: 80). Whence
arose, then, the tradition of a city so large and formidable
that a miracle was necessary to bring about its downfall?
Wright says: "... The memory of the great city which once stood
there [i.e. in the MBA] undoubtedly influenced the manner in
which the event was later related" (ibid). This is only a step
away from Noth's view (e.g. 1960: 149, n.2), which is followed
by Gray (1962: 93-4), that the story of Jericho's fall is an
aetiological legend, and that there never was an Israelite
attack as described in Jos 6, a view which the present writer
feels is inadequate to account for the growth of a tradition
which now occupies over fifty verses of narrative (Jos 2:1-24;
5: 13-6: 27, - in contrast to merely two verses taken up by
the conquest of each of the six cities mentioned in Jos 10:
28-39). Wright himself describes his own remarks as "nothing
more than suggestions" and concludes: "... At the moment we must
confess a complete inability to explain the origin of the
Jericho tradition" (1962a: 80).

We may conclude this part of our discussion by quoting one of
Kenyon's more recent statements on the problem: "It is impossible
to associate the destruction of Jericho with such a date [as is
required by a 13th century Exodus]. The town may have been
destroyed by one of the other Hebrew groups, the history of whose
infiltrations is, as generally recognized, complex. Alternatively
the placing at Jericho of a dramatic siege and capture may be an
aetiological explanation of a ruined city. Archaeology cannot
provide the answer" (1967: 273).

4.2.3 *A search for an explanation*

Various efforts have been made to account for the lack of
support which the archaeology of Jericho appears to give to the
biblical account of its destruction, without denying the basic
historicity of the account.

The most radical suggestion is that of C. Umhau Wolf
(1966: 42-51), who proposes that Tell es-Sultan may not be the
site of Jericho at all, but of Gilgal, and that Jericho must
therefore be sought elsewhere (cf. Franken 1976: 6). The present
writer does not feel that any compelling reasons exist for
doubting the identification of Tell es-Sultan with Old Testament
Jericho.

R. North has raised the possibility that the Jericho
attacked by Joshua actually lay *near* Tell es-Sultan but was not
identical with it (1967b: 70), and E. Yamauchi has suggested
that "since the excavations by Sellin, Garstang and Kenyon have
not exhausted the eight-acre site, future excavations may still
unearth the missing Late Bronze remains (1973: 53).

Such suggestions are possibilities, but belong more to the
realm of wishful thinking than to that of constructive reasoning
built on existing knowledge. A less desperate expedient would
be more welcome.

Two writers have recently attempted to reinterpret the
existing archaeological evidence in such a way as to allow for
an attack on Jericho by Israelite forces under Joshua around
1400 BC.

L.T. Wood, in an article which appeared in 1970, argues
for a return to Garstang's conclusions on certain key points.

He does not challenge Kenyon's redating of Garstang's "double wall", but argues that this makes no difference to Garstang's other conclusions: "The section of the wrongly dated wall found is far removed from the area where he located his significant material, the evidence from which has no necessary connection with the wall and is not lessened in value because of its redating" (Wood 1970: 71).

The material which Wood considers to be pivotal is "pottery found on both the mound above the spring and in the tombs which Garstang contends represents occupancy until *ca.* 1400 B.C., but which Miss Kenyon says terminated before 1500 B.C." (ibid: 72).

It is here that the evidence is most crucial for Wood's arguments, yet it is sadly also at this point that Wood loses touch with the published material and betrays a serious misunderstanding of it. The pottery to which he refers in the sentence just quoted is *not* assigned by Kenyon to the occupancy which she believes terminated in the 16th century BC; it is assigned in fact to the 14th century (cf. Kenyon 1951: 120-121, 130-33; 1957: 261). Furthermore, Wood associates this pottery with a burned layer which he wishes to argue is the result of Joshua's destruction of the city, in contrast to Kenyon who ascribes this burned layer to the "Egyptian" attack on the city at the end of the MBA (cf. Wood, 72). It is questionable, however, whether any of this pottery should be associated with the destruction layer. Kenyon's discussion (1951: 130-33) appears to treat it as chronologically quite distinct, and Wood himself describes the layer of ash as lying *below* the pottery, whereas one would expect the ash to *overlie* the pottery if the pottery really belonged to the occupation period whose termination the ash indicates. This means that Wood's arguments for dating this pottery (he refers especially to Cypriote items) to a period after 1500 BC (Wood, 72-3) have no bearing on the date of the destruction layer.

The basic weakness of Wood's argument is that while it takes account of some of the ways in which Kenyon's discoveries modify Garstang's conclusions, it fails to acknowledge other modifications which are required, particularly concerning the relationships between the various strata uncovered by Garstang's excavations at different parts of the tell.

B.K. Waltke, in an article which appeared in 1972, also bases

his reassessment of Kenyon's conclusions on the pottery
discussed by Wood, but frames his argument somewhat differently.
He points out that in Kenyon's 1951 discussion, she dated the
pottery "from the upper level above the ruins of the [MBA] store
rooms" to the first half of the 14th century BC (cf. Kenyon 1951:
121, 130-33), and that she has not yet made any statement
modifying this conclusion. Waltke therefore states: "In a word,
according to Kenyon, the latest burnt debris from the Late Bronze
Age city cannot be dated later than mid-fourteenth century B.C."
(1972: 40).

Waltke's intention is to argue that the occupation of the
tell in the LBA began some time before 1400 BC and ceased during
the first quarter of the 14th century, this break being the
result of the Israelite Conquest. To this end he tries to confine
the LBA pottery from the tell to the first half of the 14th
century and to use it to date the burnt layer. He deals with
pottery from some of the tombs, which he acknowledges must be
dated later than 1350 BC, by assigning it to a period of
sporadic habitation at the time of Eglon, king of Moab (cf.
Jdg 3: 13).

There is a non sequitur in Waltke's argument similar to the
one introduced by Wood, namely the assumption that the pottery
gives a date to the burnt debris. Nowhere does Kenyon treat the
burnt layer as deriving from the LBA city, and while her 1951
article is sometimes not very clear on this point, in her works
published after her own excavations at the tell it is quite
apparent.

In addition, it is doubtful whether Kenyon's 1951 statements
concerning the date of the LBA pottery can be held to contradict
her later conclusions that the LBA city was destroyed c. 1325 BC.
Kenyon did in fact state in 1951 that this LBA pottery from
Jericho may "just overlap" with that from Stratum VIII at
Beth-shan, dated to the second half of the 14th century (1951: 121)
in other words, while believing that this LBA pottery from Jericho
should be assigned chiefly to the first half of that century, she
was leaving open the possibility of a slight extension of the
period which it represented into the second half of that century.
There is no real contradiction between this and her later (1957)
statement that "... The latest Bronze Age occupation should, in my
view, be dated to the third quarter of the fourteenth century B.C.

In asserting that the latest pottery from Tombs 4, 5, and
13 should be dated to the second half of the 14th century, and
that it should be linked with Eglon's temporary occupation of
the site (mentioned in Jdg 3: 13), Waltke is in fact adopting
one of Garstang's conclusions (1940: 124, 127-8). Kenyon on
the other hand sees this pottery as quite in keeping with a
Canaanite occupation of the tell from c. 1400 BC down to c. 1325
BC (1957: 261) or c. 1300 BC (1971: 22).

Waltke appeals to a structure known as the Middle Building
for support for his case. He argues that this building must
post-date the burnt layer (which, as we have seen, he erroneously
dates to the first quarter of the 14th century), and is therefore
evidence of some sort of occupation subsequent to the Israelite
destruction of the city. "If then a substantial building such as
the Middle Building was secondarily introduced on the tell after
the destruction ... one has good reason to think that the few
recognizably late pottery examples from the tombs belong to this
occupation and cannot be used to date the Conquest" (1972: 42).

Apart from the fact that this argument incorporates the
error already noted concerning the burnt layer, it also hinges
on the dating of the so-called Middle Building, which is itself
notoriously difficult. No ceramic evidence has been published
from the building itself (Kenyon 1957: 261), and the evidence
from stratigraphy is uncertain. Thus Kenyon appears to have
changed her mind concerning the date of the building, first
treating it as later than its foundational material (1951: 120),
but subsequently suggesting that the debris beneath the building
may indicate the date of the building itself (1957: 261).

Since there is no certain way of dating this building, it
cannot be used in the way Waltke wishes. The building may
radically post-date the latest pottery from the tombs, and could
perhaps even date from the time of David, since from II Sam 10: 5
it would appear that there was some sort of occupation at Jericho
at that time.

Waltke (1972: 40-41) and Wood (1970: 72) both appeal to the
evidence of Egyptian scarabs from the Jericho tombs for support
for the view that occupation of the tell continued through most
of the 15th century and ceased soon after 1400 BC. The series
of XVIIIth Dynasty scarabs found at Jericho were one of Garstang's
main pieces of evidence for a date between 1400 and 1385 BC for
the end of the Canaanite city (cf. Garstang 1940: 120). This

series, which consists of scarabs from the reigns of Hatshepsut, Thutmosis III and Amenhotep III, comes to an end with the reign of the latter pharaoh; no objects datable to the reign of Amenhotep IV (Akhenaten) have been found at Jericho. Furthermore, the city is not referred to in the Amarna letters, which date mostly from Akhenaten's reign, a fact which Garstang considered as further evidence for Jericho's destruction before 1385 BC, the date after which the bulk of the letters were written (cf. Garstang 1940: 122).

As far as the scarabs are concerned, the present writer feels that Kenyon's scepticism of the value of these objects for dating is perfectly justified; as she points out, scarabs are the kinds of objects which are quite likely to become heirlooms, and they cannot be relied upon to date the strata or the tombs in which they are found except by providing an upper limit (cf. Kenyon 1951: 116-17; 1957: 260).

The silence of the Amarna correspondence concerning Jericho is perhaps a more telling point against Kenyon's view of an occupation which spanned the Amarna period. This silence will be accounted for in the scheme presented below. It does not offer much support to the theories of Wood or Waltke, however, since neither of them offers evidence for an occupation at Jericho *before* the Amarna period. It is obviously not possible to make out a compelling case for a destruction at Jericho shortly after 1400 BC without presenting evidence for an occupation of the site prior to that time, and this both writers fail to do.

Not only are the scarabs dubious evidence; there is very little pottery which can without question be dated before 1400 BC There is therefore insufficient evidence from both pottery and scarabs for the assumption that a city existed at Jericho in the 15th century /4/. More important still, neither Waltke's theory nor that of Wood attempts to attribute any buildings or fortifications to the city supposedly destroyed by Joshua. In other words, after all their theorizing, the LBA city itself still avoids detection. Waltke says nothing about this problem, while Wood simply agrees with Kenyon's conclusion that "The city mound was severely denuded of all remains of Late Bronze occupancy (i.e. after 1500 B.C.) except on the mound above the spring" (Wood 1970: 70-71), a view which we have already seen to be inadequate to account for the lack of remains.

Therefore, even if the theories of Wood and Waltke did not contain erroneous assumptions, they would still leave the most pressing problem untouched, that problem being the almost complete absence of building remains from the LBA.

4.3 *The Proposed Solution*

4.3.1 *An Alternative view: Joshua and the end of MBA Jericho*

In view of the complete failure of all attempts made thus far to resolve the problem of our "complete inability to explain the origin of the Jericho tradition" (Wright 1962a: 80), there is perhaps good reason to question whether the Israelite attack was directed against a LBA Jericho at all. Could it have been an earlier phase of the city which fell to Joshua's attack?

The various Bronze Age phases of Jericho are dated by Kenyon as follows. The EBA phase began around 3000 BC and ended shortly before 2000 BC when the city apparently fell during an invasion by hostile groups. In the following period (Intermediate EB-MB in Kenyon's terminology, MB I in Albright's) the tell was occupied by semi-nomadic tribesmen whom Kenyon suggests were Amorites. Around 1900 BC the city was rebuilt and the MBA period began (i.e. in Kenyon's terminology; in Albright's terminology this is the beginning of MB II A). During this period the city became populous and was heavily fortified with a new style of defensive system. This period ended in the first half of the 16th century BC, the city being once more destroyed in an enemy attack. This destruction was followed by a period of abandonment, and then at about 1400 BC we supposedly have the beginnings of the problematical LBA city which we have just been discussing.

Prior to the LBA, therefore, Jericho had fallen before an attacking enemy on at least two occasions. Could either of these two destructions be attributed to Joshua? In the revolutionary theory of D.A. Courville (1971) dates for all archaeological periods in Palestine are lowered by over six centuries, and the destruction of EBA Jericho is attributed to Joshua's attack, which Courville dates to *c.* 1400 BC. However, Courville's scheme depends on a revision of Egyptian chronology which, even granting that certain presuppositions underlying the present Egyptian chronology may be at fault, does not seem workable to the present writer. Even within its own framework, Courville's theory concerning the Conquest contains serious inadequacies.

The destruction which ended the EBA must therefore be ruled out. What of that which ended the MBA?

Kenyon sometimes gives the time of this destruction as *c*. 1580 BC (1970: 194), sometimes as *c*. 1560 BC (1956: 552-555; 1967: 272), and at one point says MBA Jericho was destroyed "somewhere in the period 1580-1550 B.C." (1951: 117). Her reasons for this dating will be discussed in detail below.

If Kenyon had given dates a century-and-a-half later for the end of the MBA city, we would have no hesitation (working with the early date for the Exodus) in ascribing this destruction to Joshua's attack. The archaeological evidence concerning the catastrophic end of this phase of the city provides parallels with the biblical narrative at several points.

Sometime during the MBA (about 1750/1700 BC according to current views), the defences of the city were strengthened by the addition of a huge artificial embankment running all the way round the city. This defensive system was the one in use when the MBA city finally fell. It consisted of "a wall crowning a great artificial bank, retained at a slope considerably steeper than the natural angle of the rest of the soil by a plastered surface and a massive revetment wall at the base" (Kenyon 1957: 220). All this "must have been a most imposing defence, somewhat resembling from the outside the defences of a great medieval castle" (ibid: 216). This strongly fortified city was "certainly populous" (ibid). In short, it would fit excellently as the large walled city which the biblical narrative says Joshua faced on crossing the Jordan.

Moreover, the enemy which attacked this city finally destroyed it by setting it on fire. Kenyon writes: "... The evidence for the destruction is ... dramatic. All the Middle Bronze Age buildings were violently destroyed by fire.... This destruction covers the whole area, about 52 metres by 22 metres, in which the buildings of this period surviving the subsequent denudation have been excavated. That the destruction extended right up the slopes of the mound is shown by the fact that the tops of the wall-stumps are covered by a layer about a metre thick of washed debris, coloured brown, black and red by the burnt material it contains; this material is clearly derived from burnt buildings farther up the mound" (1970: 197-8). "Walls and floors are hardened and blackened, burnt debris and beams from the upper

storeys fill the rooms, and the whole is covered by a wash from
burnt walls..." (1966a: 17). "... There is no doubt from the
scorched surfaces of the walls and floors of the violence of the
conflagration" (1957: 232; cf. Garstang 1940: 104). Kenyon is
certain that this burning was the result of a military campaign
against the city (1957: 229; 1970: 194-7; cf. Garstang 1940:
103-4). We are forcibly reminded of the fact that Joshua had
Jericho burnt to the ground after he had taken it (Jos 6: 24).

It may be objected that in the biblical account it is
related that the wall of the city "fell down flat" (Jos 6: 20),
while in some places the defences of the MBA city are well
preserved, and the summit of the rampart actually survives in at
least one place. However, the biblical account does not say that
the entire city wall collapsed. Indeed in Jos 6: 22, two verses
after it is stated that the wall fell down flat, we find Joshua
sending the two men who had formerly spied out the city to enter
Rahab's house and bring her out; since we have previously been
told (Jos 2: 15) that Rahab's house "was built into the city
wall, so that she dwelt in the wall", it is clear that the account
envisages that at least one section of the wall remained more or
less intact after the disaster. The account in Jos 6 is saying
simply that in some places breaches appeared in the defences so
that Joshua's army was able to enter the city.

An event which could cause sections of the defences to
collapse suddenly is not difficult to find. It is a fact that
Jericho lies on a volcanic rift at the northern end of a
geological fault which passes all the way along the Jordan Valley,
continuing south through the Arabah and the Red Sea, and on into
Central Africa (cf. Garstang 1940: 160). As Garstang pointed out,
the zone in which Jericho lies "is never wholly free from
earthquake shocks" (ibid: 135), and earthquakes at Jericho are
well attested in both ancient and modern times by archaeological
evidence and written records respectively (ibid: 136; cf. Kenyon
1957: 175-6, 262).

We will return shortly to the probability that a great deal
of seismic activity occurred along the Arabah and the Jordan
Valley during the period of the wilderness journeys and the
beginning of the Conquest. First I wish to direct attention to
Num 25, for here begins a series of three events which are
strikingly evidenced in the biblical narrative and the
archaeological record alike.

In Num 25 we find the Israelites encamped at Shittim, "in the plains of Moab beyond the Jordan at Jericho" (Num 22: 1; cf. 33: 48-9); i.e. the Israelite camp extended along the eastern side of the Jordan just opposite the city. The period spent at Shittim immediately preceded the attempt to destroy Jericho. It was from there that spies were sent to the city by Joshua (Jos 2: 1), and from there that the Israelites finally set out to attack it (Jos 3: 1). We read that while the camp was there, the area was affected by a severe plague. Num 25: 9 tells us that 24,000 Israelites died of this plague.

It is remarkable that a plague is evidenced at Jericho shortly before the end of the MBA city. Late in the sequence of MBA tombs at Jericho, there are several examples of multiple burials. Such burials are not a usual feature of the MBA city, and Kenyon says we may infer from them "that some catastrophe caused high mortality on an occasion very late in the history of Middle Bronze Age Jericho" (1957: 254). Since there are no signs of injury to the bodies, enemy action is not a likely cause of these deaths. Famine is ruled out by the lavish provision of food in the tombs. Kenyon therefore concludes that MBA Jericho "suffered a plague" shortly before the greater catastrophe of the city's destruction (ibid: 255) /5/.

Next we turn to the collapse of the city's walls in Jos 6: 20. Garstang wrote that "Only the miracle of an earthquake shock will justify the description of this event in the Book of Joshua" (1940: 175, cf. 135), and underlined the likelihood of this explanation by referring to numerous examples of earthquakes, ancient and recent, in the Jericho region. Further, his son, J.B.E. Garstang, collected together various biblical references which he considered indicate a series of instances of seismic activity at the time of the Exodus, the wilderness journeys, and the Conquest. He suggests that "at the time of the Exodus the whole of the geological two-fold rift from Palestine to Lake Nyasa was in a state of violent seismic and volcanic upheaval" (ibid: 160). Thus he suggests that certain of the plagues of Egypt are accounted for by volcanic activity affecting the sources of the Nile and areas further north, to the east of the Red Sea, producing clouds of ash which darkened the air. The pillar of fire and smoke may have been "a column of dust and steam and ash from the open mouth of an active volcano", and earthquake activity may have been responsible for the drawing back of the water at the sea of passage; as for the events at Sinai, "Who can read the narrative (Ex. 19: 16-19) without realising that it describes perfectly the terrific convulsions of a volcano?" (ibid: 163).

Further examples of seismic activity are the opening of the earth to swallow the rebellious host in Num 16: 27-35, and the event which temporarily stopped the flow of the Jordan in Jos 3: 14-17 (cf. ibid: 165-171, and on the latter incident also 136-7).

Garstang believed he had unearthed archaeological evidence of the earthquake recorded in the biblical narrative, in the form of fissures and dislocations in what he believed to be the walls of the city attacked by Joshua (ibid: 135-6). These, however, are the walls now assigned to the third millennium BC. Does any evidence exist for an earthquake having occurred at the end of the MBA city?

Such evidence comes not from fissured walls but from discoveries made in certain of the tombs of MBA Jericho. The tombs concerned are those containing the multiple burials. In these tombs the organic material shows a remarkable degree of preservation compared with that shown by material deposited in the EBA and earlier MBA tombs. In the earlier tombs, "The small total amount of organic matter ... disintegrated more or less completely. In contrast to this condition, the multiple burials in the MB tombs were accompanied by a wealth of mortuary equipment comprising pottery, wood, matting, basketry and food, wig-materials and textiles. Roast meat is commonly preserved, and parts of the skin and flesh of the human bodies, and occasionally hair, are preserved. The brain is very often found in the skull in a shrivelled condition" (Zeuner 1955: 125).

F.E. Zeuner, whose words these are, made a detailed study of three tombs, J14, J19, and J20, in an attempt to account for this remarkable degree of preservation. Zeuner concluded that the organic material was preserved because some while after the burials were made, natural gas containing methane and carbon dioxide entered the tombs and brought both bacterial decomposition and termite activity to an end (ibid: 128). Earth movement and resultant fissuring are suggested as the best explanation of how this gas was suddenly released into the tombs (cf. S. Dorrell 1965: 706; Kenyon 1957: 250). It is therefore significant that J14 and J20 were both found to have suffered heavy rock falls (Zeuner 1955: 125), and Kenyon writes that "One can see in the walls of the tomb shafts and chambers how the rock has been twisted and fractured" (1957: 250).

When we recall that Kenyon dates the multiple burials to shortly before the destruction of the city, and that the process of decomposition had only just begun when it was brought to a standstill, it becomes very probable that the earthquake activity which released the natural gas into the tombs occurred roughly at the time of the city's final collapse.

The third correspondence between the biblical narrative and the archaeological record has already been noted: the deliberate destruction of the city by fire.

Thus the biblical narrative and the archaeological finds at MBA Jericho point to the same pattern of events. The archaeological evidence implies a plague, followed shortly by earthquake activity and the total destruction of the city by burning. The biblical narrative gives the same sequence: a plague in the Jericho region, followed not long after by what may readily be interpreted as at least two instances of seismic activity (the first stopping the Jordan, the second destroying the city walls), followed by conquest of the city and its eventual destruction by fire.

The evidence for linking the biblical narrative with the end of the MBA city is therefore very striking. But all this remains nothing more than interesting speculation unless we can show that it is permissible to move the end of MBA Jericho from the 16th century BC into the 15th. We will now examine the reasons for the generally accepted 16th century date. There are in fact only two reasons for this date. They will be examined in turn.

4.3.2 *Jericho and the expulsion of the Hyksos*

One reason for the date currently accepted for the end of MBA Jericho has its roots in the city's assumed link with the Hyksos.

Kenyon and Garstang both connect the destruction of the MBA city with the expulsion of the Hyksos from Egypt. This event is dated variously between 1580 and 1550 BC, though some writers have offered a slightly later date, and Garstang tended to use a round figure of *c.* 1600 BC when referring to it (cf. Garstang 1940: 104).

It is known that when Egyptian armies under Amosis, founder of the XVIIIth Dynasty, drove the Hyksos out of their capital Avaris, they pursued them into Palestine. Sharuhen (Tell Farᶜah), in the extreme south of Palestine, was occupied by the retreating Hyksos and was subsequently besieged by the Egyptian armies. It fell after three years (cf. Pritchard 1955: 233).

Kenyon, like Garstang before her, supposes MBA Jericho to have been a Hyksos stronghold and therefore one of the main targets in an Egyptian campaign of liberation and revenge which destroyed all the Hyksos cities of Palestine. Thus, writing of the end of MBA Jericho, Kenyon has stated: "This destruction can be identified with very little doubt as the work of the Egyptians" (1957: 229; cf. 1951: 117; 1970: 195-7; also Garstang 1940: 103-4).

Two points need to be noted. The first is that there is no evidence whatever for an Egyptian war of retaliation in Palestine. There is no evidence that the Egyptians continued their pursuit of the Hyksos beyond Sharuhen (cf. Epstein 1966: 171). Indeed, evidence suggests that as soon as Sharuhen had fallen, Amosis turned his armies southward in an attempt to regain control of Lower Nubia (cf. Säve-Söderbergh 1951: 71). It may reasonably be asked how we can possibly envisage Egypt launching a campaign which successfully destroyed almost every large city in Palestine, when it took the Egyptians three years to reduce the Hyksos garrison nearest to their own country. In short, the whole notion of an Egyptian campaign against the Hyksos extending throughout the whole of Palestine is both improbable and largely unsupported by evidence.

We may pause to ask how the notion arose that Amosis led a massive drive into Palestine after the fall of Sharuhen. The idea originated early (e.g. Breasted 1906b: 227) as a result of an over-interpretation of a text left by one Amosis-Pennekheb, stating that he campaigned with the pharaoh Amosis in Djahy. Djahy is sometimes said to have been a geographical term used to refer to central Syria and Palestine, but according to M.S. Drower it meant the coastal plan of Phoenicia (1973: 245). Drower comments on this campaign by Amosis-Pennekheb: "... We are given no indication of the whereabouts or extent of the operation" (ibid: 431). Further support for a campaign into Palestine has been drawn from a reference in a text from late in the reign of Amosis, to the use of oxen which came from "the land of the Fenkhu" in the quarries of El-Masara. Again, according to Drower, the geographical term means the Lebanese coast (ibid: 425). In any case, T.G.H. James comments: "unfortunately an uncertainty in the reading of this text makes it doubtful whether the oxen were captured in a campaign or supplied as tribute by the Asiatics" (1965: 9).

It is amazing that a theory based on such meagre evidence should have become so widely accepted and even taken for granted. It is unlikely that it would have been so generally adopted if the destruction of Palestine's MBA cities had not been interpreted as evidence of Amosis' hypothetical activities. But the fall of Palestine's MBA cities has now become the mainstay of the theory. Thus a circular argument has been produced which loses sight of the fact that the above texts supply no evidence at all for a campaign into Palestine itself.

The second point is this: there is no reason to believe that MBA Jericho was a Hyksos fortress. If Jericho was *not* occupied by the Hyksos, there is no reason for attributing its destruction to an Egyptian army or for linking it at all with the political situation of the 16th century BC. One reason for dating Jericho's destruction to that century thus disappears.

Garstang was confident that Jericho was a Hyksos stronghold in the MBA. He describes pottery from this period as "examples of Hyksos art", and a diagram of a MBA tomb is labelled as a "section of a Hyksos tomb" (Garstang 1940: 99). He even writes of storage vessels sealed "in numerous instances with the signet of a Hyksos ruler" (ibid: 94), and of finding the scarabs of Hyksos kings (ibid: 94-5, 101-3).

All this is inference and assumption. Jericho has not yielded a single item which can truly be identified as Hyksos. In point of fact, the great majority of scarabs from MBA sites in Palestine are local products, and Kenyon describes them as "rather distant relatives" of the Egyptian scarab, bearing only "crude and meaningless copies of Egyptian hieroglyphs" (1957: 253; cf. 1970: 193). The scarabs from Jericho are no exception to this general rule. A detailed discussion of scarabs from Jericho, by D. Kirkbride, constitutes Appendix E of the detailed excavation report. Here we learn that of the multitude of MBA scarabs discovered during Kenyon's excavations, only three bear royal titles, and only one of those discovered during Garstang's

excavations bears a royal title (Kirkbride 1965: 580, 592).
Three of these four names definitely belong to non-Hyksos kings,
while the fourth belongs to no known ruler, Hyksos or otherwise
(ibid: 583).

Kenyon has attacked the practice of describing finds from
MBA Palestine as Hyksos in the following words: "Within MB II
falls the period of the Hyksos in Egypt. Such importance has been
attached to this that the period in Palestine is sometimes given
the overall name of Hyksos and the pottery and other objects
typical of this stage designated specifically Hyksos. This is
incorrect...". There is "cultural continuity from MBI to MB II"
and a "cultural continuum at this period from north to south on
the Syrian littoral.... Unless this whole new culture is to be
ascribed to the Hyksos, none of it is Hyksos" (1966a: 14-15; the
point is also made by Van Seters, 1966: 3).

And yet Kenyon herself has assumed a Hyksos occupation for
the second half of the MBA at Jericho. The reason for this is
that the defensive system of the period - the wall crowning the
artificial bank with a revetment wall at the base - is commonly
associated with Hyksos influence.

Examples of this type of defensive system appear in various
other places during the MBA, and Kenyon has associated their
appearance with the spread of the Hyksos (1957: 220-28; 1966a:
39; 1966b: 65-73; 1967: 269; 1970: 193). She says: "The
distribution of the new type of defences shows that this is the
material evidence of the Hyksos period in Palestine. Defences
of this type can be traced from Carchemish in the north-east
through inland Syria and Palestine to Tell el-Yahudiyah north
of Cairo" (1966a: 39; cf. map in 1966b: 70).

This theory is dependent on the view that the Hyksos contained
Hurrian elements which entered Palestine from the north. The
Hurri were "a people of Indo-European origin who established
themselves on the Middle Euphrates about the beginning of the
second millennium and built up the kingdom of Mitanni.... In
the course of the next centuries there was a steady expansion of
Hurrian influence towards the Mediterranean coast..." (Kenyon
1957: 222). It is suggested that by the 18th century BC a number
of towns in Syria-Palestine were under the control of Hurrian
bands from the north, and that these people became "a ruling
warrior aristocracy" whose members imposed their methods of

warfare on the land and were responsible for the defensive systems
of the MBII (Kenyon's terminology) period (ibid: 223). These
same warrior groups penetrated into Egypt and contributed to the
overthrow of the Middle Kingdom; "... To the Egyptians they were
known as the Hyksos, foreigners, Asiatics" (ibid: 224).

However, this view of the origin and spread of the Hyksos
has been undermined in so many ways in recent years that it is now
hardly tenable.

The notion that Hurrians constituted a major part of the
people which took control of Egypt has been shown to be without
firm foundation. Van Seters concludes an examination
of onomastic evidence from Egypt by saying that "not a single
name of this period can be identified with certainty as Hurrian"
(1966: 183). Van Seters concludes that the Hyksos were Amurrite
princes from the Levant (ibid: 190), and denies any connection
between the Hyksos and the MBA defences (ibid: 32-3).

There is in fact no evidence at all for the notion of a
Hurrian movement into Palestine from the north in the 18th-17th
centuries. As Van Seters points out, Hurrians are mentioned for
the first time in the annals of Thusmosis III and Amenhotep II
(15th century), and the term "land of Hurru" as a designation
for Syria-Palestine "cannot be dated to much before the Amarna
Age" (ibid: 186). As Redford says, "No evidence ... either
archaeological or epigraphic, suggests the presence of an
important Hurrian element in the Levant until the sixteenth
century; and then it appears, not in the form of a *Völkerwanderung*,
but as a state ensconced beyond the Euphrates" (1970b: 6-7; cf.
Van Seters 1966: 187).

One argument in favour of a Hurrian element among the Hyksos
has for a long time been that the Hyksos introduced the horse and
chariot into Egypt. (The Hurrian state of Mitanni appears to
have been one of the main centres of the domestication of the
horse). However, Van Seters has shown that evidence for the
Hyksos having possessed the horse and chariot is indecisive
(1966: 185). Säve-Söderbergh has made a similar point: "... There
is not the slightest evidence that the Hyksos used the horse until
the very latest part of their rule in Egypt..... Everything in
the evidence seems to demonstrate that the Hyksos never used this
war technique until possibly in the last struggles against the
Egyptians before they were expelled from the country" (1951: 59-60)

The same writer has also made strong criticisms of the
assumption that ramp fortifications of the type found at Jericho
were introduced by the Hyksos. He points out that "no certain
instance [of this fortification type] is known from Egypt, the
only country where the actual Hyksos are established·with
certainty as a political factor!" (ibid: 60). Two ruins in
Egypt, at Tell el-Yahudiyah and Heliopolis, have often been
interpreted as examples of such fortresses (e.g. Kenyon 1966a: 39;
1970: 182); "... Unfortunately", says Säve-Söderbergh, "I think
the architect Ricke is right in assuming that they are more
probably temple foundations" (1951: 60). In the work to which he
refers, Ricke makes the point that the date of both these
"fortresses" is so far quite unsettled, and that at Tell
el-Yahudiyah the gentle outer slope of the "rampart" would
actually favour attackers; in addition, this site shows no trace
of either a defensive wall or a moat, which makes it very hard
to believe that the structure unearthed had any defensive
purpose (cf. ibid: n.5).

Interestingly, it was through the discoveries at Tell
el-Yahudiyah that the rampart defences first came to be linked
with the Hyksos. It was Petrie who first examined the site
closely, and he declared it to be the remains of the Hyksos
capital Avaris (Petrie 1906: 9-10; cf. North 1967a: 87), thus
linking both the rampart-style of defence system (as he believed·
it to be) and the style of pottery which he unearthed at the
site (and which he termed Tell el-Yahudiyah ware) with the
Hyksos. Later, when it was realised that Tell el-Yahudiyah could
not have been Avaris, the link between these two things and the
Hyksos was inexcusably maintained. (The commonly assumed
connection between the Hyksos and the so-called Tell el-Yahudiyah
ware, which has also been found at many Palestinian sites, has
been strongly criticised by both Säve-Söderbergh [1951: 57] and
Van Seters [1966: 49-50]. More will be said of this erroneous
link in the Excursus.)

Van Seters' discussion of this style of fortification system
·leads him to assert:

"One criterion which should no longer be used in the dating
of these defences is their correlation with the so-called
invasion of the Hyksos from the north, or the establishment
of a Hyksos empire in Syria and Palestine. Such historical
speculation has seriously prejudiced the archaeological
evidence. Furthermore, there is no reason, from

archaeological data, to suppose that the similar development
in fortifications in Syria preceded those in Palestine or
that this style of fortification was originally derived from
regions even further north" (1966: 32). "There is no reason
whatever to postulate, for the so-called Hyksos defences,
any immigration either of a new people or of a new warrior
aristocracy in the latter part of the MBII period"
(ibid: 37).

To sum up the above material: there is no evidence for
linking the Hyksos rule in Egypt with a Hurrian migration into
Syria and Palestine; there is no evidence for any such migration
having taken place until long after the time of the Hyksos; there
is no evidence for linking the rampart fortifications with either
the Hurrians or the Hyksos. In short, Kenyon's view that the
rampart fortifications constitute "the material evidence of the
Hyksos period in Palestine" (1966a: 39) is without foundation.

Some of the facts reported by Kenyon herself actually seem
to militate against any connection between the rampart defences
and the Hyksos. She says:

"As far as Palestine is concerned, the introduction of the
new type of defence meant no break in culture. From the
first beginnings of the Middle Bronze Age down to its end,
and long past it, all the material evidence, pottery,
weapons, ornaments, buildings, building methods, is
emphatic that there is no break in culture and basic
population" (1966a: 39).

With specific reference to Jericho we have it stated: "The
Jericho evidence is emphatic that there is no cultural break" -
i.e. at the time when the new fortification system was introduced
there (1967: 269). Furthermore: "There is no uniformity in the
culture of the towns so defended" (1966a: 39). This would all
seem to imply that the rampart defences should not be associated
with any particular culture or incoming group of people, Hyksos
or otherwise. However, Kenyon takes the above facts as "evidence
of how foreign ruling aristocracies could impose themselves
without altering the existing culture..." (1967: 269). This is
clearly begging the question, as is the following, written more
recently: "From the material remains one would never deduce the
setting up of a new ruling class, with its alien Hurrian elements,
if it were not for the appearance of the new type of fortification"
(1970: 193).

Certain of Kenyon's recent works do contain indications that she may have begun to doubt the correctness of her own previous view concerning the destruction of MBA Jericho. One work, written ten years after her statement that the attack on the MBA city "can be identified with very little doubt as the work of the Egyptians" (1957: 229), contains this statement: "The destruction might be caused either by Egyptian retaliatory forays against her Asiatic enemies or by the groups dispersed from Egypt" (1967: 272). The third edition of her book *Archaeology in the Holy Land* still puts forward the view that the Egyptians destroyed the MBA cities, including Jericho (1970: 195-7), but in a slightly more recent work Kenyon appears to favour her previously offered alternative, for, writing of the numerous destructions at the end of the MBA, she says it is "likely that they were due to attacks by the groups of Asiatics displaced from Egypt at this stage" (1971: 3) - by which she presumably means the Hyksos. The fact that Kenyon avoids using the term "Hyksos" here (and in 1967: 272) obscures an important point: namely that this suggestion is incompatible with the view, put forward by Kenyon in several works, that Jericho and the other fortified cities of the MBA were *Hyksos fortresses*. Those cities would obviously not have been destroyed by the Hyksos if they were *occupied* by the Hyksos. Yet to the best of my knowledge Kenyon has nowhere retracted her picture of a Palestine ruled by Hyksos overlords from these same cities.

But even when we do dispense with such a picture, as I believe we must, it is still difficult to believe that expelled Hyksos groups were responsible for the end of MBA Jericho. There is no evidence that such groups left Egypt and travelled to that area, and it is difficult to imagine why they should have destroyed Jericho (to say nothing of all the other MBA cities which fell at the same time) even if they had.

Kenyon's belief that "a great number of the Asiatic Hyksos" poured into Palestine after the capture of Avaris by Egyptian troops, seems to be based on the testimony of Manetho, whom she cites in this connection (1971: 3). But Manetho can hardly be considered a reliable source on the expulsion of the Hyksos, since his account of this event, preserved for us by Josephus, confuses it with the Exodus of the Israelites, and appears to confuse Sharuhen with Jerusalem (Josephus, *Against Apion* I, 73-90, 227-250).

I believe, however, that Kenyon's expression "groups of Asiatics displaced from Egypt" does accurately describe those responsible for the destruction of the MBA cities - but I believe those Asiatics were the Hebrew tribes of the Conquest narratives, not hypothetical bands of marauding Hyksos, and that the time of the destructions was at least a century later than that suggested by Kenyon.

We may conclude by noting some cautionary remarks made by Van Seters: "The use of the term 'Hyksos' to designate a style or type has created great confusion in the study of the archaeology of the period [MBA]" (1966: 3). Such misuse of the term "begs the whole question of an openminded consideration of the archaeological evidence" (ibid). He notes that "Almost every instance of dating these [MBA] fortifications has been by means of a correlation with a supposed Hyksos invasion", and remarks: "Such historical speculation has seriously prejudiced the archaeological evidence" (ibid: 32 with no.8).

Yet, sadly, Van Seters himself illogically suggests that the fall of the fortress-cities "can best be understood as the activity of the Eighteenth Dynasty pharaohs and the date for the end of Middle Bronze would be about 1550 B.C." (ibid: 9). The suggestion is illogical because a view which denies any connection between the Hyksos and the fortified cities of the MBA provides no reason why those cities should have been the objects of Egyptian campaigns in the 16th century BC.

Returning to the specific problem of Jericho, our conclusions may be summarised thus: there is no evidence at all that Jericho was occupied, fortified, or used in any way by the Hyksos; if Jericho was not a Hyksos stronghold, there is no reason why it should have been a target for the Egyptian army; there is also no reason why Hyksos groups expelled from Egypt should have attacked and destroyed Jericho. In short, there is no reason to link the fall of MBA Jericho with the political situation in Egypt and Palestine in the 16th century BC. The political situation in the 16th century BC provides no explanation for the violent end of MBA Jericho, and hence it does not require that the end of MBA Jericho be dated in that century.

If the end of MBA Jericho could be placed in the following century, the Israelite attack on the city recorded in the

biblical narrative would provide an excellent explanation for
that city's sudden downfall, as we have seen. However, Kenyon
sometimes refers to a further reason for placing its destruction
in the 16th century BC, and to that we now turn.

4.3.3 *The argument from pottery*

Garstang believed that Jericho had been reoccupied almost
immediately following the destruction supposedly wrought by the
Egyptians. At the time of his excavations the pottery finds
seemed to warrant this conclusion. (Garstang classified the
restored city as a continuation of the MBA one. He placed the
change to LBA in the middle of the 15th century, there being,
he thought, a slight change in culture at that point, but no
break in occupation. See Garstang 1940: 113-14).

Kenyon's revision of Garstang's dates for the LBA city
involves a period of abandonment of 150 years or more between
the destruction of the MBA city and the beginnings of LBA
settlement. Kenyon insists that this period of abandonment
is necessary because of the evidence of the pottery:

> "When the [Garstang's] excavations were in progress, the
> true transitional pottery from MB to LB, and that of LB I,
> was in fact scarcely known in Palestine, and
> well-authenticated examples have only been provided by
> the magnificently full publication of the material from
> Megiddo and Tell Duweir. It is now quite clear that this
> material ... is completely lacking at Jericho both in the
> city and in the tombs" (1951: 115). "It must be strongly
> emphasized that the stratification of the town site shows
> a period of abandonment, and that the complete absence of
> pottery of the second half of the sixteenth century and of
> the fifteenth century B.C. makes it clear that the site
> was abandoned during this period (1967: 271-2).

I do not wish to dispute Kenyon's assertion that there was
a period of abandonment at Jericho. I wish to question, however,
the date when she says this period began, which is, of course,
the date at which the MBA city was destroyed.

The pottery which is completely absent from Jericho is the
bichrome pottery sometimes described as transitional between
the Middle and Late Bronze Ages (Kenyon 1970: 198-200; Epstein

1966: 188). This pottery is commonly viewed as having spread
to various sites in Palestine from two main centres, Megiddo
in the north and Tell el-ʿAjjul in the south. At Megiddo,
bichrome ware is confined chiefly to Stratum IX, to which
Epstein has assigned dates of c. 1575-1480 BC (Epstein 1966:
171-3). Its use is supposed to have spread southwards, having
reached ʿAjjul shortly after its first use at Megiddo (ibid).

The view expressed by both Kenyon and Epstein concerning
the origin and spread of bichrome ware, and the period for
which it was in use, will be examined in detail in the following
chapter, where it will be shown to be erroneous. It will also
emerge that while Kenyon sometimes appears to use her date for
the appearance of bichrome ware to deduce the date for the
destruction of the MBA cities, the former is actually dependent
on the latter, and not vice versa.

Here I wish simply to show that even within the framework
offered by Kenyon and Epstein, bichrome ware cannot be used to
date the fall of MBA Jericho.

There is no evidence that bichrome ware spread from Megiddo
in a south-easterly direction any further than Taanach, a
distance of less than ten miles; and from ʿAjjul it spread
eastwards only as far as the Judaean foothills. In other words,
from neither of its main centres did bichrome ware spread as
far as Jericho. Indeed, its use seems to have been quite limited.
It does not seem to have spread appreciably into the highland
regions of central Palestine, let alone as far as the Jordan
Valley. (The only highland site which has yielded bichrome
sherds to date is Beitin.) I would suggest in fact that its use
barely extended beyond a 25-mile wide strip of the Syria-Palestine
littoral. The plausibility of this suggestion is underlined by
the recent discovery that bichrome ware was not manufactured in
Palestine itself, as was previously supposed by Kenyon, Epstein
and others, but was imported into Palestine from Cyprus (cf.Artzy,
Asaro and Perlman 1973: 446-461). In other words, its spread was
from the coast eastwards, not from Syria southwards as has
commonly been supposed.

It is therefore reasonable to question whether the failure
of bichrome ware (and other types of Cypriote pottery /6/) to
appear at Jericho is of any significance at all for the chronology
of the site. If its use never extended appreciably beyond the
coastal plain, then its non-appearance at Jericho can obviously

not be taken to imply abandonment of the city.

Kenyon herself says that Jericho's geographical position may have resulted in cultural isolation. Lying east of the mountain range of central Palestine, it was "away from contacts with richer areas provided by the coastal route" (1967: 271). "... In comparison with places like Tell Ajjul, Megiddo and Beisan, in touch with the great trade route between Egypt and Syria, Jericho at this period [MBA] may have been something of a backwater" (1957: 253; also 1966a: 21). In view of these statements it is not unreasonable to ask why bichrome ware and other contemporary types of Cypriote pottery should be expected at Jericho at all.

It is very significant that "no bichrome ware is known to date" at Beth-shan (Epstein 1966: 118). Beth-shan is situated similarly to Jericho, in the Jordan Valley to the west of the river, but it lies much closer to Megiddo than Jericho does to either Megiddo or ʿAjjul. And here we have positive evidence that there was no period of abandonment. Epstein writes: "... Evidence that it was not abandoned at this period is provided by an unpublished chamber tomb, T42, which contained the funerary offerings from many burials placed in it over a long period of time and dating to both before and after the *floruit* of bichrome ware" (ibid).

This evidence makes it quite clear that the period of abandonment at Jericho cannot be dated from the absence of transitional pottery there. It could perhaps be argued that the absence of this pottery does not necessarily indicate a lengthy period of abandonment at all; however, the degree of erosion suffered by the ruins of the destroyed MBA city does indicate such a period, and I do not wish to deny that there was one. But the absence of transitional pottery tells us nothing about when this period began.

In short, the ceramic material from Jericho does not require the conclusion that the MBA city came to an end in the 16th century BC.

4.3.4 *A new working hypothesis*

We have seen that both criteria used to date the destruction of the MBA city at Jericho are in fact highly

questionable. There is no evidence which compels us to date the
destruction before 1500 BC; it could equally well have occurred
some decades after that date. I submit, therefore, that MBA
Jericho actually came to an end in the second half of the 15th
century BC, and that its attackers were the Israelites as
recorded in Jos 6.

If we date the Exodus to *c.* 1470 BC, and allow a full forty
years for the wilderness period, then we should date the
Israelite attack on Jericho to *c.* 1430 BC. We must remember,
however, that our date of *c.* 1470 BC for the Exodus is somewhat
provisional. Therefore we will not attempt to give a precise
date to the fall of Jericho, but we may reasonably suggest a
date somewhere within a decade of 1430 BC.

If the end of the MBA city is brought down to this time,
what is to be made of the archaeological material from later
periods, and how does that material correspond with information
provided by the biblical traditions?

According to the biblical tradition, when the Canaanite
city was sacked and razed, Joshua laid a curse on the site, and
the city was not rebuilt again until the reign of Ahab, in the
9th century BC, i.e. the Iron Age (cf. Jos 6: 26 and I Kgs 16:
34).

Some remains, though not many, of an Iron Age occupation at
Jericho have been found (cf. Kenyon 1957: 263-4). But what of
finds from the intervening period?

The biblical traditions do imply that temporary settlements
were occasionally made at Jericho in the intervening period.
Thus in Jdg 3: 13, we read that Eglon, King of Moab, along with
groups of Ammonites and Amalekites, took possession of Jericho
(cf. Deut 34: 3 for another example of the use of the title
"city of palms" to designate Jericho). And in II Sam 10: 5 it
appears that some sort of occupation, though perhaps only a
military station, existed at Jericho in the time of David.

The establishment of some sort of temporary settlement at
Jericho by Eglon of Moab, which would fall somewhere in the LBA,
would account adequately for all the LBA finds on the tell - the
scarabs, the pottery from the tombs and the mound, and the
scanty building remains. It seems much more reasonable to suggest

that these are the remains of a temporary, unwalled settlement
on the site than to suggest that they are all that is left of
a fortified LBA city.

It is in fact only because Kenyon believes the events of
Jos 6 "must" belong in the LBA "by any dating" (1957: 262) that
she posits the existence of a proper town in this period at all.
The archaeological finds alone certainly do not require such a
suggestion. The LBA archaeological evidence (or rather the lack
of it) is accounted for much better if it is suggested that *there
never was a city as such at Jericho in the LBA*, only sporadic
habitation. This would explain the paucity of house remains, the
complete lack of any trace of a city wall, and also the fact that
no proper LBA tombs are attested, only the re-use of certain MBA
tombs by the later settlers (cf. Kenyon 1957: 260-61; 1971: 20-21).
It would also account for the absence of references to Jericho in
the Amarna correspondence.

Concerning the settlement which seems to have existed in
David's time, we may note that according to Albright and Wright,
the so-called "hilani" building at Jericho may date to the 10th
century BC, though a date in the 9th century (Ahab's time) is
also possible (cf. Wright 1962a: 79).

It is felt that the scheme proposed here offers a more
consistent treatment of the archaeological evidence than hitherto,
as well as providing a complete explanation for the origin of the
Jericho tradition.

In the following pages we will examine evidence from various
other cities mentioned in the Conquest narratives, to see whether
this dating of the end of the MBA can operate satisfactorily at
those sites also. At these other sites a new problem arises,
however, for, unlike Jericho, they do not all lie beyond the
regions where bichrome pottery came into use. Since the
presence or absence of bichrome pottery has often been used as
a criterion for dating the fall of the MBA cities, the whole
question of when this pottery came into use and for how long it
remained in vogue must be examined in some detail. This will be
our next undertaking.

CHAPTER 5:

AN EXCURSUS: BICHROME WARE AND CERAMIC CHRONOLOGY

Chapter 5: An Excursus: Bichrome Ware and Ceramic Chronology

5.1 *Introduction*

In this Excursus we discuss a methodological problem whose ramifications extend far beyond the limits of the present work. The problem is that of constructing an absolute chronology from the ceramic record of Palestine.

We are suggesting that the date for the end of the MBA should be lowered from the 16th century to the second half of the following century. This naturally requires a lowering of the dates for the first phase of the LBA, which means in effect a redating of the pottery types characteristic of that phase. But what would be the effect of such a shift on the subsequent phases of the LBA?

The Mycenaean III A pottery found in LB II A levels in Palestine and at Tell el-Amarna in Egypt, indicates that the time spanned by those levels must include the Amarna period (c. 1380-1350 BC). Therefore, unless we abandon the conventional chronology of Egypt (as Courville does in his redating of the archaeological periods of Palestine), LB II A must be considered as firmly dated to the 14th century BC. The theories offered in the present work will be explored within the framework of the conventional Egyptian chronology. Therefore a lowering of the date for the beginning of LB I cannot be followed here by an arbitrary lowering of the dates of all subsequent periods. Is it possible, however, that the LB I period can be considerably shortened? If it can, then the placing of the LB II A period in the 14th century is no obstacle to our main theory.

The case for a reshaping of the LB I period constitutes the

argument of the following pages. It is not possible, however,
to explore every aspect of this issue in the context of the
present work. For this reason the discussion will concentrate
on the problem of dating one particular type of pottery, namely
that known as bichrome ware. This pottery is the ideal subject
for our discussion, since its appearance in Palestine is
considered the chief characteristic of the LB I period, and the
problem of dating its use illustrates how easily errors and
pitfalls can occur in the construction of a ceramic chronology.

Our arguments concerning LB I must be prefaced, however,
with a brief discussion of our redating of the end of MB II C
from the MB side of the question.

5.2 *The dating of MB II B-C*

If the date for the end of MB II B-C is to be lowered, it
follows that that period must either be extended or else redated
as a whole by the extension of one or more of the preceding MB
periods (or, of course, by a combination of both these
possibilities). All I wish to point out here is that both these
alternatives are perfectly plausible.

Lengthening the MB II C period by a full century from
c. 1550 BC would certainly not leave it distended and empty,
since it is at present described as "a brief but very eventful
and momentous period" in the history of Canaan (Mazar 1968: 96).
Dever writes concerning MB II C: "Careful stratigraphic
excavation at several sites has revealed a complex series of
building phases and fortifications that must apparently be
compressed with a period of about a hundred years, i.e. from
ca. 1650-1550 B.C." (1972b: 240). It seems reasonable to suggest
that MB II C is allowed too little time by the currently
accepted chronology. However, there is no reason why the whole
period consisting of MB II B-C together could not be dated
somewhat later than at present.

It is instructive to note the reasons for the date presently
given for the start of MB II B-C. This period is a continuation
of the basic culture of MB II A, except for "two new and rather
spectacular innovations" (Wright 1961: 88) which mark it off
from the preceding period. These innovations are the type of
pottery known as Tell el-Yahudiyah ware, and the style of
fortification discussed in the previous section. Wright

describes how these two innovations were used by Albright to date
the beginning of MB II B:

> "On the basis of Egyptian chronology, when tied to
> Palestinian stratigraphy, Albright has correlated the
> earthen fortifications with the 'Hyksos' conquest of
> Egypt and dated them in Palestine about 1700 B.C. or very
> shortly thereafter. At the same time it must be noted,
> however, that evidence from Tell Beit Mirsim, Lachish and
> Megiddo seems to prove that the new pottery shapes ...
> were introduced before the earthen embankments were
> erected. For this reason, MB II B is represented as
> beginning ca. 1750 B.C. or within the decades immediately
> thereafter" (ibid: 90).

In other words, the present dating of MB II B depends on the
supposed association of its two chief characteristics with the
Hyksos. But we have already seen that the rampart fortifications
should not be associated with the Hyksos, and we will see
subsequently that Tell el-Yahudiyah pottery should not be linked
with them either. So there is no evidence at all for
synchronizing the start of MB II B with the rise (or arrival) of
the Hyksos.

The fallacy of describing scarabs from the MB II B-C period
as Hyksos has already been noted. We may underline our previous
reservations with a further point (also made earlier but in a
different context), namely the unreliability of scarabs for
providing anything more than *termini post quem*. Hence even if
some scarabs from Palestine's MB II B-C levels could be shown to
be of Hyksos origin /1/, this would not require us to synchronize
those levels with the Hyksos period. It is salutary to bear in
mind that a scarab described as "Hyksos" was found, along with a
scarab of Thutmosis III, in Beth-shan's Level V, which probably
spans the 10th century BC (see conveniently Fitzgerald 1967: 195).

It only remains to point out that no developments *within*
the period MB II B-C have been satisfactorily correlated with any
independently dated events. Not even the transition between MB
II B and C can be dated; Mazar describes this problem as "still a
most difficult topic in Palestinian archaeology" (1968: 91). He
does, however, attempt to date the MB II C period himself by
referring to one particular innovation which took place within it,
namely the replacement of some of the earthen rampart fortifications
with walls of unhewn stones arranged in straight courses. Mazar

attributes this new development to a hypothetical group of Hurrian
and Indo-Iranian invaders who were rapidly assimilated into the
local population. He places this event in the second half of the
17th century BC (ibid: 91ff). To illustrate how unsupported this
hypothesis is, one need only point out that M. Dothan has
attributed the construction of the new defences in the south,
e.g. at Tell el-Far'ah and 'Ajjul, to the Hyksos under Apophis I
(1973: 17), while J.R. Stewart attributes the building activity
at 'Ajjul to Egyptian factions *opposing* the Hyksos (1974: 120,
n 20).

This multiplicity of explanations for the developments which
characterised MB II C shows clearly that those changes cannot be
linked satisfactorily with any event which occurred in the second
half of the 17th century BC. There is no reason why those changes
should not be dated to the 16th, or even early 15th century BC.

Having assured ourselves that no objections to a lowering
of the date for the end of MB II C are likely to come from within
the MBA itself, we may turn to the far more complex problem of
dating LB I and the appearance of bichrome ware.

5.3 *Bichrome Ware and the MBA Destructions*

We must note firstly that there is some debate as to whether
bichrome ware appeared shortly *before* the destruction of the MBA
cities or soon after.

Though there is no actual destruction level at Megiddo, the
transition between Stratum X and Stratum IX is usually taken as
marking the end of the MBA and the start of the LBA. Megiddo's
excavators, followed by Albright (1938c: 346), believed that
bichrome ware appeared at Megiddo during Stratum X, i.e. before
the end of the MBA. However, the bichrome ware attributed to
this stratum comes not from the occupation level itself but from
certain tombs. Wright (1961: 109, n 85) and Epstein (1966: 94-8)
have independently shown that the burials containing the bichrome
ware items in fact belong to Stratum IX, and that no bichrome ware
can be attributed to the previous stratum.

However, other sites have been claimed to yield bichrome
ware from before the destruction levels, notably 'Ajjul, in the
south (cf. Albright 1965: 56). Thus Epstein accepts the
appearance of bichrome ware at 'Ajjul before the destruction of

Palace I, which event she dates to between 1567 and 1564 BC (1966: 177). J.R. Stewart and others have even proposed a redating of strata at ⸀Ajjul which would place the end of Palace I at c. 1590 BC and hence the subsequent stratum, which contains the bulk of ⸀Ajjul's bichrome ware fragments, between 1590 and 1560/50 BC (Stewart 1974: 62-3). Stewart also proposes a shift in the chronology of other southern sites as a consequence of the proposed shift at ⸀Ajjul. Other writers have also stated that in the southern sites bichrome ware appeared before the wave of destructions attributed to Amosis (cf. Artzy, Asaro and Perlman 1973: 446). Kenyon, however, takes a totally different view. Discussing the appearance of bichrome ware during the Palace I phase at ⸀Ajjul, Kenyon treats its presence as evidence that the building known as Palace I continued in use "into the first stages of the Late Bronze Age", since, according to Kenyon, bichrome vessels "are not elsewhere found in Middle Bronze Age levels" (1971: 29).

This illustrates the subjectivity to which interpretations of the ceramic evidence are susceptible. If one begins with the assumption that the destruction of Palace I at ⸀Ajjul marks the end of the MBA city, then the presence of bichrome ware in the Palace I level proves that it appeared at ⸀Ajjul before the end of the MBA. But if one begins with the assumption that bichrome ware did not appear until LB I, its appearance in the Palace I level merely proves that Palace I was not destroyed until after LB I had started.

It makes no difference to the main theory put forward here whether bichrome ware appeared in Palestine before the end of the MBA or not. It is important, however, to note that the question is not yet settled, and that the way one settles it depends (in the present uncertain state of the evidence) on one's prior assumptions /2/. We shall see below that the same is true of various other problems concerning bichrome ware.

5.4   *Megiddo*

Megiddo and ⸀Ajjul are the two main centres at which bichrome ware has been found and from which it has long been assumed to have spread. ⸀Ajjul will be the subject of a subsequent section. Megiddo will introduce our discussion of bichrome ware's chronology, since it is here that "we encounter

in full force the problem ... of what boundaries to place on
the Bichrome repertory" (Artzy, Asaro and Perlman 1973: 461).

Megiddo figures prominently in the pioneering study of this
pottery by W.A. Heurtley (1939: 21-34), and in the study by
Epstein (1966). Most of Heurtley's views have for some time
been unacceptable in the light of subsequent discoveries (cf.
Epstein 1966: 20), though his theory concerning a single
artist-potter who produced the ware while living chiefly at
ʿAjjul is still to be found occasionally in recent works (e.g.
Negev 1972: 249). Since Epstein's work has superseded
Heurtley's as the most important contribution to the study of
this pottery, Epstein's thesis will form the starting-point for
our discussion.

At Megiddo bichrome ware is found almost exclusively in
Stratum IX, with a very slight overlap into the beginning of
Stratum VIII. The period for which bichrome ware was in use is
therefore tied up with the dating of Stratum IX at Megiddo.

Epstein writes: "The end of Stratum X and the beginning of
Stratum IX was dated by the excavators to 1550 B.C., presumably
on the basis of a date in the mid-sixteenth century for the
expulsion of the Hyksos from Egypt" (1966: 171). Epstein
herself rejects this basis for dating Megiddo's strata. She
points out that there is no evidence of any destruction between
Stratum X and Stratum IX, "such as would undoubtedly have left
its mark had the city been involved in any way in the final
clash between Egyptians and Hyksos" (ibid: 172; cf. also Kenyon
1970: 197). She also draws attention to the point made above
in our discussion of the Jericho problem, that there is no
evidence that the Egyptians pursued the Hyksos any further
north than Sharuhen, in the south (ibid: 171); there is thus no
reason to believe that any of the more northerly cities were
involved in or affected by events surrounding the expulsion of
the Hyksos.

Epstein herself wishes to link the appearance of bichrome
ware with the arrival of a Hurrian element in the population of
Palestine; she believes that "Palestinian bichrome ware" shows
the assimilation of

"... a decorative approach introduced by the Hurrian
element in the population. Thus it could only have
evolved *after* the arrival of the Hurrians. By postulating

some quarter of a century during which one generation could achieve adulthood in the new places of settlement, a date of 1575 is arrived at, and it is this date which is here proposed for the beginning of Stratum IX at Megiddo and as a *terminus post quem* for the beginning of bichrome ware there" (173).

This is obviously extremely speculative. It will be criticised in detail shortly. Also very speculative is Epstein's date for the *end* of the use of bichrome ware at Megiddo. She writes:

"As for the duration of Stratum IX, it would seem that it came to an end not long before the battle of Megiddo in 1481, though ... it must be stressed that neither the Egyptian records nor the results of excavation provide evidence for the destruction of the town by Thutmosis III". "By allowing a few years following on the battle of Megiddo for true bichrome ware to die out, the date of *c.* 1475 is arrived at, giving a very slight overlap in Stratum VIII" (ibid).

Hence Epstein suggests that bichrome pottery was in use for "no more than a century" at Megiddo, and says in addition that there is " no evidence for its use longer elsewhere" (ibid).

As our discussion proceeds, we will see that Epstein's arguments concerning both the beginning and the end of Stratum IX at Megiddo, and for the period for which bichrome ware was in use, are without foundation.

The chronology of Megiddo's LBA strata is a complex problem. Stratum VIII began c. 1479, according to the chronology adopted by the excavators (cf. Loud 1948: 5 table), and ended 1350/1300 BC (cf. ibid; also Schofield 1967: 319; Negev 1972: 204). Stratum VII is divided into two periods, A and B, of which B is the earlier.

The dates normally given to Stratum VII are 1350/1300-1150/ 1130 BC (Loud 1948: 5 table; Negev 1972: 204). From Stratum X down to the end of VIIB, there are no signs of wholesale destruction, only of partial rebuilding as individual structures collapsed and were replaced (cf. Epstein 172-3). However, VIIB is divided from VIIA by a violent destruction of the city (cf. conveniently Schofield 1967: 318). In the framework of the

chronology of Megiddo which has been generally in use until
recently, this destruction would have to be dated to either the
12th or 13th century BC.

However, Kenyon has recently proposed a drastic reshaping
of the previously worked-out scheme for Megiddo. This revision
places the end of what has been called Stratum VIIB in area BB
at c. 1480 BC, over 200 years earlier than the dating given by
the conventional chronology for the site.

Kenyon considers that the destruction between Stratum VIIB
and Stratum VIIA was followed by a gap in occupation, and writes:
"It would be natural to expect that the gap at Megiddo comes
with its historical destruction by Thotmes [Thutmosis] III,
c. 1480 B.C." (1969: 60; cf. also 1971: 8-10). However, it is
only "natural to expect" this to be the case if a destruction
of the city by Thutmosis can actually be shown to have taken
place, whereas in fact it cannot. It is true that Kenyon writes
of "the historically-recorded destruction" by Thutmosis III
(1969: 53), but we should remind ourselves of Epstein's point
(1966: 154, 173) that Egyptian records provide no evidence
whatsoever for a destruction of the city by this pharaoh. What
is recorded is how Megiddo was besieged following an incident
in which a group of kings forming a coalition against Thutmosis
took refuge within its walls. The city capitulated and was not
destroyed (cf. Pritchard 1955: 235-40; Drower 1973: 449-50).
Fisher actually suggests that it was essential for Thutmosis to
preserve Megiddo as a base for further operations and as part of
a chain of posts along his road northwards from Egypt (Fisher
1929: 13-16). There is no "historically-recorded destruction" of
Megiddo by Thutmosis III.

It is true that Kenyon argues her case also from the pottery,
but she writes: "The pottery evidence for this date for the end of
Stratum VIIB is, however, so scanty that it would not stand alone
The historical probability is much the most important factor, and
the two together are reasonably conclusive" (1969: 60). But
without written evidence for the city's destruction by Thutmosis
III, it is not correct to speak of this "historical probability";
it simply does not exist.

A brief detour to the site of Tell Abu Hawam (or Huwam), on
the coast to the northwest of Megiddo, provides us with further
interesting, if confusing, facts. The earliest stratum at this
site is Stratum V. Basing his reasoning partly on the discovery

of a scarab of Amenhotep III in this stratum, the excavator of
this site, R.W. Hamilton, concluded that the settlement was
founded "soon after 1400 B.C." (Hamilton 1935: 67). Amiran,
after remarking that bichrome ware "flourishes mainly in LB I, that
is, Stratum IX at Megiddo", adds that vessels of the same style
"still occur in LB II A, for instance in the lower phase of
Stratum V at Tell Abu Hawam and Stratum VIII at Megiddo" (1970:
154, also pl. 48, nos. 14-16). Since Amiran dates the start of
LB II A at c. 1400 BC (cf. ibid: 12), she clearly accepts
Hamilton's date for the founding of Tell Abu Hawam, and hence
assumes a much later date than does Epstein for the end of the
use of bichrome ware. Also, the transition between Stratum IX
and Stratum VIII at Megiddo, dated by Epstein to c. 1480 BC, is
dated to c. 1400 BC by Amiran (cf. ibid: 154 and table on 12)
/3/.

Further confusion is introduced by the fact that Mazar has
proposed a revision of the dates given to strata at Tell Abu Hawam
on the basis of a comparison of the pottery from those strata
with pottery from Megiddo (Mazar 1951: 21-5). Thus he argues
that the pottery of Stratum V at Tell Abu Hawam is contemporary
with that assigned to Stratum VIIB at Megiddo. This synchronism
requires placing the founding of Tell Abu Hawam as late as c. 1300
BC. (Mazar actually suggests that the site was founded by Seti I
as a base for the Egyptian navy.) However, while Mazar adopts a
date of c. 1300 BC for the start of Megiddo's Stratum VIIB, this
is the Stratum whose *end* Kenyon wishes to place at 1480 BC /4/.

My main aim in presenting these facts is to illustrate how
fluid and open to interpretation the ceramic evidence is. I do
not intend to put forward a case supporting any one of these
schemes, nor do I intend to offer an alternative of my own. I
wish simply to draw two conclusions from what we have seen; one
general, the other specific. The general conclusion is the very
obvious one that the division and dating of LBA strata at Megiddo
is uncertain to an extraordinary degree. Differences between
various views can be measured in centuries. The full seriousness
of this confusion becomes apparent when one appreciates the
extent to which the chronology worked out for Megiddo's strata by
the original excavators has been used for constructing a dating
sequence for LBA pottery throughout Palestine and beyond (cf.
Albright 1938c: 346; 1956: 29; Schofield 1967: 316; Kenyon 1970:
198-200; and cf. the above example of Mazar's chronology for
Tell Abu Hawam).

The specific conclusion is this: with the chronology of LBA
Megiddo so uncertain, there is at present no way to give a date
to the end of Stratum IX and hence to the end of the use of
bichrome ware. With no evidence, either from Egyptian records
or from the archaeology of Strata IX-VIII, for a destruction of
the town by Thutmosis III (cf. Epstein 173), a date of c. 1480 BC
(or one a decade later on the Egyptian chronology employed by
Albright) for the end of Stratum IX is purely arbitrary. But
equally arbitrary is a date at the very beginning of the 15th
century, as appears to be required by Kenyon's revised scheme,
and the same applies to Amiran's much later date of c. 1400 BC.

Here we reach an important point which will be elaborated on
shortly. The chronology of Megiddo, far from being an independent
guide to the chronology of other sites, is itself adrift.
Megiddo was not destroyed at the end of the MBA. Its chronology
can only be anchored when it is tied to the chronology of those
towns which were destroyed at that time. But *their* chronologies
only acquire a fixed point when we succeed in dating their
destructions. As has already been suggested in the section on
Jericho, this has not yet been done in a reliable fashion.

This means that any date offered at present for the time
when bichrome ware went out of use must be treated as unreliable.
Suitable means for controlling the data do not exist. This point
has been made by the writers reporting the new discoveries which
prove the Cypriote origins of the pottery. They call for "a
careful re-examination of stratigraphic information and for
chemical analyses of a larger array of pottery of these [LBA]
periods" (Artzy, Asaro and Perlman 1973: 446), and state: "For
the present, we believe that there are still questions of typology
and chronology which cannot be answered satisfactorily" (ibid:
460).

5.5 *The "Hurrian Migration" and the Appearance of Bichrome Ware*

Emphasis has so far been on the difficulty of dating the *end*
of the use of bichrome ware in Palestine. We turn now to the
problem of when bichrome ware first made its appearance in
Palestine.

As we have seen, Epstein's date for the start of the use of
this pottery at Megiddo is c. 1575 BC, this being based on the
assumption that it was introduced into Palestine by a movement of

Hurrians which supposedly took place c. 1600 BC. This is also
Kenyon's view. Hence she writes of bichrome ware's "certain
affinities in style to Hurrian decorated pottery", and states
that it "may be taken as evidence for renewed northern contacts,
and probably the continuance of the infiltration of new groups
from that direction" (1970: 200).

    As early as 1951, Säve-Söderbergh had warned against linking
bichrome ware with the Hurrians (1951: 58), describing this view
(first put forward strongly by Engberg 1939) as "a rather wild
guess". Similarly, Van Seters warned: "The ascription of this
ware as Hurrian is questionable. The ware is far more
characteristic of coastal Syria, Palestine, and the Eastern
Mediterranean than it is of distinctively Hurrian regions"
(1966: 52-3). In addition he pointed out that there is no
evidence whatever for a Hurrian migration into Palestine before
the late 15th century BC (ibid: 186-7).

    This scepticism of the Hurrian theory has been shown to have
been entirely justified by the recent discovery that bichrome ware
entered Palestine as an import from Cyprus. This fact has been
demonstrated beyond all doubt by neutron activation analysis of
the clay used in its manufacture. M. Artzy, one of the
researchers involved in this discovery, has made this interesting
comment: "The reliance of the scholars of the Hurrian migration
southward and on the political upheavals caused by the Hyksos
defeat disregards the stratigraphical data of the appearance ...
of the Bichrome Ware, which seems to have been produced regardless
of the political situation in the Near East" (Artzy 1973: 9).

    This serves as a warning against the perennial tendency of
archaeologists to interpret their discoveries within a framework
based on supposed political events. Sometimes those events
themselves are not even known for certain to have taken place,
and in some cases (for example, the supposed destruction of
Megiddo by Thutmosis III, and the supposed arrival of Hurrian
groups c. 1600 BC) the evidence, when carefully examined, suggests
that they may *not* have taken place.

    With the appearance of bichrome ware thoroughly severed from
a hypothetical Hurrian migration, is there any other criterion
which can be used to date the beginning of its use in Palestine?

<u>5.6</u>   *The Problem of Circular Arguments*

An early discussion by Albright treated the chronology of
LBA strata at Megiddo as "decisive" for the chronology of
bichrome ware (Albright 1938c: 346), and proceeded on that basis
to adduce dates for the pottery which were then used to date
strata at ʿAjjul (ibid: 347-9).

Albright naturally dated bichrome ware by dating Megiddo's
Stratum IX, and he did this by assuming (a) that the city of
Stratum X was destroyed by the Egyptians after the expulsion of
the Hyksos, and that the city of Stratum IX was rebuilt soon
afterwards; he therefore agreed with the excavators in placing
the start of Stratum IX at c. 1550 BC (ibid: 346); he also assumed
(b) that the end of Stratum IX indicated the taking of the city by
Thutmosis III, which (following the then new Borchardt-Egerton
chronology) he dated at 1468-7 BC, some twelve years later than
the date followed by the excavators (ibid).

We have already seen that there is no reason to link the
transition between Stratum IX and Stratum VIII with the so-called
battle of Megiddo. We may also recall that there is no reason
to link the transition between Stratum X and Stratum IX with the
expulsion of the Hyksos; not only is there no trace of a
destruction between these strata (on the contrary there is "a
marked continuity" - cf. Epstein 172), there is no evidence that
the expulsion of the Hyksos resulted in Egyptian campaigns
throughout Palestine.

Since the chronology of Stratum IX at Megiddo cannot itself
be controlled, it is quite useless for controlling the chronology
of bichrome ware. Epstein realises this, and uses her date for
the introduction of bichrome ware to date the beginning of
Stratum IX at Megiddo, rejecting the excavators' (and Albright's)
date of c. 1550 BC and offering an alternative of c. 1575 BC.
But she arrives at this latter date on the sole basis of the
theory which links bichrome ware with a migration of Hurrians.
Since this theory is now seen to be false, the dating of the start
of Megiddo's Stratum IX remains a moot point.

That the starting-date for Megiddo's Stratum IX is dependent
solely on the date for the appearance of bichrome ware and not
vice versa becomes quite clear in some of Kenyon's recent works.
Thus in the *Levant* article in which Kenyon attempts her redating

of all Megiddo's LBA strata, she seeks to date the introduction
of bichrome ware first, and then goes on to use her conclusion to
date the beginning of Megiddo's Stratum IX (Kenyon 1969: 50-51).

The method which Kenyon uses to date the introduction of
bichrome ware is worth examining. In the *Levant* article Kenyon
describes the appearance of bichrome ware as "the diagnostic
feature which is taken as defining a stage later than the
destruction of Middle Bronze Age Jericho and Tell Beit Mirsim"
(ibid: 50). As was explained in the section on Jericho, bichrome
ware has not been discovered at that site, a fact which Kenyon
takes as indicating that its introduction occurred after MBA
Jericho had been destroyed. Bichrome ware is also absent from
Tell Beit Mirsim, a fact which Kenyon interprets in the same way,
and with more justification than in the case of Jericho, since
Tell Beit Mirsim lies much nearer the coast, in the region where
bichrome ware is commonly found. She goes on:

> "The exact chronological date for the appearance of bichrome
> ware depends on whether it is accepted that the destruction
> of Middle Bronze Age Jericho and Tell Beit Mirsim marks the
> effect of the re-establishment of Egyptian power at the
> beginning of the XVIIIth Dynasty, *c.* 1560 BC., or whether
> it is claimed that these sites end at an earlier date"
> (ibid: 51).

This is a remarkable statement for two reasons. Firstly, it
admits that the destruction of these two cities at the end of the
MBA may have had nothing to do with the expulsion of the Hyksos,
and yet, for no apparent reason, it suggests that the destructions
may have occurred *before* that event, and does not appear to
countenance the possibility that they occurred later.

The second point, however, is the significant one for our
present discussion. In other works, Kenyon has used the fact
that no bichrome ware appears at Jericho to date the fall of the
MBA city, assuming a date in the first half of the 16th century
BC for the introduction of bichrome ware (cf. 1951: 115; 1967:
271-2; 1970: 195-200). But in the statement just quoted, we find
precisely the opposite method employed. There the date for the
appearance of bichrome ware is made dependent on the date for the
destruction of MBA Jericho, not vice versa. Thus we find ourselves
presented with a circular argument. What is dependent on what?

We must anticipate the contents of a later section here to
point out that the destruction of Tell Beit Mirsim does not

provide a fixed point for dating either the appearance of bichrome
ware or the destruction of Jericho. Like Jericho, this site shows
a violent destruction at the end of the MBA, followed by a period
of non-occupation until after the end of LB I, and has similarly
been assumed to have fallen when the Hyksos were expelled from
Egypt (cf. conveniently Albright 1967: 214-15). Several of the
points made concerning Jericho in the previous section apply
equally to Tell Beit Mirsim; in other words, there is no reason
to link its destruction with the expulsion of the Hyksos; like
Jericho, it may well have fallen in the following century, and
if Albright is correct in identifying it with Old Testament Debir,
we may suggest that the fall of this MBA city was also the work of
Israelite forces, as recounted in Jos 10: 38-9 (cf. Jdg 1: 11-13).

In short, once one has admitted (a) that the date given to
the appearance of bichrome ware does not fix the time of the
destruction of MBA Jericho and Tell Beit Mirsim, but is in fact
dependent upon it, and (b) that their fall may have had nothing
to do with the re-establishment of Egyptian power at the start of
the XVIIIth Dynasty - and Kenyon's *Levant* article admits both
these things - then no reason remains for dating their fall in the
16th century BC. Yet Kenyon chooses so to date it, and hence also
dates the appearance of bichrome ware in that century: "... It can
be accepted that the appearance of the ware belongs to the
sixteenth century B.C." (1969: 51). This is quite illogical.

Is the date for the appearance of bichrome ware dependent
on the date for the fall of the MBA cities, or vice versa? This
is now seen to be the vital question.

Kenyon's fullest statement concerning the establishment of a
ceramic chronology for Palestine at the start of the LBA is quite
unequivocal. It makes it perfectly clear that the ceramic
chronology is dependent on the date given to the fall of the MBA
cities, and not the other way round.

In chapter XI of the second volume of the revised *CAH*,
Kenyon explains that "The dating of the stages of occupation in
the Palestinian towns of the Late Bronze Age is almost entirely
dependent on pottery", and that scarabs and other datable Egyptian
objects can only provide *termini post quem*; "It is therefore
necessary to build up a corpus of pottery groups that form
recognizable assemblages, to which a chronological framework can
be given by historical evidence or external contacts" (1971: 4-5).

What Kenyon describes as "the starting point" for this
chronological framework is the break which occurs at many sites
at the end of the MBA, "a break", says Kenyon, "which can be
ascribed either to Egyptian campaigns at the beginning of the
Eighteenth Dynasty or to the Asiatics expelled from Egypt after
the fall of Avaris and pushed back into Palestine. The
outstanding examples of this are Tell Beit Mirsim and Jericho"
(ibid: 5). Three pages later she returns to this topic and says
that "There are no certain criteria for connecting the
stratigraphical sequence in most sites with the reconquest of
Palestine by the Egyptian rulers of the Eighteenth Dynasty", but
that it is

> "... reasonable to suppose that the destruction of Jericho,
> Tell Beit Mirsim and Shechem is associated with that event,
> and that the pottery of the final stages at Jericho and
> Tell Beit Mirsim *can be used as a yardstick for dating
> levels elsewhere,* with the reservation that new forms may
> begin to appear slightly earlier at important sites such
> as Megiddo and Tell el-Ajjul than at these sites" (ibid: 8,
> my emphasis).

The last quotation actually introduces a discussion of the
chronology of LBA Megiddo, and therefore contrasts strikingly
with a statement made elsewhere by Kenyon concerning the first
phase of the LBA (i.e. the phase represented at Megiddo by
Stratum IX), that "The chronology of the pottery depends almost
entirely on Megiddo..." (1970: 198). There can be no doubt,
however, that the fuller statement reflects the true nature of
the problem. We have seen above that the chronology of Megiddo,
far from being an independent guide to the dating of Palestine's
LBA pottery, must itself be treated as one of the last links in
the deductive chain.

We see therefore that *the date given to the fall of the MBA
cities, especially Jericho and Tell Beit Mirsim, is the key to the
ceramic chronology of Palestine at the beginning of the LBA.*
Everything depends on the presuppositions which lie behind the
dating of their destruction. Is it really, as Kenyon states,
"reasonable to suppose" a link between their collapse and the end
of Hyksos rule in Egypt? We have seen already that in the case of
Jericho it is not, and the same reasoning can be applied at many
other sites.

Not only is there a complete lack of evidence for linking the

MBA cities with the Hyksos, there is also a lack of adequate
evidence from the Egyptian side for a campaign to "reconquer"
Palestine in the period immediately following the Hyksos
expulsion. In fact the main evidence for an "Egyptian reconquest
of the country" (Wright 1961: 91) consists of the MB II C
destruction levels. But they can only be interpreted as evidence
for this event if they can be independently dated to the appropriate
time. This cannot be done.

This is another area where circular arguments tend to occur.
Thus Wright, speaking of the end of the MBA, says: "Every
excavated city of the time in Palestine shows evidence of
destruction in the same era /5/. How far north ... Amosis
managed to go in his conquest of the Mediterranean coastland is
unknown and consequently debated. The Palestinian evidence
suggests that a positive appraisal of his achievement is probably
in order" (1965: 75). In other words, we have no reason to believe
in an extensive Egyptian campaign into Palestine by Amosis unless
we choose to interpret the fall of Palestine's MBA cities as
evidence of such a campaign. But the only reason for dating the
fall of those cities to the time of the Hyksos expulsion is the
assumption that their fall was the result of extensive Egyptian
reprisals against the Hyksos. It is this assumption that we
believe to be groundless.

To return to the fact which is of prime importance for the
theory offered in the present thesis: the ceramic chronology of
Palestine in LB I is not an obstacle to a lowering of the date for
the fall of the MBA cities, because it is itself dependent upon
the date given to that event.

5.7 *Previous Redatings of the Appearance of Bichrome Ware*

There have been attempts by some writers to place the
appearance of bichrome ware earlier than the date suggested by
Epstein. The efforts of Stewart and Kempinski to revise 'Ajjul's
chronology provide one example, and will be examined shortly.
Here I wish to highlight a trend to *lower* the date for the
appearance of this pottery, since this trend leads in the
direction of the theory put forward here.

A date later than that adopted by Epstein and Kenyon for the
appearance of bichrome ware has been suggested partly because of
new and later dates given by some Egyptologists to the expulsion

of the Hyksos, and partly because of a suggestion that a period
of abandonment should be assumed between the destruction of the
MBA cities and the appearance of bichrome ware in the subsequent
strata.

In his 1938 article on the chronology of strata at ʿAjjul,
Albright established a chronology of c. 1550-1450 BC for bichrome
ware (on the basis of assumptions which we have seen should be
considered invalid). In an article which appeared in 1956,
Albright was able to refer to this dating of bichrome ware and
say that he had followed it "consistently ever since" (1956: 29,
n 11). However, shortly after that time he did revise his
opinion concerning the beginning of the bichrome ware phase.

In 1962, Albright noted a tendency among Egyptologists to
lower the date for the expulsion of the Hyksos. Thus he wrote:

"This event is being dated by more and more scholars about
1550 B.C., toward the end of the reign of Amosis (1570-1545)
.... It is very improbable that Palestine was conquered
before the very end of the reign of Amosis or early in the
reign of Amenophis I. The end of the Middle Bronze
occupation therefore fell ... somewhere in the third
quarter of the sixteenth century (i.e. 1550-1525 B.C.),
just before the *floruit* of the panelled bichrome ware
(*c.* 1525-1450)" (1962: 41-2) /6/.

Albright subsequently continued to cite late dates for the
expulsion of the Hyksos and the end of the MBA cities, and to
lower the date for the appearance of bichrome ware. Some of the
authorities cited by Albright actually date the accession of
Amosis in the decade 1560-1550 BC, and place the defeat of the
Hyksos late in his reign, close to 1530 BC (cf. Albright 1973b:
17-18). (Note that in the chronology worked out for Egypt by
E.O. Forrer, the expulsion of the Hyksos is dated as late as
1519 BC; cf. Schaeffer 1948: 607-8.) In 1965, Albright placed
the destruction of Palestine's fortress-cities between 1540 and
1520 BC, and dated the appearance of bichrome ware to "shortly
afterwards" (1965: 56). In 1967 Albright wrote that the span of
bichrome ware "is to be placed between *c.* 1500 and 1450 B.C.,
contrary to some recently expressed views" (1967: 214) /7/.

Wright also adopted a late date for the defeat of the
Hyksos, and, on this basis, a later date for the end of the MBA
cities, though he admits: "... The evidence is not yet clear as

to precisely when the Middle Bronze Age should be conceived as
ending and the Late Bronze beginning" (1961: 91). Most
significant is this sentence: "Because of the violence of the
Egyptian conquest, it is not certain that we have any deposits
that must be dated solely in the second half of the sixteenth
century, following the first and main wave of the conquest in
the middle decades of that century" (ibid). Wright specifically
mentions Stratum IX at Megiddo and the contemporary stratum at
ʿAjjul (Stratum II and Palace II), referring to these strata as
fixing chronologically the bichrome ware phase. Wright considers
that these strata "belong, for the most part, to the first part of
the fifteenth century", and says: "Whether or how far these
strata go back into the sixteenth century is unknown" (ibid).
Speaking specifically of bichrome ware he says: "Hitherto, the
ware has been dated between 1550 and 1450 B.C., but in my judgement
there is thus far no clear evidence which requires that it be dated
before 1500 B.C." (ibid).

5.8 *The Length of LB I and the Use of Bichrome Ware*

While Kenyon has in one place suggested classifying the bulk
of the bichrome ware period as transitional between MBA and LBA,
and dating the start of LB I proper at 1500/1480 BC (1970: 197,
200, 202), it seems more sensible to use the label LB I for the
whole period which extends from the destruction of the MB II C
cities to the beginning of LB II A, as is done for example by
Amiran (1970: 12, 124) and in the tables in Avi-Yonah 1975 and
1976.

In Amiran's view, Megiddo Stratum IX fills the whole of this
LB I period (cf. Amiran 1970: 154). This stratum, as we have
noted previously, roughly defines the time for which bichrome ware
was in use, though the ware overlaps slightly into Stratum VIII,
and Amiran believes that at least one bichrome ware item from
Megiddo belongs to Stratum X (ibid). Since Amiran dates LB I
(and hence Megiddo IX) as 1570/1550-1410/1400 BC (ibid: 12, 124),
she allows bichrome ware a period of about 170 years.

To recall Epstein's dating in order to compare it with this:
Epstein places the beginning of the pottery's use at *c.* 1575 BC,
and dates the end of Megiddo IX to *c.* 1480 BC, so that the slight
overlap of the ware into Stratum VIII extends its use to *c.* 1475
BC, thus allowing it "no more than a century" (1966: 173).

The shortest period suggested for bichrome ware comes with
Wright's dating. Unlike Amiran, Wright rejects the view that any
bichrome ware from Megiddo belongs to Stratum X (Wright 1961: 109,
n.85). He doubts whether Stratum IX dates back before 1500 BC
(ibid: 91), and dates the end of that stratum to the battle of
Megiddo, which, following the Borchardt-Egerton chronology for
Egypt, he dates to 1468 BC (ibid; also 1965: 75, n.21). This
chronology in effect allows bichrome ware a span of only about
30 years. This would be reduced to a mere 20 years if the date
of 1481 BC for the end of Megiddo IX (as is followed by Kenyon and
Epstein) were to be combined with Wright's date of *c*. 1500 BC for
the beginning of the phase.

We see, therefore, how subjective is the process by which the
length of an archaeological period, the *floruit* of a pottery style,
or the time represented by a stratum of debris and building remains,
is estimated. The time for which bichrome ware was in use could
be extended to cover 170 years or compressed to a mere 30 or even
20 years. The same necessarily applies to the archaeological
period which the ware characterises, LB I.

Thus we have arrived at the proposition set out at the
beginning of this Excursus: that the LB I period can be
considerably shortened, to allow the placing of the destruction
of the MBA cities in the second half of the 15th century BC.

5.9 *The Surrounding Regions: Egypt*

So far the discussion has concentrated entirely on bichrome
ware within Palestine. We must now examine the occurrence of
bichrome ware in the neighbouring areas of Egypt, Cyprus and
Syria to see whether evidence from these confirms or contradicts
our proposed reshaping of LB I.

Bichrome ware has been discovered at the Egyptian sites of
Abusir el-Malak, Kaw (Qaw el-Qebir), and Sedment, and this might
be expected to help establish a chronology for the pottery, since
Egyptian chronology is generally considered to be a well
established and proven structure.

Unfortunately the historical context of the Egyptian bichrome
ware finds is a hotly debated point. Thus Åström maintains that
"the repeated occurrences of Hyksos scarabs, and no later objects,

in these tombs [containing examples of bichrome ware] strongly
suggest that the tombs really belong to the Second Intermediate
Period" (1957: 273; cf. also Kantor 1965: 23), while Hennessy
writes: "The supposed occurrence of Bichrome Wheel-made ware in
pre-XVIIIth Dynasty contexts in Egypt ... does not bear close
examination" (1963: 54).

Concerning the "Hyksos" scarabs which the excavators of the
Mayana cemetary, near Sedment, reported finding in the burials
containing bichrome ware, Epstein warns: "... It should be
remembered that at the time of writing, this term was used
generally to cover scarabs which might today be considered
post-Hyksos and in any case scarabs alone cannot be used as
reliable dating evidence" (1966: 139).

We also need to remind ourselves that it is extremely
difficult to identify any Egyptian strata with certainty as
"Hyksos". Thus Van Seters writes: "... There has been as yet
no site excavated in Egypt that can be identified with the
foreign cultural phase of the Hyksos period. The nearest one
can come to such a site in Egypt are the Delta sites of Tell
el-Yahudiyeh and Ezbet Rushdi-Khataᶜna. Both sites give some
evidence of actual settlements of foreigners, but the data
even from these sites is quite limited" (1966: 4). (Since this
was written, finds made at Tell ed-Dabᶜa have been identified as
remains of Avaris [Bietak 1975a, 1975b]. In the present writer's
view the identification is questionable, but the problem is too
involved to be entered into here). We have already noted that the
two criteria for identifying Tell el-Yahudiyah as a Hyksos site
are invalid.

Concerning the examples of bichrome ware found in Egypt
Van Seters remarks that all this pottery is dated on the basis
of typology, and that nothing speaks against an XVIIIth Dynasty
date (ibid: 52).

R.S. Merrillees, in a recent article, disagrees strongly with
this kind of argument, and attempts to confine all Egyptian
bichrome ware finds to the Hyksos period (1970: 3-26). His
reasoning, however, is defective, as a brief examination of it
will show.

His conclusion is derived partly from the belief that
Tell el-Yahudiyah ware does not occur in Egypt after the end of
the Hyksos period. Thus any occurrence of bichrome ware alongside

Tell el-Yahudiyah ware is taken to indicate a date for the former
at the end of the Hyksos period at the very latest. But his
belief that Tell el-Yahudiyah ware is confined to the Hyksos
period is itself based on the assumption that it is "the
characteristic product of the Hyksos" (ibid: 16). We will see
this to be an incorrect assumption when we discuss bichrome ware
and Cyprus.

More important, and more basic to his conclusion, is
Merrillees' acceptance of Epstein's theory that bichrome ware
spread into Palestine from Syria as a result of Hurrian migrations.
Thus he writes: "Bichrome Wheel-made ware was therefore being
manufactured in Palestine by the same Asiatic race of people to
whom the Hyksos, then occupying Egypt, also belonged" (ibid: 17).
We should recall here two points made previously: there is no
evidence for a Hurrian migration into Palestine at the start of
the 16th century, and there is no evidence for a Hurrian element
among the Hyksos. However, Merrillees considers that the (purely
hypothetical) connection between the Hyksos and the Hurrians of
this (purely hypothetical) migration "makes the transmission of
the Bichrome style to the Nile Valley ... a readily comprehensible
event" (ibid). This leads to the crux of his argument:

"... This very association, when seen against the background
of Egyptian campaigns against the Asiatics at the beginning
of the XVIIIth Dynasty, makes it a priori improbable that
any direct commercial links with the home of the Ware should
have been maintained by the Egyptians after the Hyksos, or
at least their leaders, had been expelled from their land and
forced to retreat into Palestine" (ibid).

This argument, extremely shaky to begin with, is completely
undermined by the discovery that bichrome ware originated on
Cyprus.

There is therefore no reason to reject the view of Hennessy
and Van Seters, that the contexts in which bichrome ware has been
found in Egypt can all be considered post-Hyksos. It is
interesting to note Epstein's conclusion concerning the bichrome
ware finds in Egypt, since it is strongly at variance with that
of Merrillees. She considers that the finds reflect "the
growing contact with the north which resulted from Egyptian
expansion under the Eighteenth Dynasty" (1966: 141).

The precise historical dating of the Egyptian contexts in

which the ware has been found must await more accurate dating of
other pottery types found within them, such as Kerma Ware (which
Merrillees admits may have been produced in Nubia during the
first half of the XVIIIth Dynasty, 1970: 16), and Tell
el-Yahudiyah ware, of which more will be said shortly.
Furthermore, since these contexts also include Cypriote Black
Lustrous Wheel-made Ware, which appears during LB I in Palestine
(cf. Kenyon 1971: 5), their dating is ultimately dependent on
Palestine's ceramic chronology. The Cypriote origin of this
last-mentioned pottery does not affect the validity of this
statement, as we shall now see.

5.10 *Cyprus*

The Cypriote origin of bichrome ware is now a scientifically
proven fact. It might therefore be expected that dates for the
use of the ware on Cyprus would provide indications of the limits
which should be set on its use in Palestine.

This, however, is not the case, because the dates assigned
to the period in which bichrome ware occurs on Cyprus, the Late
Cypriote Period, *depend on the ceramic chronology of Palestine
and Syria*. This is perfectly clear in almost all the discussions
of the chronology of this period which pre-date the discovery of
bichrome ware's Cypriote origin. Prior to that discovery,
examples of this pottery found on Cyprus were naturally regarded
as imports from the mainland. Therefore the earliest examples of
the ware to occur on Cyprus, which date from the very beginning
of LC (Late Cypriote) I A, could not be placed earlier than the
ware's first appearance in Palestine /8/.

Special mention must be made, however, of an article by
Merrillees which attempts to date the opening phase of LC I
other than by reference to the ceramic chronology of Palestine.

Merrillees here takes Oren (Oren 1969: 137ff) to task for
treating Palestine as "the arbiter of the island's relative
chronology" (Merrillees 1971: 73), and sets out to date the end
of LC I A with reference to Egypt. He notes the occurrence,
ignored by Oren, of Tell el-Yahudiyah ware in LC I A contexts at
various sites on the island. (Oren claims that Tell el-Yahudiyah
ware disappeared from Cyprus before the end of the preceding
period, MC [Middle Cypriote] III.) Merrillees then proceeds with
the following argument: "Now as Tell el-Yahudiya Ware evidently

ceased being made in Egypt after the expulsion of the Hyksos, the end of L.C. I A must be coterminous with the end of the Second Intermediate Period in Egypt" (1971: 73). He goes on to deduce from "this chronological finding" that "eastern Cyprus' trade relations with Egypt and cultural exclusivity underwent a sudden and drastic change when the Egyptians drove the Hyksos from their country" (ibid).

Since the earliest examples of bichrome ware on Cyprus come from the beginning of LC I A (cf. Artzy, Asaro and Perlman 1973: 451), Merrillees' synchronizing of the *end* of LC I A with the expulsion of the Hyksos from Egypt obviously places the appearance of bichrome ware earlier than their expulsion. However, what Merrillees describes as a "chronological finding" is in fact a mistaken deduction.

Merrillees, like Albright, Engberg, and others, assumes that Tell el-Yahudiyah ware is "the characteristic product of the Hyksos" (1970: 16, 23-4). It has often been assumed that the appearance of Tell el-Yahudiyah ware in Palestine marks the arrival there of the southward-moving groups which later reached Egypt as the Hyksos (cf. Engberg 1939: 18, 25ff; Wright 1961: 88-90). However, as long ago as 1951, Säve-Söderbergh warned against treating Tell el-Yahudiyah juglets as Hyksos products. He pointed out:

"In Egyptian territory they were introduced long before the arrival of the Hyksos, and are found in tombs in Lower Nubia dating from a time when the Hyksos had hardly even reached Middle Egypt.... It should also be stressed that these jugs *were used in Egypt after the unpopular Hyksos had been expelled*" (1951: 57, my emphasis).

Furthermore it has recently emerged from the analyses done by Artzy and her associates that Tell el-Yahudiyah ware did not reach Egypt from Palestine but was actually an Egyptian product/9/, a fact which fully accounts for its use in Egypt both before and after the Hyksos Period. (It should be noted that while wishing to dissociate this ware from the Hyksos, Säve-Söderbergh assumes a Palestinian origin for it; ibid; cf. Van Seters 1966: 49-52). Tell el-Yahudiyah ware was produced in Egypt regardless of the presence or absence of the Hyksos.

We should also note that its use in the post-Hyksos period was not confined to the *early* XVIIIth Dynasty; an item of the ware

from Abydos was found with a scarab of Thutmosis III (cf.
Åström 1957: 233, n.6, 239).

We must therefore reject Merrillees' assumption that the
disappearance of Tell el-Yahudiyah ware from Cypriote sites is
to be associated with the expulsion of the Hyksos from Egypt.
If the ware continued to be produced in Egypt after the end of
the Second Intermediate Period, there is no reason why the end
of the island's LC I A period should be synchronized with that
point. LC I A may well have extended some way beyond the end of
the Hyksos domination of Egypt; indeed, I can see no reason why
its *start* should not be dated after the expulsion of the Hyksos.
This is in fact the important point: it is perfectly reasonable
to place the transition between MC III and LC I A (and therefore
the first appearance of bichrome ware on Cyprus) during the
XVIIIth Dynasty. I see no reason why the origin of bichrome ware
on the island should be dated before 1500 BC.

Since "Cypriote trade with the Levant was pursued during
M.C. III and L.C. I A on a considerable scale" (Merrillees 1971:
77), it is in fact logical to assume that the   appearance of
bichrome ware on Cyprus be dated no earlier than 1460 BC. The
reasoning behind this is as follows: our date for the Exodus
requires that the Conquest began in the decades around 1430 BC,
as has been explained previously, and it is to that time,
therefore, on the basis of the theory offered here, that I date
the fall of the MBA cities. If we follow the majority opinion,
and date the appearance of bichrome ware in Palestine to shortly
before the fall of the MBA cities, we may tentatively date its
arrival there to *c.* 1450 BC. The emergence of the bichrome style
on Cyprus is best dated on these grounds to the second quarter
of the 15th century BC.

This means in effect synchronizing LC I A roughly with the
period of the Israelites' wilderness wanderings, a synchronism
which is confirmed to some extent by certain odd features of
LC I A.

A number of writers have noted that LC I was a period of
considerable unrest of some kind. Some Cypriote sites which had
been major centres in MC III went into a sharp decline, almost
to the point of complete desertion in some cases (cf. Schaeffer
1948: 400; Åström 1957: 278; Merrillees 1971: 77). Evidence from
several graves dating from the second half of LC I A and the
beginning of LC I B shows that hurried mass burials became common

at this period (Schaeffer 1948: 367; Merrillees 1971: 75). Such
burials have no antecedents in the EC and MC periods.

The two main explanations offered for these events are
warfare and plague. Merrillees, after discussing the various
theories offered (ibid: 75-6), decides in favour of warfare,
suggesting, like other writers before him, some connection
between events on Cyprus and the expulsion of the Hyksos from
Egypt (ibid: 77-8). He does not suggest, however, that the
hypothetical Egyptian "war of liberation" against the Hyksos
actually reached Cyprus (as is suggested by Sjöqvist 1940: 100,
199), but rather that the defeat of the Hyksos affected the
trading status of the eastern end of the island (whose trade
he mistakenly supposes involved the *importing* of bichrome ware
from Palestine in exchange for Tell el-Yahudiyah ware from the
Hyksos), and led indirectly to an economic and social revolution
in which the western end of the island gained ascendancy over the
eastern end.

The theories of both Sjöqvist and Merrillees are really
quite tenuous, since there is no reason why Egyptian reprisals
against the Hyksos should have spread to Cyprus, and no reason
why the expulsion of the Hyksos should have resulted in a decline
in the trading strength of the eastern half of the island.

Against the view that the mass burials indicate the outbreak
of war is the fact, pointed out by Schaeffer (1948: 367, 400), that
no wounds are evident on the skeletons, and that the grave-goods
do not suggest that the graves are those of warriors. Schaeffer
therefore preferred the view that most of these burials had
resulted from plague. If we follow this interpretation, which
seems to be more true to the evidence, then the dating of LC I A
proposed above means that plague broke out on Cyprus during the
same period in which it seems to have been a recurring problem
on the mainland.

We have already seen archaeological evidence that a plague
struck Jericho shortly before the end of the MB II C city. And
if the biblical narrative is given credence, the Israelites were
hit by plague no less than five times during the period of their
wilderness wanderings, sometimes with a very high death-toll
resulting (cf. Ex 32: 35; Num 11: 33; 14: 37; 16: 46-50; 25: 9);
in addition, Egypt was affected by plague just before the Exodus
took place (Ex 9: 8-12). In view of the trading links which
Cyprus seems to have had with both Palestine and Egypt during

LC I A, it is perfectly logical to suggest the spread of plague
from either Egypt or the Levant to the eastern end of Cyprus in
this period.   Furthermore, if the eastern end of the island was
more severely affected than the west, this would explain the
later ascendancy of the west and the spread of western wares
eastwards (cf. Merrillees 1971: 78), as people from the western
end moved into the decimated areas after the end of the epidemic.

This theory is certainly no more speculative than those of
Sjöqvist and Merrillees, and the evidence for plague breaking out
on Cyprus during LC I A strengthens to some extent the dating
scheme offered above.

5.11 Syria

Syria is another region which might be expected to provide
evidence for fixing chronologically the bichrome ware phase.
The sites of Alalakh and Ugarit (Ras Shamra) have yielded an
enormous amount of inscriptional material, some of it bearing on
links with the Hittite Empire, which is itself dated fairly firmly
through thoroughly documented contacts with Egypt.

But even here, the evidence, when examined closely, turns out
to be sparse and much open to subjective interpretation.

Both Alalakh and Ugarit have actually yielded very few
examples of bichrome ware, a fact which is quite extraordinary in
view of their close proximity to the home of this pottery (Cyprus
is visible on a clear day from Ras Shamra).

At Ugarit recorded bichrome sherds from the occupation levels
are few and far between, and no complete assemblages can be
isolated as at Megiddo (cf. Epstein 1966: 121). Schaeffer, the
site's excavator, says that archaeological remains are extremely
rare for the period which he dates between 1700 and 1550 BC
(1948: 39). He believes that at c. 1600 BC activity came to an
end in the greater part of the city, the population being
drastically reduced either by plague or by emigration to escape
some other natural disaster (ibid: 28). This sudden lapse in
the life of Ugarit marks the end of Middle Ugarit 3, the phase
which is represented by level II, 3. The next phase, comprising
the periods Late Ugarit 1-2, is represented by levels I, 1 and I, 2
and is dated by Schaeffer c. 1600-1365 BC (ibid: 39), though we
should remember that for the first part of this the finds are

comparatively scanty.   (However, Epstein [1966: 127, cf. also
121] disagrees with Schaeffer's picture of a partially abandoned
city, suggesting there may be "an extensive contemporary
occupation level in the town of Ugarit ... yet to be revealed by
the excavator's spade".)

Bichrome ware is also extremely scarce at Alalakh.   It is
true that the excavation report for Alalakh (Tell Atchana) gives
the impression that bichrome ware is quite common in Levels VI-V
of that site (cf. Woolley 1955: 387), but Epstein points out that
this

"... is not borne out by the published drawings, by the
Field Pottery Register, or by the residual material. All
these sources together yield a total of five fragmentary
vessels decorated in the bichrome style. One of these is
from Level VI and four are from Level V". "Apart from
these four sherds, there is no record of any other bichrome
ware in Level V, so that it is difficult to understand the
excavator's statement concerning the frequency of its
occurrence in this stratum" (1966: 134, 135).

Levels VI and V were in fact difficult to distinguish at
many points during the excavations (cf. Woolley 1955: 315).
Inscriptional material is lacking, and these two levels may
therefore be considered together as representing a "dark age" in
the history of the city.

What dates should be assigned to the strata yielding bichrome
ware at Ugarit and Alalakh? The dates given to these
archaeologically poor levels depend on the dates given to the
richer preceding ones.

Schaeffer dates Alalakh VII as c. 1900-1700 BC on the basis
of a comparison with Ras Shamra II, 2-3, which he dates c. 1900-
1600 BC (Schaeffer 1948: 101-7). These dates for Alalakh VII are
slightly lower than Sidney Smith's, but themselves need to be
lowered further.

Van Seters has pointed out that Schaeffer's dating of
material from Ras Shamra II, 2-3 is typological, and depends
ultimately on the dating of finds at Kahun, in Egypt. Schaeffer
followed Petrie's dating of c. 1900-1875 BC for foreign sherds at
this site, but Petrie had wrongly associated the occupation of
the site with the building of the pyramid of Sesostris II.

According to Van Seters, the remains from Kahun date from the end
of the XIIth Dynasty and from the Hyksos Period, "at least a
hundred years later than Schaeffer's upper limit" (Van Seters 1966:
26). That is, the upper limit of Alalakh VII and Ras Shamra II,
2-3 should be lowered by at least a century from Schaeffer's date
of *c*. 1900 BC. Van Seters synchronizes Ras Shamra II, 2-3 with
Palestine's MB II B-C, i.e. *c*. 1750-1550 BC (ibid), and places
Alalakh VII *within* MB II B-C; i.e. MB II B-C "begins before and
ends after" Alalakh VII (ibid: 24).

The history of Kahun can actually be traced beyond the Hyksos
Period and into the XVIIIth Dynasty (cf. Åström 1957: 212-13).
Pottery from the site which Petrie referred to in the 1890's as
XIIth Dynasty is now considered to be much later (at that time
Petrie considered Tell el-Yahudiyah ware to be XIIth Dynasty, i.e.
early 19th century BC); Smith assigns a great deal of it to the
17th and 16th centuries BC (Smith 1940: 8). Since no
stratification is preserved for Kahun, and no indication of floor
levels (cf, Åström 1957: 213), the dating of the foreign pottery
from the site depends ultimately on Palestine's ceramic chronology.

Ras Shamra II, 2-3 have also been lowered by Åström, to a
degree similar to that suggested by Van Seters (1957: 260-264).
An even more drastic revision has been proposed by A. Perkins,
who dates Ras Shamra II, 2 (Middle Ugarit 2) *c*. 1750-1500 BC; she
reduces the succeeding levels, Ras Shamra II, 3 and I, 1 (Middle
Ugarit 3 and Late Ugarit I) together to a period of only 50 years,
c. 1500-1450 BC (Perkins 1950: 52). This revision is noteworthy,
as it is only slightly short of what is needed to harmonise the
dating of strata at Ugarit with the dating of Palestine's MB II
C-LB I proposed above. A lowering by a further one or two
decades of the end of Ras Shamra I, 1 would be sufficient to allow
the small quantity of bichrome ware found in that level to have
reached Ugarit from Cyprus after the pottery began to be
manufactured there (i.e. on the dates for its use suggested above).
This scarcity of bichrome ware at both Ugarit and Alalakh is a
mystery which has not yet been adequately explained.

We have already seen that the chronology of certain of
Alalakh's strata is tied to that of the Ras Shamra levels, and
hence ultimately to the ceramic chronology of Palestine. But even
leaving aside links between Alalakh VII, Ras Shamra and Kahun, we
still find that the dating of Alalakh VI and V (the levels
containing the few bichrome ware fragments from the site) depends
on synchronisms with Palestinian sites. Thus Albright dates

levels VI and V by comparison with Megiddo IX and Tell el-ʿAjjul
Palace II (1956: 29).

Is there any reason why these levels should not be dated in
accordance with the chronology proposed above for Palestine's
MB II C-LB I strata?

We have already seen that according to Van Seters Alalakh
VII ended before the end of MB II C, which on his chronology for
Palestinian strata means before c. 1550 BC. Previously Albright
had dated the end of Alalakh VII within the century c. 1650-1550
BC (Albright 1957b: 30), a good deal later than the date of
1750 BC proposed by Sidney Smith (cf. Woolley 1955: 396-9).
"Level VII ended in complete disaster, all the public buildings
being sacked and burned" (ibid: 386). How long it took for the
city to recover is not known. This means in effect that we need
not concern ourselves with the exact date for the end of Level VII.
Suffice it to say that its end probably came later than Van Seters
suggests, in view of the redatings we have proposed above for
Palestinian strata and for Ras Shamra /10/.

The important question here is the dating of Alalakh VI-V.
As was stated above, these strata are devoid of inscriptional
material. The subsequent stratum, however, Alalakh IV, has
yielded a wealth of inscriptions, which might be expected to
produce a fairly precise date for this stratum and hence a
criterion for dating the lower limit of VI-V. In fact this is
not the case, for the inscriptional material has produced a range
of dates as wide as any based on purely ceramic evidence.

Alalakh IV has been dated as early as c. 1550-1473 BC (cf.
conveniently Wiseman 1967: 120). Since this is the period to which
bichrome ware is conventionally dated, this dating appears to
ignore the fact that the site's only examples of bichrome ware
belong to the *previous* periods. However, it has also been dated
c. 1483-1370 BC (cf. ibid), 1447-1370 BC (cf. Woolley 1955: 399;
Negev 1972: 21), and even 1435-1370 BC (cf. Woolley 1955: 388-9).

This latest date is perfectly acceptable from the point of
view of the revised ceramic chronology put forward in the present
work. It is arrived at from an application of the chronology
worked out for Babylon and the Hittite kingdoms by Albright,
van der Meer, and others (cf. ibid: 388). Woolley rejects this
date, however, but he rejects it *on the basis of the ceramic
content of Levels VI-V, making specific reference to bichrome ware*

(ibid: 389). He objects that elsewhere in Syria and Palestine
the pottery found in these levels occurs earlier than it would
at Alalakh if this chronology is adopted. In the context of
the revised ceramic chronology proposed above, Woolley's objection
does not stand /11/.

I would suggest that Alalakh VI and V together be dated
c. 1550/1500-1435 BC, the former representing a longer period than
the latter (as it does, in fact, in the scheme worked out by Smith)
reaching to the time of the earliest arrival of bichrome ware in
Syria, thus explaining the occurrence of a single fragmentary
bichrome vessel in this level. The four vessels from Level V
would thus date between c. 1450 and 1435 BC. As at Ras Shamra,
the scarcity of these vessels, but the presence of other
contemporary types of pottery (cf. Epstein 1966: 137), is a
very odd circumstance.

The chronology of Ugarit and Alalakh is a very complex issue,
and no effort has been made here to outline the problems underlying
it (cf. conveniently Smith 1940; Woolley 1955: 377-99; Albright
1956: 26-30; 1957b: 27ff; Åström 1957: 257-73). I have tried to
show, however, that the uncertainties behind the chronology of
these two key sites (and hence behind the chronology of Syria as
a whole) are as great as those behind the chronology of Palestine
which we are attempting to revise.

5.12   Tell el-ʿAjjul

Finally we return to Palestine to discuss the chronology of
strata at Tell el-ʿAjjul. This is a very confused issue which
will not be dealt with at length; I wish only to point out that
evidence from ʿAjjul can readily be interpreted in harmony with
the theory outlined in the previous discussions.

Until recently the most widely accepted chronology for
ʿAjjul's strata was that worked out by Albright. This was set out
by him in an article which appeared in 1938 (Albright 1938c:
337-59). In Albright's scheme, the destruction of the building
which Petrie named Palace I is dated close to the hypothetical
Egyptian invasion of Palestine after the Hyksos expulsion, an
event which Albright then dated to c. 1560 BC. The destruction
of Palace I is treated as contemporary with the burning of the
southeast section of the city (Level III). Petrie reckoned there
was a gap of six centuries between the end of Palace I and the

building of Palace II (Petrie 1932: 1, 5), believing such a gap
to be attested by three feet of wash resulting from erosion.
Albright deduced that this wash represented a gap of no more
than five years. The end of Palace II (and Level II in the SE
area) was dated by Albright to between 1470 and 1450 BC. This
phase of the city is therefore dated roughly 1560-1460 BC.

It is from this phase that most of ʿAjjul's bichrome ware
derives. The unresolved problem of whether bichrome ware came
into use before the end of the previous phase or not has already
been mentioned. The various conflicting views on this will not
be outlined again here, but it is important to note that the date
given to the arrival of bichrome ware at ʿAjjul depends on two
things: (a) whether or not it arrived before the end of Palace I,
and (b) the limits set on the period of Palace II.

Views have recently been expressed which differ drastically
from Albright's. Stewart, Kempinski and Tufnell (J.R. Stewart
1974: 62-3); A. Kempinski 1974: 145-52; Tufnell 1975: 52-60) have
all suggested dating the end of Palace II, rather than Palace I,
to coincide with the expulsion of the Hyksos. Since all three
writers accept early dates for the end of Hyksos rule (i.e.
1570/60 rather than 1540/30 BC), this means they place the end
of Palace II a full century earlier than Albright's date for
that event.

The basis for his earlier dating, as outlined by Kempinski
and Tufnell, is the location of Hyksos scarabs in the redated
strata /12/. Taken in isolation, this evidence for the earlier
dates appears sound. However, those dates run into severe
difficulties when checked against other material.

Albright (1938c: 339ff) and Epstein (1966: 177) have both
synchronized, on the basis of pottery, the last phase of ʿAjjul's
Palace I with the last phase of Stratum D at Tell Beit Mirsim, and
the ceramic chronology worked out for the latter has become a
cornerstone for ceramic chronology throughout Palestine. Kempinski
does not deny this synchronism between Palace I and Tell Beit
Mirsim D. Instead he simply says that "since it is now possible
to date the end of Tell Beit Mirsim Stratum D to the second half of

the seventeenth century B.C., Albright's view [concerning ʿAjjul]
can be corrected" (1974: 148). But on what grounds is it "now
possible" to re-date the end of Tell Beit Mirsim D in this way?
In a footnote to the above statement, Kempinski simply says: "In
southern Palestine, after the middle of the seventeenth century
B.C., the piriform juglet is replaced by the cylindrical
flat-based juglet. In Tell Beit Mirsim the juglet still exists
in stratum D". But we have already seen that the chronology of
the Palestinian pottery forms is dependent on the dates given to
the fall of the MBA cities, and that it is not legitimate to
reverse this dependence /13/. Furthermore, there exists a
concrete obstacle to Kempinski's proposed redating of Tell Beit
Mirsim D.

Albright reports that in Stratum E_2 at Tell Beit Mirsim there
was found "a secondary scarab of the first known Semitic Hyksos
ruler, Yaʿqub", proving that "this phase is later than the early
seventeenth century B.C." (Albright 1967: 213). Albright
elsewhere dates the start of E_1 (which precedes E_2 chronologically)
to after 1700 BC (Albright 1975: 175). Åström (1957: 268) also
asserts, on completely different grounds, that Tell Beit Mirsim's
Strata G-F "come down to at least the first quarter of the
seventeenth century B.C.". With this dating it is impossible to
place the end of Stratum D as early as the second half of the
17th century BC, unless Strata E_1, E_2 and D are all compressed
within a period of about 50 years (when Albright assigned them
over 150 years).

Further, the dating of Yaʿqub assumed by Albright is not the
only one possible. While Albright places this Yaʿqub *before* the
main Hyksos rulers of Dynasty XV, Egyptologists have tended to
place him later. Säve-Söderbergh, following Stock, assigns this
Yaʿqub to Dynasty XVI, and hence says that the *start* of Tell Beit
Mirsim's Stratum D "can hardly be dated before 1600 B.C." (1951:
62, n.5). This view completely precludes Kempinski's dating of
the *end* of Stratum D to the second half of the 17th century.

Yet without Kempinski's redating of the ceramic chronology
of Tell Beit Mirsim, the early dating of strata at ʿAjjul is
difficult to maintain. It would be quite unreasonable to treat
ʿAjjul in isolation from other Palestinian sites. Not only is
the end of ʿAjjul's Palace I synchronized with the end of Tell Beit
Mirsim's Stratum D; Tell Beit Mirsim D is synchronized on the
basis of pottery with the end of MBA Jericho (cf. Kenyon 1966a: 31)
which is likewise synchronized with the end of MBA Hazor (ibid: 25)

In fact the early dating proposed for ʿAjjul requires an earlier
dating than at present for strata throughout Palestine /14/.
There is no need to enter into detail here concerning the problems
which would arise from such a redating, but a few brief indications
can be given.

As stated above, bichrome ware at ʿAjjul is found chiefly in
the Palace II level. Apart from a few items from Palace IIIA
(Stewart 1974: 63), which followed immediately after the end of
Palace II, bichrome ware is not a characteristic of the following
phases. Kempinski dates the beginning of Palace IIIA to the start
of Egypt's XVIIIth Dynasty, for which he accepts a date of *c.* 1570
BC. Kempinski's scheme therefore places the end of bichrome ware's
use at ʿAjjul in the period long accepted as the time when it first
came *into* use (*c.* 1575/50 BC). Because ʿAjjul cannot be treated
in isolation from other sites, this requires in effect that LB I,
the period characterised by bichrome ware, be shifted back into
the Hyksos period.

The facts opposing such a move have already been touched upon:
the fixing of MB II B levels by the Yaʿqub scarab at Tell Beit
Mirsim (Stratum E_2 = MB II B), and the apparent impossibility of
compressing the MB II C period; we have already seen that this was
a very full period for which the century currently assigned to it
is seemingly too short. It should also be noted that the required
redating would place the destruction of the MB II C cities
throughout Palestine at *c.* 1600 BC or shortly after, where such
widespread destruction would be left without any feasible
explanation.

Until these problems have been faced and satisfactorily
resolved by the proponents of the early dates for ʿAjjul, those
dates will remain very difficult to accept, and the Hyksos
scarabs on which they are based must be regarded as providing only
termini post quem.

To emphasize further the uncertainty surrounding the dating
of ʿAjjul's strata, we may finally note Kenyon's recently proposed
revision of Albright's view. Kenyon suggests that Palace I was
actually destroyed in the campaigns of Thutmosis III (1971: 29).
This is the phase which Albright believed came to an end at the
close of the Hyksos period, and which Kempinski, Tufnell and
Stewart believe was destroyed *during* the Hyksos period, well over
a century earlier than the date required by Kenyon's view. Kenyon
analyzes the pottery from phases II and III of the "Palace"

building as belonging to what her classification calls Group C,
which she dates 1475/50-*c*.1400 BC (cf. ibid: 29, 6). This is
drastically different from the dating given to these phases by
the above writers, namely 1600/1590-1570 BC for II, and *c*. 1570-
1450 BC for III. (We may also note that Schaeffer proposed
dating the transition between Palaces I and II as late as 1500 BC;
1948: 158-63).

Further confusion is introduced by Kenyon's statement that "a
considerable number of fragments of Bichrome ware" were found in
the wash resulting from the destruction of Palace I (ibid: 29).
According to Kempinski, bichrome ware pieces assigned to Palace I
"are mostly from the big central courtyard area which was in use
in palaces II and III and should be regarded as intrusive" (1974:
148, n.18). He states that the bichrome ware from Palace II
"belongs mostly *to the last phase* of this city" (ibid, my emphasis
- i.e. city II *in* Kempinski's scheme, which comprises Palace II
and Level II in the SE area. In other words, Kenyon and Kempinski
not only differ drastically concerning the dating of the strata,
but also concerning the strata to which the appearance of bichrome
ware should be attributed. We have previously noted differences
of opinion concerning whether bichrome ware appeared at the end of
Palace I or the beginning of Palace II, but Kempinski's view seems
to place its appearance *late* in Palace II, not at the beginning.

I do not intend to offer yet another alternative chronology
for ʿAjjul, but it should be clear that to do so, and to make
that chronology harmonize with the redating of LB I proposed in
this thesis, would be very simple. If Palace I and Level III
came to an end *c*. 1450 BC, which is only slightly later than
Kenyon's suggested date, and if bichrome ware did not appear at
ʿAjjul until either the very end of Palace I (with Kenyon and
Stewart but against Kempinski) or the start of Palace II, ʿAjjul's
chronology would be perfectly in keeping with the dating of
bichrome ware proposed here. (Since ʿAjjul was a port in contact
with Cyprus, it would in fact be plausible to suggest that
bichrome ware reached ʿAjjul from there, along with other Cypriote
wares, slightly before it reached any other site in Palestine).
But I do not wish to press this possibility. My main aim above
is simply to show how subjective are the methods employed in
dating ʿAjjul's strata, and to emphasize yet again the
uncertainties of Palestine's ceramic chronology.

5.13 *Conclusion: the Problem of Methodology*

The above discussion may seem inadequate in certain areas.
It concerns itself almost entirely with one type of pottery, and
though it explores something of the consequences which the
proposed redating of this pottery in Palestine has in other areas,
it does not pretend to do so in any great breadth or detail. It
should be borne in mind, however, that this discussion has been
undertaken to illustrate a methodological problem which extends
into areas far outside the limits of the present work.

Lowering the dates for bichrome ware necessarily means
lowering the dates for all contemporary pottery. Lowering the
dates for the last MBA and first LBA strata in Palestine means
lowering the dates for strata in other areas which can be proved
contemporary with these.

This is the point I wish to stress: it is not simply the
dates for certain strata in Palestine that I am suggesting should
be redated, nor even simply the MBA-LB I strata *throughout*
Palestine, but also related strata on Cyprus, in Syria, and
beyond /15/. This means that the current dating of strata in
these regions *can not be used as a basis for objecting to the
proposed redating of strata in Palestine*. And I have tried to
show above that related strata on Cyprus and in Syria can be
appropriately redated.

Dates given to strata in Palestine have for a long time
(though perhaps often unconsciously) been treated as the key for
dating strata elsewhere. Hence Albright wrote in 1954:
"Palestinian dates ... form the only reliable pivots in our
system of southwest-Asiatic archaeology in the Middle Bronze Age"
(in Ehrich 1954: 33), a statement which also holds true for LB I.
However, Albright and others have often been far too confident
about the firmness of the Palestinian dates. Thus Albright, in
the same passage just quoted, describes the Palestinian dates as
"very well established relatively, and solidly pegged down at key
points by the astronomically fixed chronology of contemporary
Egypt" (ibid). As Åström points out after quoting this same
passage: "This is a half-truth, for the Egyptian key points in the
Middle Bronze Age are only indirect, and the Palestinian Middle
Bronze Age chronology is not so firmly established as Albright
claims" (Åström 1957: 265).

On the other hand, it is not legitimate to employ dates for sites beyond Palestine to date strata *in* Palestine, unless the former have been independently and reliably dated. Hence it is not legitimate to use Cypriote ceramic chronology to support a redating of strata at ʿAjjul, as Stewart does (1974: 62-3), because the Cypriote chronology is not independently fixed. The latter, as noted already, can only be "fixed" by comparisons with Palestinian stratigraphy.

Writers often overlook this kind of interdependence, so that circular arguments tend to occur. Stewart's chronology for ʿAjjul is explained on the basis of Cypriote chronology (ibid), but is actually employed by Åström as one of the criteria by which the latter dates the beginning of Late Cypriote I via associations with Palestine and Syria (Åström 1957: 273). Åström also employs the occurrence of bichrome ware at Ras Shamra (in a tomb assigned by Schaeffer to Middle Ugarit 2) as another criterion for dating the start of Late Cypriote I (ibid), but elsewhere in the same work uses comparisons with Cypriote ceramics to revise Schaeffer's dating of Middle Ugarit 2-3 (ibid: 262-4) /16/.

Circular arguments also tend to occur on a much larger scale. As an example we may note the following: Stewart offers a redating of ʿAjjul and Megiddo on the basis of Cypriote chronology; the dating of Late Cypriote I which he uses is proposed by Åström on the basis of finds at Ras Shamra and elsewhere; Alalakh is the key to the dating of Ras Shamra and other Syrian sites; Albright's dating of Alalakh, which Åström accepts, is arrived at by comparison with ʿAjjul and Megiddo.

Because a number of circular arguments in effect underlie Åström's chapter "Absolute Chronology" in his *The Middle Cypriote Bronze Age*, the title of the chapter is really a misnomer. All Åström succeeds in doing in this chapter, which includes discussions of the dating of Alalakh, Ras Shamra, Megiddo and Tell Beit Mirsim in an effort to establish a chronology for Middle Cypriote I-III, is to demonstrate the numerous interrelations which exist. It is a clear fact that no one of these sites could be redated without affecting the others. It is also a fact (but this time an obscured one) that certain related strata at these sites can all be redated together.

I have tried to argue in this Excursus that the Palestinian strata contemporary with the *floruit* of bichrome ware can be redated to allow the end of the MBA cities to be placed in the 15th century BC. Whether these strata *should* be redated in this way depends on the strength of the arguments put forward in the preceding chapter on Jericho and in the chapters which follow. The important fact to be borne in mind is that the date given to the destruction of Palestine's MB II C cities decides the ceramic chronology for the MB II C-LB I periods, not the other way round.

In short there are no obstacles to dating the first appearance of bichrome ware in Palestine to *c.* 1450 BC at the earliest. Its period of use need not have been more than 50 years, and probably ended *c.* 1400 BC, as Amiran has already suggested.

CHAPTER 6:
HAZOR

Chapter 6:   Hazor

6.1 *Introduction*

Hazor features as the last city to be destroyed in the long account of the war of conquest in Jos 1-11. By the end of the tenth chapter the Israelites under Joshua have conquered the major parts of the central hill country, the Negeb, and the coastal plain. Then we read in chapter 11 of an alliance of northern kings forming in order to oppose the conquerors. This coalition of kings of the northern hill country is headed by one Jabin, king of Hazor, and Hazor is described as "formerly the head of all those kingdoms" (11: 10). Joshua and his men come upon the coalition forces at the waters of Merom and defeat them (11: 7-9). Hazor is subsequently taken and burned (11: 10-11).

The account of the defeat of the coalition and the destruction of Hazor occupies fifteen verses (11: 1-15), and therefore, like the account of the end of Jericho (though to a lesser extent), falls into a different category from the two-verse accounts of the taking of various other cities in Jos 10: 28-39).

We must also note that in Jdg 4-5 Hazor and its king reappear. There we read of "Jabin king of Canaan, who reigned in Hazor" as an oppressor of Israel, who kept Israel in subjection for 20 years (Jdg 4: 2-3). This reappearance of Hazor and Jabin has raised a complex set of problems which will be discussed below. These problems arise because the current interpretation of the archaeological evidence does not allow for a resurgence of Hazor after its destruction by Joshua. With the alternative scheme put forward here, this problem disappears.

We turn first, however, to a brief survey of excavations at the site of this city.

6.2 *Excavations at Hazor: Garstang and Yadin*

At Hazor the first excavations of importance were carried out
by Garstang. As in the case of Jericho, the site was excavated
again in the 1950's, and these more recent excavations made
necessary several changes to Garstang's conclusions.

The identification of Hazor with Tell el-Qedah was first
suggested by J. L. Porter in 1875. The same identification was
made by Garstang in 1926, without his being aware of Porter's
earlier suggestion. The identification is now undisputed (cf.
Yadin 1972: 13-14, 201).

The site is a very large one. The tell is roughly
bottle-shaped with an area of some 25 acres. Extending to the
north is a vast enclosed plateau, roughly rectangular, with a
total area of about 200 acres.

Garstang's work consisted of soundings which were made in a
period of just over three weeks. He concluded that the large
plateau had been a "fortified camp", in contrast to the
"permanent city" on the tell (Garstang 1931: 184-5). He believed
that in the MBA, at *c*. 1800 BC, some permanent houses had been
built inside the camp, but he wrote of "more normal conditions"
returning in the 15th century, which he considered to be the time
of Joshua; he considered that then the plateau was occupied only
by temporary structures, tents or huts (ibid: 185). This surface
occupation, he concluded, was terminated around 1400 BC "by a
general conflagration" (ibid: 383). Garstang arrived at this
date because he found no Mycenaean pottery on the site; Mycenaean
pottery should have been present if the city had continued to be
occupied much beyond 1400 BC. He attributed the destruction to
Joshua, in keeping with his view that the Exodus occurred
c. 1440 BC and the Conquest some 40 years later.

The James A. de Rothschild expedition of the 1950's and
1960's, led by Y. Yadin, soon made discoveries which overthrew
Garstang's conclusions.

Excavations on the plateau showed that this area had been a
properly built city, not just a fortified encampment, and that
it remained so to the end of Hazor's LBA period. As a result of
this discovery, the area on the plateau is now referred to as the
Lower City instead of "the enclosure".

The new excavations also produced a quantity of Mycenaean pottery, showing that Garstang's date for the final destruction of the city had been erroneous.

The destruction wrought by the Israelites led by Joshua is dated by Yadin to the second half of the 13th century (e.g. Yadin 1967: 258), which is in keeping with the popular dating of the Exodus. This date saw the end of LBA occupation at Hazor and, according to Yadin, the end of the Canaanite phase. The next inhabitants of the site are theorised to have been Israelite settlers of the early Iron Age (ibid: 258-9).

Unlike the situation at Jericho, the one at Hazor seems quite clear-cut. Thus Yadin writes: "The excavations have shown in a decisive manner that the great Canaanite city was destroyed by fire and was never rebuilt, in the second part of the thirteenth century B.C.... This destruction must be attributed to the one described so minutely in the book of Joshua" (ibid: 258). De Vaux writes of "positive evidence" being "at last brought by the excavations at Hazor" (1965: 27), and E. Yamauchi has written of Hazor as providing "unambiguous evidence for Joshua's campaign" (1973: 50). While there have been dissenters from this view (notably Fritz 1973), this seems to represent the opinion of most supporters of a late date for the Exodus. It is an attitude which was fostered by Yadin himself as early as 1957, when he wrote of the excavations as "of paramount importance" in solving "the vexed problem in biblical archaeology of fixing the date of the Exodus and the occupation of Canaan by the tribes of Israel under Joshua" (1957: 35).

In the case of Jericho we found that the problem involved in associating LBA remains with the destruction recorded in the book of Joshua was so great as to cast doubt on the whole notion that the biblical account refers to the (hypothetical) LBA city. At Hazor, though problems do exist (and will be discussed below), they are not of the same magnitude. Here we will start not by examining the problems involved in the current view, but by testing at Hazor the scheme worked out in our examination of Jericho. Then the problems raised by Jdg 4-5 will be discussed in relation to both the current and the new interpretations to see which offers the most satisfactory solution.

6.3 *A Short Survey of MBA and LBA Hazor*

In what follows, Albright's terminology, as employed by the excavators, will be used for the various phases.

MB I began with a semi-nomadic settlement on the tell (Yadin 1972: 120-21), contemporary with Kenyon's transitional EB-MB period at Jericho. At this time the Lower City had not yet been founded. This settlement was either destroyed or abandoned *c.* 1850 BC (Yadin 1967: 260 table). The MB II A period which followed saw only meagre occupation of the tell (Yadin 1969: 54-5; 1972: 121-2). Then, at around 1750 BC (MB II B), the Lower City was founded and activity on the tell also increased (Yadin 1969: 54 table; 1972: 108). This was the beginning of Hazor's period of greatest size and prosperity. For the rest of the MB II period the tell was "densely populated and highly fortified" (Yadin 1972: 121). The Lower City was also densely populated at this time, and was fortified by the creation of ditches and an earthen ramp.

The city continued to flourish throughout the MB II B-C period, which is represented by Strata 4 and 3 of the Lower City, and by Strata XVII and XVI on the tell. At the end of MB II C, the whole city was violently destroyed, both Upper and Lower (Yadin 1967: 248). Of the Lower City Yadin writes: "Stratum 3 came to its end as a result of a violent conflagration, and a thick layer of ashes separated it from the one which followed" (1972: 31); "... The walls of Stratum 2 were laid afresh with no relation to those of the stratum below them" (ibid: 32; cf. also 1960b: 92). Stratum XVI on the tell was simultaneously destroyed: "The end of MB II came as a result of a violent destruction" (ibid: 124). The tell was occupied for a time by "squatters" before the city was rebuilt in the LBA (ibid: 125; 1969: 55).

The next city is that of LB I, represented by Stratum 2 of the Lower City, Stratum XV on the tell. This city was also destroyed. The following city of LB II (Stratum 1b of the Lower City, XIV on the tell), was also destroyed, somewhere around 1300 BC according to the excavators (Yadin 1960b: 159). The final LBA city, LB III (Stratum 1a of the Lower City, XIII on the tell), was destroyed around 1230 BC, and it is this destruction which is attributed by the excavators to the Israelites under Joshua. This destruction marked the permanent end of the Lower City. The tell, however, was re-occupied in the early Iron Age, and the city there was rebuilt by Israelite hands in the Solomonic period.

Thus we find that from the end of MB II C to the end of the
LBA, Hazor was destroyed no less than four times. Does the
attack of Joshua have to be associated with the last of these,
or is this association arrived at subjectively from an assumed
late date for the Exodus?

6.4   *Wood and Waltke on Hazor*

This question has been raised by Wood and Waltke, both of
whom wish to support a date of *c.* 1440 BC for the Exodus, and
hence a date of *c.* 1400 BC for the Conquest. We will briefly
examine their views before offering our own alternative.

Firstly the view of Wood. His main point is as follows:

"... Yadin found no indication of burning in connection
with the destruction of the thirteenth century (Stratum
I on the plateau), whereas Joshua 11: 11 states definitely
that the city destroyed by Joshua was burned. At Stratum
III below, however, Yadin did find evidence of burning....
It may very well be that the city of Stratum III was really
the one Joshua destroyed and not that of thirteenth century
Stratum I" (1970: 74).

(See below for an explanation of Wood's nomenclature for the
strata. His Stratum III is the Stratum referred to above as
Stratum 2, and his Stratum I is the one referred to above as
Stratum 1a.)

Hence Wood wishes to date the end of what he refers to as
Stratum III to *c.* 1400 BC and to associate this destruction and
not the later one with Joshua. Yadin has actually suggested
dating the end of this stratum about half a century earlier than
Wood requires, but only very tentatively (cf. Yadin 1957: 44), so
this itself does not constitute a problem for Wood's view.

However, Wood's argument that the 13th century destruction is
not associated with signs of burning and therefore should not be
attributed to Joshua does not accord with the facts. It is true
that the preliminary excavation reports do not make it clear that
Hazor was burned in the 13th century. But in 1967 Yadin stated
quite clearly: "The excavations have shown in a decisive manner
that the Canaanite city was destroyed by fire ... in the second
part of the thirteenth century B.C..." (1967: 258). There are

also references to "destruction by fire" and to "a violent
conflagration" at the end of the LBA city on other pages of the
same work (252, 253; cf. 1972: 37; also Aharoni 1967: 207).
Wood's error appears quite astonishing, since elsewhere in his
article he shows familiarity with this work (Wood 1970: notes
35, 40, 41, 44 and 50).

The situation is in fact far more complex than Wood's
argument assumes. The complexity of the problem becomes apparent
in an examination of Waltke's argument (Waltke 1972: 42-6).

Waltke begins by pointing out that all three strata of the
Lower City of the LBA end with a destruction. As we have seen,
Yadin believes that the *last* of the LBA strata was the one
destroyed by Joshua. In the Lower City this is numbered Stratum
1a, and its end is dated *c.* 1230 BC. The stratum underlying
this one is 1b, which also shows signs of a destruction, dated
by Yadin to *c.* 1300 BC. Yadin actually suggests that Seti I was
responsible for this destruction (1960b: 159). The report states
that Stratum 1b is "the stratum of the El-Amarna age at Hazor"
(ibid). The next stratum down is labelled Stratum 2, and again
we have a destruction layer between it and the one above:
"Stratum 1b was built after Stratum 2 had been completely
destroyed" (ibid: 92).

Waltke dates the destruction of Stratum 2 to "about 1400
B.C.", simply on the basis that it is the stratum which "belongs
to the Pre-Amarna Age" (1972: 43). The excavators have not given
an exact date to the end of this stratum. It is this stratum
which Waltke wishes to claim was destroyed by Joshua. (It is
in fact the same stratum which Wood attempts to link with Joshua's
attack. Confusion has arisen over the terms for the various
strata because, apparently, the excavators have not consistently
employed one simple nomenclature. General Stratum III [roman
numerals] is in fact the same as Stratum 2 [arabic numerals];
General Stratum II = Stratum 1b; General Stratum I = Stratum 1a.
Cf. Yadin 1959a: 74-88.)

Waltke's argument contains a serious flaw. In order for the
archaeological evidence to tally exactly with the biblical account,
there has to be evidence of burning in connection with the end
of Stratum 2. However, the excavation reports which Waltke cites
contain no references to burning in this context. Therefore
Waltke brings into his discussion a destroyed gateway excavated
in Area K of the Lower City. In one of the preliminary reports

Yadin wrote that this gate "must have been destroyed in a violent conflagration, traces of burnt bricks of its inner walls and the ashes of the burnt beams still cover the floors in thick heaps" (1959b: 8-9). These lines are quoted by Waltke (1972: 43). The preliminary report gives no date for this gate; it states only that it was built "on the foundations of the earlier MBA II gate" and before the final destruction of Hazor in the 13th century (Yadin 1959b: 8-9). The report actually adds, after the lines which Waltke quotes: "The evidence suggests that this destruction occurred before the final destruction of Hazor [in the 13th century] by the Israelites, *but this problem remains to be studied*" (ibid: 9, my emphasis). Waltke is therefore constructing an argument out of unsafe material when he writes of the destruction of this gate as "presumably belonging to the destruction of about 1400 B.C." (1972: 43).

His assumption does not appear to have been correct. In a much later work than the one which Waltke quotes concerning this gateway, Yadin gives it as his opinion that this gate belongs after all to Stratum 1a, and that its destruction therefore dates to the end of the Canaanite city, *c.* 1230 BC (1972: 63). Yadin explains that the late I. Dunayevsky, who was one of the team of excavators, believed otherwise; Dunayevsky "ascribed the layer of ashes to 1b, and claimed that the city gate went out of use in this period" (ibid: n.3). In other words, Dunayevsky linked the burning of this gate with the destruction of Stratum 1b, which is dated, as we have seen, to *c.* 1300 BC. Therefore while Dunayevsky and Yadin disagree over the destruction of this gate, one dating it to *c.* 1300 BC, the other to *c.* 1230 BC, there seems to be no support for its being dated to *c.* 1400 BC and the end of Stratum 2.

This burnt gate must therefore disappear from the discussion, leaving us with no reason to believe that the end of Stratum 2 was accompanied by burning. Without evidence of burning at the end of Stratum 2, neither Waltke nor Wood has any reason to identify the destruction of this stratum with Joshua's attack. (Waltke's date of 1400 BC for the end of Stratum 2 is purely arbitrary).

We must conclude that both Wood and Waltke fail to produce a working hypothesis which convincingly fits Hazor into the theory of an early date for the Exodus without at the same time contradicting part of the biblical account.

6.5 *A 15th Century Date for the End of MBA Hazor*

We now turn our attention to the end of the MBA city. We
have already seen that the destruction which brought to an end
the MB II C city was accompanied by burning. The stratum in
question in the Lower City is Stratum 3. "Stratum 3 was destroyed
by conflagration.... Stratum 2 lies atop a thick layer of ash (of
the destruction of Stratum 3)..." (Yadin 1967: 248; also 1960b:
92, quoted previously). The destruction was total and included
the Upper City (the tell) as well (Yadin 1969: 54-5).

When did this destruction take place? It is a very
interesting fact that Yadin changed his mind on this issue during
the excavations. In 1957 he suggested that the destruction of
the MBA city may have been the work of either Thutmosis III or
Amenhotep II (1957: 44), which means that he then considered a
date in the second half of the 15th century to be quite plausible.
It also appears that Yadin then placed the beginning of the next
city (LB I, Stratum 2) in the 14th century (ibid). A year later
Yadin placed the end of the MBA city at "*ca*.1400 B.C." (1958: 31).
Dates of this order would be perfectly in keeping with the view
proposed here, that MB II C Hazor was destroyed by Joshua at a
time somewhere between 1430 and 1400 BC (i.e. during the first
few decades which followed the destruction of Jericho).

However, we find that in all subsequent publications an
earlier date is offered. Thus in 1969 Yadin placed the end of
the MBA city in the middle of the 16th century, i.e. *c*. 1550 BC
(1969: 55). Along with this earlier date, Yadin adopted the
theory that the MBA city was destroyed by Amosis (1967: 260
table; cf. 1975: 268), thus linking its destruction with Egyptian
reprisals against the Hyksos.

In Yadin's most recent statements a date in the 16th century
for the end of the MBA city is maintained, and the LB I city
(Stratum 2) is dated as 16th-15th centuries (1972: 32, 200; 1975:
275 table).

What was the reason for this shift to an earlier date for the
destruction of the MBA city? The shift was made necessary by a
redating of the stratum above it, Stratum 2, representing the
LB I city. And such a redating was made necessary *by the
discovery in this stratum of several examples of bichrome pottery.*

Bichrome ware did not begin to turn up at Hazor until the later stages of the excavations, in season 4 (1959) and season 5 (1969). Thus Epstein writes: "Although the excavations of the areas dug in the Lower City at Hazor reached a level at which bichrome ware could be expected to occur, it was only during the last two seasons that vessels and sherds began to be found in sufficient quantity to warrant the inference that here, too, it formed an integral part of the contemporary repertoire" (1966: 113).

"Its profusion indicates that Hazor was densely populated in the latter part of the sixteenth century and the first half of the fifteenth century" (Yadin 1972: 45). It was Stratum 2 which produced this profusion of bichrome vessels (ibid), and the discovery therefore necessitated a redating of this stratum; whereas Yadin once considered that Stratum 2 began in the 14th century BC (1957: 44), he now sees it as "representing the sixteenth-fifteenth centuries in Hazor" (1972: 32).

This redating of Stratum 2 is entirely dependent on the traditional dating of the use of bichrome ware, i.e. from 1575/1550 to 1475/1450 BC. We have seen in the preceding section that no evidence exists which requires this dating, and that bichrome ware's period of use was probably much shorter than a century.

The redating of Stratum 2 occasioned by the discovery of bichrome ware is the only reason for redating the end of the MBA city to the 16th century. No other reason exists for making the MB II C phase synchronous with the Hyksos Period. Although scarabs which have been described as "Hyksos" have been found in the MBA strata of the city, not one of them bears a royal name (Yadin 1975: 39), and they carry only "pseudo-hieroglyphs" (ibid); like the scarabs discussed in the section on Jericho, they need not be linked at all with the Hyksos.

The view that the MBA city at Hazor was destroyed by Amosis (cf. Yadin 1967: 260 table; 1975: 268) is just as lacking in evidence as is the view that MBA Jericho was destroyed by that pharaoh. Hazor has been classed as a Hyksos stronghold (cf. Garstang 1931: 184), but there is no basis for this. It is true that the MBA city was fortified with the artificial embankment style of defences often associated with the Hyksos (cf. Kenyon 1970: 181; Yadin 1975: 129-41, 266-8), but we have already seen that it is quite wrong to treat this style of fortification as a sign of the presence of Hyksos overlords.

In short, no reason exists for the view that the MBA city was destroyed in the 16th century BC. Yadin shifted the end of the MBA city to this earlier date without cause. There is in fact no reason to prefer this earlier date to Yadin's original view, which allowed the destruction to be placed in the second half of the 15th century.

If the MB II C city was destroyed during the final decades of the 15th century, there is still room to place the LB I city (Stratum 2) between its end and the beginning of the stratum which contains pottery attributed to the Amarna age (Stratum 1b). It is interesting in this connection that Kenyon has suggested a period of short duration for Stratum 2, at "the end of the fifteenth century" (Kenyon 1970: 342; cf. 1971: 12) /1/. This would be quite in keeping with the dates for bichrome ware suggested in the previous section, allowing time for the ware to spread to Hazor from the coastal cities.

In conclusion, a late 15th century date for the end of MB II C Hazor is perfectly plausible, and it is therefore feasible to suggest that this was the city destroyed by the Israelites under Joshua.

6.6   *The problem of Judges 4-5*

According to Yadin, the destruction of LBA Hazor which took place towards the end of the 13th century BC put a complete end to the Canaanite city. The next settlement on the site, dated to the 12th century BC, is diagnosed as a temporary settlement by semi-nomadic Israelites. There was further (but still meagre) Israelite settlement in the 11th century BC, and the mid-10th century saw the building of the Solomonic city of Hazor. These three Israelite phases are represented by Strata XII-X on the tell (the Lower City was never rebuilt after the destruction at the end of the LBA), and all three fall in the Iron I period (cf. conveniently 1967: 258-60; 1975: 274-5).

This archaeological evidence has been noted by several writers as posing a problem for an historical understanding of the biblical references to Hazor. For after its destruction by the Israelites in Jos 11, Hazor reappears as a centre of opposition to the Israelite tribes in Jdg 4. Here it is related that Israel was oppressed cruelly for twenty years by "Jabin king of Canaan, who reigned in Hazor" and the commander of his army, Sisera, who dwelt in Harosheth-ha-goiim (Jdg 4: 2-3).

Two problems have been pointed to in connection with Jdg 4. The lesser one is that Jos 11: 10 relates that Jabin, king of Hazor (cf. verse 1), was killed by Joshua. At first this may seem to make nonsense of the reappearance of Jabin as king of Hazor in Jdg 4. However, it is quite possible that the same name was shared by several kings of Hazor. A letter by Shamshi-Adad, king of Assyria, in the Mari archives, refers to a king of MB II B Hazor as Ibni-Adad, which is "the Akkadian form of the West Semitic name Yabni-Hadad" (Yadin 1972: 5, where he also notes that Ibni-Adad is mentioned several times in other documents which have not yet been published; cf. also ibid: 207). Albright has pointed out that the Old Testament name Jabin "is an easily explicable phonetic development from a more original *Yabn(i)*. The name *Yabn(i)* itself is a typical short form of an original *Yabni-El* or *Yabni-Hadad*" (1963: 102, n.83). In other words, the Old Testament form of the name may well be simply a hypocoristicon of the full theophoric name. "If this is true, it is possible that the name Yabin was a royal dynastic name of the Kings of Hazor" (Yadin 1972: 5). It is therefore perfectly plausible that several kings of Hazor bore the name Jabin (cf. also Kitchen 1966: 68).

A more serious problem is the reappearance of Hazor itself, which is quite impossible on the current interpretation of the archaeological evidence. With the city destroyed by Joshua currently identified with the last LBA city, and the following settlements identified as Israelite, the archaeological evidence does not allow for a resurgence of Canaanite Hazor.

There have been many attempts to resolve this problem. Kitchen has suggested that the later Jabin may have had "a small fortified residence somewhere on (or near) Tell el-Qedah that has not yet been touched by the excavators", or perhaps he "still ruled the *state* of Hazor but from a different town in the area" (1966: 68). A. D. Crown has recently reasoned that in Jdg 4 Hazor as an occupied site is not mentioned, "and there is no necessary connection between the King and his city". He suggests that the Jabin mentioned there was not ruling from Hazor as such, but was "living with military friends led by one Sisera i.e. at Harosheth. Thus the account can be readily reconciled with the archaeological data" (1973: 114).

Suppositions such as these, unsupported by any evidence, and purely *ad hoc,* do not commend themselves to the present writer. In particular, it is difficult to see why Jdg 4: 2 should describe Jabin as the "king of Canaan who ruled in Hazor" if he was in fact the king of Hazor who ruled in Harosheth (or elsewhere).

Albright suggests that Jdg 4 contains a confusion of traditions. He states that the prose narrative in this chapter is based on the Song of Deborah in ch. 5, "which it sometimes misunderstands" (1963: 39). He suggests that the appearance of a Jabin as the king of Hazor in Jdg 4 is the result of confusion between the Jabin who ruled Hazor in the time of Joshua, and "a later Canaanite prince of the same name who ... was probably involved in the coalition against Israel described in Jdg 5" - i.e. a hypothetical Jabin who was *not* a king of Hazor (ibid: 102, n.83). In other words, Albright would remove the references to Hazor (verses 2 and 17) from Jdg 4. Albright therefore has no wish to argue that Hazor, or even a displaced king of Hazor, existed at the time of the battle of Jdg 4-5. (Albright's dating of this battle to *c.* 1125 BC has already been discussed.)

Aharoni has raised certain objections to Albright's view. In Aharoni's opinion, a comparison of the prose account (Jdg 4) with the Song (Jdg 5) points to the view that "the prose passage does not depend upon the poem but furnishes various independent details which fit together to form a logical picture" (1967: 201). Albright's suggestion fails to explain the origin of the tradition which makes Sisera the commander of Jabin's army, which is attested not only in Jdg 4 but also in I Sam 12: 9 and Ps 83: 9 (ibid). Also, the removal of Hazor from Jdg 4 leaves Harosheth in an elevated position, and this is a further problem: "It seems still more difficult to understand the rise of Harosheth-ha-goiim to the head of the Canaanite alliance, a place completely unknown in all other sources, both biblical and non-biblical" (ibid). Aharoni actually suggests that Harosheth-ha-goiim is not a place-name at all, but a term referring to the forested regions of Galilee, a suggestion supported by the LXX reading of Jdg 4: 16, *heōs drumou tōn ethnōn* (cf. ibid: 203). He suggests further that the statement that Sisera dwelt (*yšb*) in Harosheth-ha-goiim (Jdg 4: 2), i.e. in the Galilee forests, "means that he ruled that area as a governor and tyrant, just as Joab, the commander of David's army, 'dwelt' (*yšb*) in Edom (I Kgs 11: 16) and Omri, King of Israel, 'dwelt' in the Mishor of Moab (Mesha Stele, line 8)" (ibid).

Aharoni prefers the following suggestion for resolving the problems posed by Jdg 4-5: "... A better solution to the difficulties is perhaps to accept the descriptions of the two battles [of Jos 11 and Jdg 4-5] as they are but to reverse the order of events. According to this theory the two wars do not belong to the first stage of penetration but to a later period, and the battle of Merom [Jos 11] was eventually associated with Joshua and all of Israel..." (ibid). In other words, the account of the final destruction of Hazor in Jos 11 really refers to an event which came some time *after* the battle of Jdg 4-5, and Joshua should not be associated with either event. This theory was first offered by Mazar (1952/3: 83ff).

This theory runs into difficulties of its own, however, because in Yadin's opinion it requires an untenable interpretation of certain archaeological finds. The events of Jdg 4-5 can only be placed some time before the final destruction of Hazor if it is postulated that the occupation of the northern territory by the Israelites took place a considerable time before the city was destroyed. This must be so, because Jdg 4-5 contains indications that the events related there do not belong to the initial stages of Israelite settlement; Deborah's battle was preceded by a period of oppression, and Barak seems already to be settled in Kedesh of Naphtali (cf. Aharoni 1967: 203; also Gray 1966: 39). In accordance with this evidence, Aharoni has claimed that certain Iron Age settlements in Upper Galilee predate the fall of Hazor and constitute evidence of Israelite penetration into the unsettled hill country a generation or so before Hazor was attacked (ibid: 200-201; cf. Yadin 1972: 131).

Yadin, however, has discovered the culture of these Iron Age settlements in Stratum XII at Hazor, and since this is the stratum which *post*-dates the fall of the LBA city, Yadin considers it proof that the destruction of Hazor *preceded* the Israelite settlement:

"The settlements in Galilee as well as Stratum XII represent the same situation: the settlement of the semi-nomadic Israelites *after* the fall of the Canaanite cities" (1972: 131; cf. also 1975: 254-5). "The theory that the archaeological evidence of the Galilee survey supports the view of a peaceful infiltration of the tribes of Israel, prior to the destruction of the Canaanite cities - at least as far as Hazor is concerned - seems, therefore, to collapse" (1967: 259).

Furthermore, the fact that "no true city actually existed" at Hazor in the 12th-11th centuries BC "eliminates the possibility of shifting the description in Joshua xi and placing the events mentioned there within the time frame of Deborah's activities" (ibid).

Some writers, such as Mazar and Rowton (cf. Yadin 1972: 131), have suggested, in the light of the Hazor excavations, dating Deborah to the 13th century BC, thus retaining the view that her battle preceded the final destruction of Hazor. This date, as Yadin remarks, "encounters great difficulties" (ibid), not least of which is the fact that the Iron Age settlements must still be dated later than the fall of Hazor (cf. ibid: 132 with n.1), which leaves no archaeological evidence to justify the view that Israelite penetration occurred earlier than the destruction of the city. Furthermore, placing Deborah considerably before the fall of Hazor would not fit well with the usual late date theory of the Exodus, since Yadin insists that the fall of Hazor must belong to the 13th century BC, and can on no account be moved into the 12th, as Aharoni (1970: 263) has implied (cf. Yadin 1972: 132).

On these grounds, Yadin has rejected the view of Mazar and Aharoni, and has adopted the view that "there was no Jabin, king of Hazor, in the time of Deborah", and that the mentions of Jabin in Jdg 4 "must be attributed to a later editor" (ibid); "... In Judges iv there is a later effort to interrelate Sisera with Jabin" (1967: 259; cf. Fritz 1973 for references to other writers who consider the appearance of Jabin in Jdg 4 to be secondary). Thus he admits that the archaeological evidence is in "apparent contradiction with Judges iv" (1972: 200 table and 198; also 1975: 275 table), a contradiction which is only resolved by assuming the work of an editor. One can only say in reply to this that it is difficult to see why an editor should have wished to link Sisera with Jabin, if the two were in fact separated in both time and place.

We must note that the above difficulties only arise through adherence to a late date for the Exodus. They disappear if an early date is adopted.

So far as I am aware, M. B. Rowton was the first to suggest that the destruction of Hazor in the 13th century should be linked with the events related in Jdg 4-5 instead of with Jos 11 (Rowton 1962: 67-9). Rowton does not, however, suggest a very clear scheme of events. He considers it premature to attempt a

date for the Exodus, and says /2/ that more evidence is needed
to decide whether there was one Exodus or two. But he "very
tentatively" offers the view that Barak should be dated to the
second half of the 13th century, and the Exodus, if there was only
one, some three or four generations previously, its background
being either the Amarna period "or the aftermath of that period".
He adds that "In that case the Conquest really gathered impetus
only some two centuries later" (ibid: 69).

Rowton therefore does not attempt to date the initial influx
of Hebrew tribes, and does not seem to consider the possibility
that cities were attacked and destroyed at the time of the
initial influx. He certainly does not consider the possibility
that any of the pre-13th century destructions at Hazor were the
work of the Israelites. The only destruction between the Amarna
period and the 13th century is that which Yadin has dated to
c. 1300 BC, and Rowton agrees with Yadin's suggestion that Seti I
was probably responsible for this (ibid: 68). Rowton's view
therefore offers no historical background for the destruction of
Hazor by Joshua related in Jos 11.

The scheme proposed here, however, makes possible a very
close correspondence between archaeological evidence and the
biblical traditions.

We have already proposed dating the destruction of the MBA
city to the second half of the 15th century BC and viewing it as
the work of the newly-arrived Israelite invaders, as recounted in
Jos 11. If the biblical traditions are in a trustworthy order,
some five or six generations must be allowed between the war of
conquest and Barak's battle, which would indicate a gap of
something slightly less than two centuries between the two events
(cf. Jdg 2: 10; 3: 8-11, 14 and 30). Thus if Joshua's battle
took place in the final decades of the 15th century, Barak's must
be dated to roughly the middle of the 13th century. The prose
account of the battle ends with the words: "So on that day God
subdued Jabin the king of Canaan.... And the hand of the people
of Israel bore harder and harder on Jabin the king of Canaan,
until they destroyed Jabin king of Canaan" (Jdg 4: 23-4). This
final "destruction" of Jabin, who ruled in Hazor (4: 2), can
therefore be equated with the final destruction of the LBA city
in the second half of the 13th century.

This last point has already been made by Waltke (1972: 45-6),
who also draws attention to the fact that Aharoni says Hazor

suffered "a sharp decline" before its final destruction (Aharoni
1967: 207). This decline "is especially noticeable in the lower
city which evidently ceased to be fortified in the last stratum.
Its temples were abandoned and apparently plundered, being
rebuilt afterwards in a very poor and temporary form". This
last LBA town was "concentrated mainly on the high tell in an
area of about fifteen acres..." (ibid). Aharoni himself suggests
that "the sharp decline which preceded the final collapse ... came
as a consequence of the war of Deborah" (ibid). We need not
agree with Aharoni's view that Jos 11 relates to the final
destruction of the Canaanite city in order to agree with this
last-quoted statement. The decline may be assumed to have begun
with the defeat of Sisera's forces, and to have continued as
"the hand of the people of Israel bore harder and harder on Jabin
the king of Canaan", resulting in the final destruction of the
city, which is not recorded in the biblical narrative, but is
perhaps referred to implicitly in Jdg 4: 23-4).

I would suggest, therefore, that the scheme presented here
offers a much more satisfactory understanding of the biblical
material referring to Hazor than does the current view which
places the Conquest in the 13th century and links the end of the
LBA city with Jos 11. Such a view is unable to account
satisfactorily for the reappearance of the city in Jdg 4-5.
The city attacked and destroyed by Joshua's forces was in fact
the final phase of the MBA city. Hazor was subsequently rebuilt
(perhaps after a period of abandonment; cf. Kenyon 1971: 12), and
continued to flourish, though with less importance than it
possessed in the MBA (cf. Aharoni 1967: 206-7; Malamat 1960:
12-19), until the 13th century, when it finally succumbed to the
Israelite pressure which followed the defeat of Sisera's troops.

CHAPTER 7:
OTHER CONQUEST TRADITIONS AND THE END OF THE MIDDLE BRONZE AGE

Chapter 7: Other Conquest Traditions and the End of the Middle Bronze Age

7.1 *More Problem-Cities for a Thirteenth Century Conquest*

We have already seen that Jericho poses a serious problem for a 13th century date for the Conquest. Ai is also a notorious difficulty, and is to be discussed separately. De Vaux (1965: 27) and Mendenhall (1965: 33) have both pointed out, in discussing evidence for a Conquest in the 13th century, the irony of the fact that the only two detailed narratives of the destructions of cities are those concerning Jericho and Ai, while archaeological evidence shows both sites to have lacked any significant population at the appropriate time.

De Vaux's comment, that "the negative results of archaeology at Jericho and at Ai demand a reappreciation of the first chapters of Joshua" (1965: 27), is hardly satisfactory. The length of the narratives devoted to the end of these two cities should itself give us pause before rejecting their historicity. But more important than this, there are several other cities which create problems for a 13th century Conquest. Indeed, those which create problems for that date outnumber those which do not.

This section will concentrate first on the other cities which do not provide evidence for a Conquest in the 13th century, but which do provide evidence which supports, or is at least compatible with, a Conquest at the end of the MBA.

7.1.1 *Hebron*

According to Num 13: 22, Jos 14: 15, 15: 13 and Jdg 1: 10, 20, at the time of the Israelite Conquest, Hebron was occupied by the greatly feared Anakim. The defeat of the city was, however, accomplished. It is by no means certain whether Hebron was taken by Joshua (Jos 10: 36-7), by the tribe of Judah (Jdg 1: 10), or by Caleb and a group other than the Judahites (Jos 14: 15; 15: 13-14; Jdg 1: 20), but this confusion need not mean that the tradition of the city's defeat is not historical.

However, excavations at Hebron have uncovered no remains from between the end of the MBA and a relatively late period of Iron I (P. C. Hammond 1965: 267-70; 1966: 566-9; 1968: 253-8; Campbell 1965: 30-32; De Vaux 1971: 500), a fact which makes it extremely difficult to see any historical core at all in the tradition of Hebron's defeat, if the Conquest is placed at the close of the LBA. The archaeological evidence does, however, permit the defeat of Hebron to be placed at the end of the MBA, since there is evidence of a populous town, with rampart fortifications (described as "Hyksos" in the reports), existing down to the end of MB II.

We may offer here a suggestion as to the meaning of the statement in Num 13: 22, that Hebron was built seven years before Zoan (= Tanis) in Egypt. Many incorrect assumptions have been made concerning this statement, owing to the mistaken identification of Tanis with Avaris and Pi-Raᶜmesse. Thus Albright (1935b: 16) took the statement to mean that Hebron was founded shortly before the establishment of Avaris by the Hyksos. Winnett (1937: 21-9) understood it to refer to the capture of Hebron by Caleb seven years before the rebuilding of Avaris-Tanis by Israelite forced labour under Rameses II, a view which Rowley also favoured, suggesting that the verse would then "carry some memory of the fact [sic!] that Hebron was captured by Caleb while the tribes which Moses led were still in bondage in Egypt" (1950: 76-7).

In the light of the discovery that Avaris and Pi-Raᶜmesse should probably both be located at Qantir, not Tanis, and Van Seters' view that Tanis may not have been founded until the XXIst Dynasty (1085-935 BC), we may make the suggestion that Num 13: 22 refers to the building of Israelite Hebron, not to the building of Kiriath-arba, the pre-Israelite city (cf. Jos 14: 15; Jdg 1: 10). This would fit well with the archaeological evidence for a rebuilding of Hebron late in Iron I (Iron Age I B = c. 1150-1000 BC) /1/.

In any case it is difficult to see how the verse could refer
to the founding of Kiriath-arba, an event of which the Israelites
would probably have known nothing. The verse could on no account
relate to the original settlement at the site, since it was
occupied as early as Chalcolithic times. By far the most likely
view, therefore, is that Num 13: 22 refers to the founding of
Israelite Hebron.

If the Conquest is placed at the end of the MBA, we have
precise harmony between the archaeological record and the
biblical traditions. The archaeological evidence shows a gap
between the end of the MBA and the second half of Iron I; the
Bible records the destruction of Hebron (Kiriath-arba) at the
time of the Conquest, and makes no mention of it again until the
early monarchic period (I Sam 30: 31; II Sam 2: 1 etc.), which is
what we would expect if, as both archaeology and Num 13: 22
indicate, Israelite Hebron was not built until the 11th century
BC.

7.1.2 *Hormah*

According to Jdg 1: 17, prior to its destruction by the
tribes of Judah and Simeon this city was called Zephath. The
incident described here may be the same as the one related
briefly in Num 21: 1-3, where Hormah appears to have been taken
during Israelite reprisals against the king of Arad, who had
previously defeated Israel. The king of Hormah is listed
alongside the king of Arad in the list of kings killed by Joshua
in Jos 12: 14.

Hormah has been identified in recent years as Tel Masos
(Khirbet el-Meshâsh), eight miles east of Beer-sheba (cf. Aharoni
and Amiran 1975: 88). Excavations at Tel Masos have revealed a
much eroded MB II earth rampart, a widely spread out Iron I
settlement (described as early Israelite and dated to the 12th
century BC), and an Iron Age II fortress (cf. Aharoni, Fritz and
Kempinski 1972: 243; TAUIA 1974: 13-14).

Again there is no trace of any town built between the end of
the MBA and the first phase of the Iron Age, which poses a
problem for the mentions of the place in Num 14: 45; 21: 3, and
Jdg 1: 17 if the Conquest is placed in the 13th century BC. If it
is placed at the end of the MBA, however, the problem disappears,

for the remains of an earth rampart dating from MB II are evidence
that a fortified town existed here at that time /2/.

7.1.3 *Arad*

The king of Arad is mentioned as opposing Israel in Num 22:
1 and 33: 40. It may be that from 21: 2-3 we should deduce his
subsequent defeat by the Israelites. A later tradition records
his death at the hands of Joshua (Jos 12: 14).

Excavations at Tel Arad have revealed nothing between the
EBA and the Iron Age, a fact which poses problems for the view
offered here as well as for the conventional view. When, after
five seasons' excavations, it became apparent that no finds were
going to interrupt this 2000-year gap, Aharoni wrote that the king
of Arad had "become a very real problem" (1968: 3).

It has been suggested, however, that Canaanite Arad should
not be sought at Tel Arad but at Tel Malhata (Tell el-Milḥ),
roughly eight miles to the southwest (cf. Aharoni and Amiran
1964: 146-7; 1975: 88). Excavations were carried out at this
site in 1962 and 1967, and remains of a MB II city were discovered,
with "strong Canaanite fortifications" (id. 1964: 146-7).

The 1967 excavations revealed evidence of a conflagration
towards the end of MB II, which it is tempting to connect with the
clash between Arad and the Israelites in Num 21: 1-3. The site
was immediately resettled in the closing phase of MB II C
(cf. Kochavi 1967: 272-3), showing that its destruction did not
occur at the very end of the MBA, but very slightly before. Since
the Israelites' clash with Arad occurred shortly before the main
wave of their attacks on the central Canaanite cities, this
destruction would correspond well with the time of their clash
with the city if the main wave of the Conquest is dated to the end
of MB II C.

The identification of Tel Malhata with the site of Canaanite
Arad therefore removes the problem of Arad from the view offered
here. It does not, however, remove the problem from the
conventional view, which would place Israel's clash with Arad in
the LBA. No LBA remains have been found at Tel Malhata; Iron Age
remains from the 10th-9th centuries BC lie above the final MBA
remains (cf. Kochavi 1967: 272-3; 1968: 392-5; de Vaux 1971: 500).

Arad is therefore another site where the archaeological finds
do not make sense in the context of the currently prevalent dating
of the Conquest. On the view offered here, however, there is no
problem once it is allowed that Canaanite Arad is to be identified
with Tel Malhata /3/.

7.1.4 Gibeon

It is related in Jos 9-10 that the city of Gibeon was not
destroyed by Joshua, because the Gibeonites tricked the
Israelites into making a covenant with them. Its population was,
however, enslaved by the newcomers (9: 22-27).

Gibeon was at that time, according to Jos 10: 2, "a great
city, like one of the royal cities ... greater than Ai". Yet
excavations at the site (el-Jib) have shown that during the LBA
there was no significant occupation on the tell.

At the close of the 1960 season, some items of LBA pottery
were discovered in seven tombs on the west side of the tell, and
a report in The Illustrated London News for Sept 24th of that year
(pp 518-19) stated: "The Late Bronze tombs have provided the
first evidence for the Canaanite city which is described in
chapters nine and ten of the book of Joshua". But during the
fifth season (1962), when the Bronze Age cemetery was cleared, no
more LBA items were found. Pritchard writes:

"Alas, there were in the large cemetery of fifty-five
rock-cut tombs, no more burial deposits of the Late Bronze
Age. When the contents of the tombs were studied more
carefully for publication, it was clear that the seven
deposits of Late Bronze material had been made in tombs
hewn from the rock in the Middle Bronze period, and not
one of the tombs containing this later material had been
prepared especially for the Late Bronze burials" (1965: 318).

Trenches cut out into areas of the mound not previously
explored, in the hope of discovering traces of a LBA city,
produced nothing from that period. Thus Pritchard concludes:

"... There was no extensive city on the tell from the end of
Middle Bronze until the beginning of the twelfth century.
The Late Bronze tombs of the fourteenth century belonged
either to a very small settlement, limited to some small

section of the mound as yet untouched, or to the temporary camps in the vicinity. There can be no doubt, on the basis of the best evidence available, that there was no city of any importance at the time of Joshua" (ibid: 319; cf. also E. M. Good 1962: 993; Blenkinsopp 1972: 6).

This last sentence assumes, of course, that Joshua should be placed late in the LBA.

It is not surprising, therefore, that we find Gibeon mentioned alongside Jericho and Ai as one of the cities where archaeological evidence upsets the picture of a 13th century Conquest (e.g. de Vaux 1970: 76-8; Hyatt 1971: 40).

However, if the Conquest is placed at the close of the MBA, the problem is considerably reduced. It is true that no traces of city walls have been found which could be dated to the MBA, but remains of house walls, pottery and tombs, indicate occupation in that period (cf. Reed 1967: 235). Indeed, MB II pottery has been recovered from very widely separated areas of the tell, causing Pritchard to remark that "the area of occupation must have been extensive in this period" (1962: 154). There is therefore no reason to doubt that a large city like that described in Jos 10: 2 existed at Gibeon during MB II.

If the MBA city was without defences, as appears to have been the case, this would explain why, even though it was large, it sought to make peace with the Israelites rather than oppose them, and also why it begged help from the Israelites when threatened by the Amorite alliance (Jos 10: 6). The abandonment of the city at the end of the MBA may be viewed as a result of the removal and enslavement of much of its population by the Israelites, or as a result of Amorite hostility.

7.1.5 *Dan*

The final city to be discussed in this section is the northern city of Dan, whose end is described in Jdg 18: 27. The name Dan was, however, only given to the city after its resettlement by the Danites; prior to its destruction by that tribe, it was called Laish (Jdg 18: 7, 14, 27, 29) or Leshem (Jos 19: 47).

Before discussing archaeological evidence from Laish-Dan, we must look briefly at the question of the migration of the tribe of Dan and its relation to the Conquest and other traditions.

This is a complex problem and I do not intend to discuss it in detail or to refer to all of the numerous attempts to resolve it. Scholars who have examined the problem have shown, by arriving at widely divergent conclusions, that it involves so many unknown factors that a definitive solution is impossible.

Does Jos 19: 47a (which reads literally "the border of the children of Dan went out from them") mean, as in the RSV translation, that "the territory of the Danites was lost to them"; or is the expression meant to indicate, as Yadin suggests (1968: 10-11), that Dan was without an inheritance among or within the tribes of Israel from the beginning? Such verses as Jdg 18: 11-12 and 13: 25, referring to a "camp of Dan", may indicate that this tribe remained nomadic longer than other Israelite groups and therefore was without territory after other groups had begun to settle. This is certainly the implication of Jdg 18: 1. On the other hand Jos 19: 40-46 could be taken to indicate the possession of territory which was later lost (cf. the RSV translation of 19: 47); but the list of towns contained in these verses may be late and hence provide no real support for such a view.

If we suppose Dan to have once held territory in the south, bordering on the coast, was the tribe displaced by Philistine pressure, as Rowley has argued (1950: 81-6), or by pressure from the Amorites, as is stated in Jdg 1: 34? Does the reference to Dan in Jdg 5: 17 refer to a time when the tribe held territory in the south (cf. Yadin 1968: 13ff), or to a period when Dan was in the north (cf. Mayes 1969: 355, n.1)?

These are some of the unresolved problems which surround the history of this tribe. It is, however, necessary for a number of proposed solutions to be laid aside.

As mentioned above, Rowley argues that the Danites were displaced northwards by Philistine pressure (also Soggin 1972: 17). As the Philistine expansion is dated to the 12th century BC on the basis of extra-biblical material, Rowley dates the Danite migration to the middle of that century. The story of the migration involves a grandson of Moses (Jdg 18: 30), which indicates that it cannot have taken place very much after the main wave of the Israelite Conquest; and since Rowley fixes the migration in the middle of the 12th century, the Exodus and Conquest must, he says, be dated in the 13th century.

This reasoning is employed by Rowley as an argument against
a 15th century date for the Exodus (1950: 81-6). It is, however,
seriously inadequate. There are no grounds for linking the
Danite migration with the Philistine expansion; the biblical
tradition itself cites the Amorites, not the Philistines, as the
people who caused problems for the Danites (Jdg 1: 34). Rowley's
attempt to acknowledge this verse within the context of his
theory, by suggesting that the Philistine incursion "dislodged
the Amorites, who in turn pressed the Danites" (ibid: 85) begs the
question.

In short, Rowley fails to produce any reason for placing the
Danite migration in the 12th century. If the cause of Danite
restlessness was Amorite pressure, there is no reason why the
northward movement should not have occurred very soon after the
initial Israelite penetration into the land, since the Amorites
were among the peoples whom the Israelites found in Canaan when
they first arrived.

We may note here another reason offered for placing the
Danite migration in the 12th century. Yadin has stated:

"From the Biblical account it is clear that the conquest of
Laish took place at a time when Sidon, which should have
helped the inhabitants of Laish, had been completely
weakened and did not have the strength to do its duty.
This situation could only have been round about the end
of the twelfth century (near the year 1100), both following
the victory of Ashkelon over Sidon and as a result of the
campaigns of Tiglath-Pileser I" (1968: 21).

In Jdg 18 , however, we read nothing of Sidon having a duty
to protect Laish, nor of Sidon being weak; what we *do* read is
that when the Danites attacked the people of Laish, "there was no
deliverer because it was far from Sidon, and they had no dealings
with anyone" (18: 28; cf. verse 7). The implication of this is
that it was *not* Sidon's duty to protect Laish, because there was
no effective contact between the two cities. It is therefore
unnecessary to place the conquest of Laish in a period of Sidonian
weakness.

The differences of opinion over the reference to Dan in Jdg 5:
17 show that it is not possible to use that verse to date the

northward movement relative to Barak's battle with Sisera.
Because the import of the verse is not clear, it does not tell
us whether the tribe of Dan was in a northern or southern locality
at the time of the battle. Furthermore, there is, as Rowley
points out, "no reason to believe that the whole tribe migrated"
(1950: 83).

For this reason we cannot assume, simply because Samson comes
from a Danite family (Jdg 13: 2ff) and carries on exploits in
Philistine territory, that the northward migration did not occur
until after Samson's time. Samson's family could well have
belonged to a part of the tribe which did not take part in the
move to Laish. Alternatively, if the whole tribe remained
nomadic for slightly longer than the other Israelite groups, it
is possible that the settlement in the north and the settlement
in what subsequently became Philistine territory, were
simultaneous settlements by two groups which went their different
ways shortly after the tribe's initial entry into the land.

Further speculation on this point would not be profitable
here, but I mention these various possibilities to prepare the way
for the reasoning which follows.

Jdg 18: 30 records that when the Danites resettled Laish and
called it Dan, they set up there the graven image made by Micah,
and made Jonathan, son of Gershom, son of Moses, their priest. It
is added that Jonathan's descendants were priests to the Danites
"until the day of the captivity of the land". While it is
possible that for "Moses" one should read "Manasseh" here, it is
more probable that Moses is spoken of. According to Ex 2: 22,
Moses' son Gershom was born before the Exodus. Therefore, if these
traditions are historically reliable, the incident of the setting
up of Micah's image in the new city cannot be placed very much
later than the main wave of Conquest, and we must assume that the
destruction of Laish was not separated appreciably in time from
the destruction of the other Canaanite cities. In other words, on
the basis of the biblical traditions themselves, we should expect
the end of Laish to be dated archaeologically to approximately the
same time as the end of the other cities which fell to the
Israelite tribes. In the framework offered here, we should
therefore find evidence for the destruction of Laish at the end
of MB II C.

It is therefore gratifying to find that excavations have
revealed that the MB II C city, incorrectly described as "Hyksos"

(e.g. Biran 1966: 145) like many other cities of that period, was
"destroyed in a massive conflagration" (Biran 1969: 121). It is
specifically stated in Jdg 18: 27 that the Danites destroyed
Laish by burning it.

Since the biblical record implies that the Danites
re-settled the site immediately, we should expect some evidence
of LB I reoccupation, and this also has been discovered, though at
present it appears to be scanty (cf. Biran 1969: 122-3; 1974: 34).

Evidence for the Danite destruction of Laish within the
conventional framework is in contrast very poor. Biran points out
that if the Exodus is placed in the 13th century BC, the capture
of Laish must be placed in the first half of the 12th century
(because of the involvement of a grandson of Moses), at the end
of the LBA (1974: 37-8). Yet Biran specifically states that there
is no evidence whatever of a conflagration at the end of Stratum
VII, the last LBA stratum (ibid: 35). There was, however, a change
in the level of material culture, and it is this which Biran sees
as an indication that an Israelite tribe had occupied the site.
This is because Stratum VI, the first Iron Age stratum at Tel Dan,
contains pottery similar to that in Stratum XII at Hazor, the
stratum which Yadin has claimed represents the first Israelite
settlement there (ibid: 35, 38). Since there is no real
justification for identifying this Iron I pottery as Israelite,
there is naturally no reason to place the arrival of the Danites
at Laish at the transition between the LBA and the Iron Age. The
most telling fact, however, is that no conflagration layer
separates Strata VII and VI, while the biblical tradition relates
specifically that Laish was burnt by the Danites /4/.

In short, the archaeological finds at Dan provide evidence for
placing the burning of Laish by the Danites at the end of the MBA
rather than at the end of the LBA.

7.2 Other Cities Destroyed at the End of the Middle Bronze Age

Jos 10: 28-39 lists six cities destroyed by the Israelites:
Makkedah, Libnah, Lachish, Eglon, Hebron and Debir. De Vaux
remarks concerning these verses that "the redactional character of
these lists is shown by literary criticism" (1965: 27; also 1970:
77), and implies that they possess little historical value. It
is true that they present a somewhat schematized view of the
Conquest, and probably attribute to Joshua, as leader of all
Israel, successes which were actually achieved by smaller groups

under other leaders. It is noteworthy that Jdg 1: 11-15 (cf. Jos 15: 15-19) records the taking of Debir by the Calebites, while the taking of Hebron is attributed to Judah in Jdg 1: 10 and to Calebites in Jos 15: 13-14 (cf. Jdg 1: 20). For the present discussion the important thing is that tradition does record the defeat of these cities by Israelite and allied groups. It must remain uncertain which tradition is nearer to the historical truth, but it hardly seems reasonable to doubt, on the grounds provided, that Debir and Hebron were destroyed during the war of conquest.

We should perhaps attach less certainty to the other four cities in the list of Jos 10, since their capture is recorded here and nowhere else. But the examples of Debir and Hebron give us reason to believe that, schematized though this list may be, it need not be considered pure fiction.

To this list of six cities Jdg 1 adds a further six: Jerusalem Hormah, Gaza, Ashkelon, Ekron and Bethel. Of this total of twelve cities, Hebron and Hormah have already been dealt with; the remaining ten will be discussed here.

Debir is commonly identified (following Albright) with Tell Beit Mirsim. Some have expressed reservations about this identification, pointing out that while there is "nothing to disprove Albright's identification of the site ... there is no compelling reason so to identify it" (Gray 1962: 95). Some have actually proposed alternative locations for Debir (e.g. Kochavi 1974: 2-28), but the majority of scholars continue to accept Tell Beit Mirsim as the correct site, and this identification will be followed here.

At Tell Beit Mirsim the MB II C city (Stratum D) "was completely destroyed and the site was then abandoned for a comparatively long time..." (Albright 1967: 214). This destruction involved a conflagration, since Stratum D was covered with a layer of ash (cf. Kenyon 1970: 197).

Lachish is identified confidently with Tell ed-Duweir. In the opinion of the excavators, the last phase of the MBA city was deliberately destroyed (cf. Tufnell 1958: 34-5, 48-9). Again the destruction involved a violent conflagration.

We will see below that the identification of Bethel with Beitin may be erroneous. However, adopting this generally

accepted location here, we find there is clear evidence for the
destruction of the MB II C city (cf. Albright 1968a: 46-7),
including some evidence of conflagration (ibid: 24-7). Pottery
for the following period is scanty, suggesting that the site was
abandoned for a time (ibid: 28, 47).

Eglon is often identified with Tell el-Hesy, though Tell
en-Nejileh (or Nagila) has also been suggested (Lilley 1962: 337).
Both these sites were destroyed at the end of the MBA.

The final phase of the MBA is represented at Tell el-Hesy by
what Bliss, the site's excavator, labelled Sub-city II (Bliss
1894: 1-17). Schaeffer has proposed a relabelling of Hesy's
strata so that cities Sub-II and II of Bliss become Hesy III and
Hesy IV respectively, and shows quite clearly that at the end of
Hesy III there was a destruction followed by a hiatus (cf.
Schaeffer 1948: 200-204, and Table 4). It is not clear whether
the destruction was accompanied by burning or not. The MBA city
possessed a glacis and a tower "typical of the time of the Hyksos"
(Negev 1972: 145), and the tower shows "traces of conflagration"
(Amiran and Worrell 1976: 516), but it appears to be uncertain
whether these traces are to be associated with the end of the MBA
city (cf. ibid).

At Nejileh during MB II B-C there was a large city with
fortifications of the type commonly described as "Hyksos" (Amiran
and Eitan 1965: 113-123). This city was violently destroyed and
burned at the end of MB II C (Amiran and Eitan 1964: 220).
According to Wright, the site remained unoccupied after the end
of the MBA apart from a Judaean fort (1971: 85). Other writers
mention some finds of LBA pottery from the site, but no building
remains, and occupation is considered to have been very sparse
between the MBA and the Iron Age (cf. Amiran and Eitan 1963:
143-4, 333-4; 1965: 115; C.F. Pfeiffer 1966: 572).

Libnah has commonly been identified with Tell es-Safi (or
Safiyeh), though some writers now prefer to identify either Gath
(cf. G.A. Smith 1931: 193, 222; Negev 1972: 277) or Makkedah
(Albright 1924: 9; V.R. Gold 1962: 228) with this site.
Alternatives suggested for Libnah are Tell Bornat (Albright 1924:
9) and, more recently, Tell el-Judeideh (cf. Negev 1972: 176).

Safi was excavated by Bliss and Macalister in 1898-1900, but
no clear stratification of the site is recorded, and it is
impossible to say whether or not this city was destroyed at the

end of the MBA (cf. Bliss and Macalister 1902: 28-43). However, the excavations yielded pottery which shows that the site was at least occupied in both MBA and LBA periods (ibid: 35; cf. Negev 1972: 277). At Tell Bornat occupation does not appear to have begun until the LBA (Wright 1971: 83), so this site does not support the present thesis if its identification with Libnah is correct.

However, Tell el-Judeideh, which is now favoured as the site of Libnah, following the rejection of its earlier identification as Moresheth-Gath (Negev 1972: 176), may well have fallen at the end of the MBA. The Tell was excavated by Bliss and Macalister, 1899-1900, but the excavations concentrated on the city of the Roman period, and there was penetration of pre-Israelite levels only in six pits dug in the northern part of the tell. In this area, immediately beneath an "Israelite" or "Jewish" (i.e. Iron Age) stratum, Bliss and Macalister found a stratum characterized by what they termed "early pre-Israelite" pottery. This pottery is of types which would now be classified as EBA and MBA. LBA types, called "late pre-Israelite" by the excavators, were represented by only "a few specimens"; "... The absence of a distinct stratum characterized by this ware is noticeable. This leads us to conclude that Tell el-Judeideh suffered an interruption in its history" (Bliss and Macalister 1902: 51). It is not possible to be certain of this point on the basis of the excavators' report, but it seems very probable that this interruption came at the end of the MBA. The excavators also state that "Signs of conflagration were visible in many places" in the six clearance pits (ibid: 50), but it is impossible to ascertain whether any of these were associated with the start of the hiatus just mentioned.

Makkedah, as mentioned above, is identified by some with Tell es-Safi. We have already seen that this site was at least occupied during the MBA, but beyond that nothing relevant to our discussion can be deduced from the old report. Others suggest identifying Makkedah with Khirbet el-Kheishum, an apparently unexcavated ruin to the north-east of Azekah (cf. Lilley 1962: 773; also Grollenberg 1956: 156).

In the case of Jerusalem, we must note that the traditions themselves are not consistent. Although Jdg 1: 8 records the destruction and burning of the city, 1: 21 states that the Jebusites were not driven out of Jerusalem, and it appears to have remained a Jebusite stronghold until the time of David. It is also

notable that although the king of Jerusalem figures as the head
of the league which opposes Joshua in Jos 10, Jerusalem is not
included in the list of cities conquered after the defeat of the
league in 10: 28-39.   There are therefore strong hints in the
text that Jerusalem was not in fact taken by the Israelites at
the time of the Conquest (cf. further de Vaux 1971: 502-3 on the
dubious worth of Jdg 1: 8).

Only a small portion of the wall of the MBA city has been
uncovered, and shows no sign of burning.   Kenyon actually
believes that this wall, built in MB II A, remained in use until
David's capture of the Jebusite city and even beyond (cf. Mazar
1975: 3; Kenyon 1976: 594).   Evidence of a city flourishing at
Jerusalem to the end of the MBA consists of finds from tombs on
the Mount of Olives and other adjacent sites (Kenyon 1971: 22;
Mazar 1975: 3).

The tradition concerning Gaza, Ashkelon and Ekron is also
ambiguous, because the LXX negates the MT's statement (Jdg 1: 18)
that Judah took these cities.   Ancient Gaza was originally
identified by Petrie with Tell el-ʿAjjul, but it is now thought
to have occupied the same site as the medieval and modern cities
of Gaza.   Excavations carried out here by W.J. Phythian-Adams in
1922-3 revealed traces of various walls, the earliest two of
which were designated the Grey and Green walls.   One or both of
these may date back as far as the MBA, but Phythian-Adams was
unable to associate any pottery with them in order to date them
precisely (cf. A. Ovadiah 1976: 411-2; also Garstang 1931: 375-6).
Ashkelon (Tell el-Hader) was certainly occupied in the MBA and
was violently destroyed at the end of that period (cf. Schaeffer
1948: 208-9 and Table 4; Avi-Yonah and Y. Ephan 1975: 125).   The
exact location of Ekron is unknown (cf. Stinespring 1962: 69;
Negev 1972: 98).

Many of the MBA cities mentioned above have rampart
fortifications of the type wrongly associated with the Hyksos,
and have been described by various writers as Hyksos cities.   Thus
their destructions have frequently been seen as the work of
Egyptian armies following the expulsion of the Hyksos from Egypt.
The points made in reply to this view in relation to Jericho
apply equally to the other destroyed MBA cities.   The theory which
dates their destruction to the 16th century BC and associates it
with the Hyksos defeat is not supported by the evidence.

We have now considered every city mentioned as destroyed by
Israelite groups in the Conquest narratives, except for the city
of Ai. The following section is devoted to the special problems
posed by this city.

7.3   The Problem-City of Ai

The conquest of Ai is reported in great detail in Jos 8: 1-29,
immediately after the narrative of the fall of Jericho. Ai has
been omitted from our discussion until now because of the
possibility, a strong one it seems to the present writer, that
the long held identification of this city with Khirbet et-Tell may
be erroneous.

Excavations at et-Tell have shown that site to have been
desolate from the end of the EBA to the early Iron Age. There was
no city at et-Tell at all during the intervening periods. Thus
the absence of LBA remains has made the site an embarrassment to
both early and late date schemes for the Exodus (cf. remarks in
Rowley 1950: 20; Callaway 1968: 312), and the absence of remains
from the MBA means that the theory offered in the present book
does nothing to resolve the difficulty.

There have been various attempts to account for the anomaly
of Ai apart from the assumption that the narrative in Jos 8 is
an aetiological fiction (Noth 1953). Albright suggested in 1934
that Ai became confused with Bethel in the traditions, so that
what is recounted in Jos 8 is really the conquest of Bethel, whose
destruction by the Josephites is reported in Jdg 1: 22-25 (1934:
11). There are problems with this view. The events surrounding
the conquest of Ai in Jos 7-8 bear little relation to the fall of
Bethel in Jdg 1. There is also the fact that Bethel is mentioned
as well as Ai in Jos 7: 2; 8: 12 and 17.

Père Vincent suggested in 1937 that though Ai was not a city
at the time of the Conquest, the people of Bethel erected there a
bulwark against the encroaching Israelites, and that nothing
remains of this outpost because it was hastily established and
its buildings only flimsy structures (Vincent 1937: 258-266). A
similar view has been put forward more recently by Harrison (1970:
121-2). Such theories, designed to do the maximum possible
justice to both the biblical narrative and the archaeological
evidence, really fail to account for certain of the narrative's
features, such as the appearance of a king of Ai (Jos 8: 1-2, 23,

29) and the apparent existence of a city gate (7: 5), which implies the existence of fortified walls.

It is of course *possible* that the story really refers to Bethel or a military outpost thereof, but to the present writer such views seem unsatisfactory in the absence of supporting archaeological evidence and of any hints to this effect in the narratives.

The suggestion of Callaway, that the Israelite attack was actually directed against the earliest Iron Age village on the site, has already been criticised in Part One, and will not be discussed again here.

The possibility that the identification of Ai with et-Tell is mistaken holds out the hope of a more satisfactory solution to the problem, and it is on this possibility the following discussion will concentrate.

How was the identification Ai = et-Tell arrived at? Edward Robinson remained uncertain about the location of Ai, being unable to decide between et-Tell and Khirbet Haiyan (Robinson 1856: II, 313), both being sites close to Beitin, which he identified as Bethel (ibid: I, 449-50). In 1851-2 Van-de-Velde identified Ai with et-Tell on the basis of the meaning of the name et-Tell ("the mound") and the biblical reference to Ai being made "a heap forever" by the destruction wrought by Joshua (Jos 8: 28) (cf. Grintz 1961: 202). In 1878 Kitchener published the suggestion that Ai should be located at Khirbet Haiy, a mile southeast of Mukhmas. He objected to the identification with et-Tell on the grounds that its proximity to Bethel (Beitin) would have made impossible the ambush described in Jos 8: 12 (cf. ibid: 202-3). In 1881 Guerin offered Khirbet el-Kuhdeira, a ruin southeast of Beitin, as yet another possible site (cf. ibid: 203).

Albright was convinced at an early stage of the correctness of locating Ai at et-Tell (cf. 1922/3: 141-9). Sherds were found at the site which at that time were believed to date to the Middle and Late Bronze Ages (cf. ibid: 141, 146-7; Garstang 1931: 355), and this made the site's identification with a city involved in the Israelite Conquest all the more likely. Indeed, the existence of these sherds was a factor which prompted the excavation of the site (cf. Grintz 206).

Excavations were carried out for two years, 1933-5, headed by Judith Marquet-Krause. During these it emerged that the site had

been abandoned from the end of the third millennium to the 12th
century BC. Sherds which had previously been thought to be Middle
Bronze were found to be Early Bronze, and those described as
"early Late Bronze" were found to date from the Iron Age occupation
of the 12th century (cf. Albright 1934: 11). In the light of
these discoveries, Marquet-Krause herself suggested that the
Conquest narratives of Jos 1-8 consisted merely of legend (1935:
325ff).

Other researchers have reacted by objecting that et-Tell
cannot be Ai and that the biblical city should be sought at one of
the other ruins in the area around Bethel. We will look at some
of the relevant arguments below.

Soundings were made at the possible alternative sites during
excavations carried out at et-Tell in the 1960's. A sounding was
made at Khirbet Haiyan in 1965, and revealed no architecture
earlier than Islamic (cf. Callaway 1965: 16, n.4; Callaway and
Nicol 1966: 12-19). In 1966 Khirbet el-Kuhdeira (Khudriya) and
fifteen tombs discovered in the nearby Wadi Asas were examined.
Callaway reports that neither Khudriya itself nor the tombs
yielded anything to suggest the identification of this site with
Ai (1969: 5). Khirbet Haiy (or Hai) was also examined. "Nothing
that could be dated before Byzantine was found on the small,
unfortified site" (Callaway 1968: 315). Callaway refers to these
findings as confirming Albright's conclusion that et-Tell is the
only possible site for Ai (ibid).

However, the affirmation that no other alternative exists can
only be made in the context of the identification of Bethel with
Beitin. Bethel and Ai lay close together, and it is true that if
Bethel should be located at Beitin, then et-Tell is the most
plausible site for Ai, since the other nearby sites are even less
suitable in view of their archaeological remains. The
identification of Beitin with Bethel has, however, been questioned,
and in the light of this we may note some of the objections which
have been raised to the location of Ai at et-Tell.

Grintz has noted that the opinion "that et-Tell is a
translation of Ai cannot be maintained" (1961: 208). He points
out that the name et-Tell is by no means a unique phenomenon. "It
is a designation quite common throughout the country. The list of
ruins and tells compiled by the Antiquities Department of the
Mandatory Government enumerates six tells with this name in
Western Palestine alone.... Should we assume that all these places

once bore the name Ai? We have exact identifications for a
number of them and we know for a fact that that is not the case"
(ibid: 208-9). He goes on to show that there are also several
examples of the name Ai, or variations thereon, "and they always,
so far as they are known to us, indicate a settled town and never
designated an actual ruin" (211). He asserts therefore that the
name Ai "does not have the meaning of 'ruin' (either in Arabic or
Hebrew)" (210). Furthermore, the use of the definite article
before the name should not be taken to indicate this meaning (i.e.
"the ruin", a ruin of particular significance in the area), since
this use of the article before place names is quite common. In
Jos 18, "of the twenty-six place names listed in the territory of
Benjamin, ten appear with the definite article *Ha-*..." (210). He
thus concludes that the name Ai should not be treated as a noun
used to designate a ruin, nor should et-Tell be considered an
Arabic rendering of the name. In other words he asserts that,
contrary to popular opinion, there is no linguistic evidence for
the identification of Ai with et-Tell.

Grintz further objects that et-Tell is too close to Beitin
(which he accepts as the site of Bethel) to be Ai, and also
argues that the lack of any remains at et-Tell from the period of
the Conquest (on either the early or late date view) is itself
evidence that this is not Ai /5/. He also assembles a detailed
argument for identifying et-Tell with biblical Beth-aven (212-16),
thus attempting to preclude the possibility that et-Tell is Ai /6/.

Grintz does not propose a firm alternative for Ai, though he
suggests Khirbet Haiy as a possibility (216). This is one of the
sites excluded from the argument by the soundings of the 1960's.
But Grintz is not so much concerned to establish the true site for
Ai as to make the point that et-Tell *cannot* be Ai. This he
appears to do very effectively. But while the true site is sought
in the vicinity of Beitin, its location remains a complete mystery.
No objections to the location of Ai at et-Tell, however strong,
can be expected to receive a hearing while no alternative site
appears to exist.

D. Livingston has recently produced an alternative site, but
only at the expense of abandoning the traditional identification of
Bethel with Beitin. This move cannot be expected to be received
with much enthusiasm, because the traditional identification has
become so popular. But before examining Livingston's proposed
shifting of Bethel, we may note the objections which he raises to
the identification of Ai with et-Tell.

According to the biblical information, Ai lay "beside" Bethel
(Jos 12: 9), and to the east of it (Gen 12: 8). Beth-aven lay
"beside" Ai and east of Bethel (Jos 7: 2; cf. Brown, Driver and
Briggs 1952: 110; Livingston 1970: 26), which implies that
Beth-aven lay east of Ai. Michmash lay east of Beth-aven (I Sam
13: 5). A mountain lay between Bethel and Ai and therefore to
the west of Ai (Gen 12: 8). If Beitin is assumed to be Bethel,
the identification of Ai with et-Tell does not fit very well with
this picture. It places Ai north of Michmash when it should be
west of it, and there is no mountain, but rather a valley,
between et-Tell and Beitin (Livingston 1970: 27, 38). There is
a small hill to the northwest of et-Tell, but this could hardly
be said to be *between* it and Beitin (ibid: 38, n.69).

Like Grintz, Livingston sees the lack of remains from the
periods to which the Conquest is normally assigned as further
evidence that et-Tell cannot be Ai.

But the core of Livingston's argument concerns his relocation
of Bethel. He points out that until Edward Robinson identified
Bethel with Beitin in the last century, the location of Bethel
was unknown. In Robinson's day, the monks of Jerusalem actually
believed Bethel had been some distance further north than Beitin.

Livingston examines the various grounds on which the
identification was made and is now upheld, pointing out certain
weaknesses and then offering his alternative identification.
Livingston believes that Bethel should be identified with
el-Bireh, about an hour's walk southwest of Beitin. Bireh was
earlier identified as the site of biblical Beeroth, but this is now
acknowledged to be incorrect, and the site of Beeroth is thought
to be either Nebi Samwil or Khirbet el-Burj, near modern Biddu;
Livingston actually suggests that Biddu itself may be the correct
location (ibid: 40, n.79; cf. Negev 1972: 46).

Livingston's identification of Bethel with Bireh enables him
to propose an alternative site for Ai. One and a half miles from
Bireh lies a small tell, and it is here that he suggests Ai should
be sought. The tell is presently unnamed and has not yet (or at
least, at the time Livingston was writing his article, had not)
been excavated (Livingston 43). The topography of the region
certainly seems correct. A large mountain, called et-Tawil, lies
between Bireh and this ruin. The ruin is to the southeast of
Bireh. Placing Ai here requires a site for Beth-aven west of
Michmash, where it should be, not north of it, as is the case with

et-Tell (Livingston 42-3).

Livingston's arguments concerning the location of Bethel have
recently been strongly challenged by Rainey, who insists that
Beitin is the only possible site for this town. It will be
convenient here to consider Livingston's arguments and Rainey's
answers together.

Robinson felt the identification of Bethel with Beitin to be
confirmed decisively by the form of the modern name (1856: I,
449-50). He found several parallels to support the idea that the
change from Hebrew *el* to Arabic *in* was a common one. Livingston
suggests that the name Beitin has nothing to do with Bethel. In
Arabic, Beitin means "two houses", and he suggests that it became
the name of the site because two ruined buildings were a prominent
feature there before the site was resettled in the 19th century
after being abandoned for a considerable time (Livingston 32, n.46).
He also notes a point made by Albright (1939: 14), that names of
towns and villages are sometimes known to have been displaced over
a considerable local area, so that even if the derivation of
Beitin from Bethel was an assured fact, it would not be conclusive
proof that the place now bearing that name is the site of
biblical Bethel.

Rainey objects to this by arguing that enquiring after the
meaning of Beitin in Arabic is a wrong approach which creates "an
artificial ambiguity" and "falsifies the evidence" (Rainey 1971:
177), though it is by no means made clear in what way this is so.
He insists: "The oral tradition which produced *Beitîn >—Bêṯ-ʾēl*
is perfectly clear", and says the name constitutes evidence which
is "virtually conclusive in itself" (ibid). Thus he seems to miss
Livingston's point that although such a derivation is *possible*, it
is not *proven* etymologically, and that in any case a displacement
may have occurred /7/.

Rainey's second main objection to Livingston's view concerns
archaeological evidence for equating Bethel with Beitin.
Livingston makes the point that the identification is not proven
archaeologically, i.e., it remains unconfirmed by any inscriptional
evidence. Rainey argues that the archaeological evidence is
sufficient to prove the accepted identification: "... The fact
that *Beitin* is one of the few sites in the area north of Jerusalem
with Middle and Late Bronze Age stratification is extremely
important" (ibid: 178). It is "the one site with sufficient
archaeological remains to satisfy the biblical and post-biblical

sources" (ibid: 179). But if the ability of a site to satisfy
the sources is a main criterion for identification, why was not
the identification of Ai with et-Tell abandoned long ago? And
surely on these grounds, the finding of a satisfactory site for
Ai would play an important part in deciding the extent to which
any proposed location for Bethel "satisfied the sources". Even
more important, Livingston makes the point concerning Bireh that
"no excavating has been done, and there has been no archaeological
survey of the area undertaken" (41). Since Rainey nowhere
contradicts this, we may conclude that nothing had been undertaken
to make Livingston's remark obsolete before Rainey penned his own
article. So how can Rainey be sure that Bireh will not yield
"sufficient archaeological remains to satisfy the biblical and
post-biblical sources" at some date in the future? Only when
sufficient excavation has been done to test Livingston's theory
can we decide whether Beitin deserves to remain the site of
Bethel. Rainey's contention concerning the archaeological evidence
from Beitin therefore sounds somewhat hollow.

The arguments and counter-arguments concerning topography
are rather complex and will be simplified here.

Livingston makes several points in this respect. The first
is that Bethel seems to have been a road junction. It was on the
main north-south trade route, and also served east-west traffic
(cf. Livingston 29 with notes 33-36). He points out that other
towns with this characteristic which were visited by Abraham
(Shechem, Hebron and Beer-sheba) have never ceased to be "living
towns", and are still busy places today (though Tell Beer-sheba
lies just outside the modern city). Beitin never seems to have
occupied such a favourable position, and was in fact completely
deserted in Robinson's day when its identification with Bethel
was first proposed. Bireh on the other hand, is a "living town",
and occupies the natural cross-roads of that area. Furthermore
it has been for a very long time the traditional limit of the
first day's journey northward from Jerusalem.

Rainey objects that "Though one of the prerequisites for a
major town in antiquity was association with routes of some
importance, proximity is one thing, immediate continuity is
another. It was always better from the point of view of security
for the city to be located some distance away from the main
route". He cites Jerusalem, Gezer, Megiddo and Taanach as
examples of important cities thus situated. "Therefore *Beitin's*
location vis-à-vis the roads in her vicinity is just what we would

expect of the most important city north of Jerusalem" (Rainey 181).

This is a valid point which weakens the objections
Livingston makes on topographical grounds to the identification of
Beitin with Bethel. On the other hand it does nothing to weaken
Livingston's arguments *for* locating Bethel at Bireh. It remains
a fact that some towns *were* located on the main routes rather than
some way off them, and that Bethel seems to have been one such
town (cf. Jdg 21: 19).

The same can be said of Rainey's reply to Livingston's second
topographical argument. Bethel was a border town between Ephraim
and Benjamin (cf. Jos 16: 1, 2; 18: 12, 13). Livingston notes
that boundaries are often formed by natural formations, and points
out that one such is the geographical rift which forms the valley
of Aijalon. But this natural dividing line lies a full two miles
south of Beitin, so that if Bethel is located there, the location
requires an abnormal northward bulge in the border.

Rainey's reply concentrates on the position of the border
between Israel and Judah during the period of the divided monarchy.
He argues that the border during this troubled period would
certainly *not* pass close to a royal strongpoint, which is what
Bethel was (Jeroboam's temple stood there). Under Asa the border
seems to have been set near to Geba and Mizpah, since these towns
appear to have guarded it on the south (cf. I Kgs 15: 22). Just
north of Tell en-Nasbeh, which Rainey takes to be Mizpah, lies a
prominent ridge, which Rainey suggests was the border from Asa's
time until 722 BC. Beitin lies north of this. Rainey says all
this makes perfect sense only if Beitin = Bethel (184).

However, Rainey's argument effectively hinges on the
assumption that Bethel, being a royal strongpoint, must have been
north of the border rather than on it. This leads him to suppose
that natural topographical border must be sought between Bethel
and Mizpah (Tell en-Nasbeh), and hence that Beitin, lying north
of the ridge near Mizpah, is confirmed as Bethel. His basic
assumption overlooks a point made by Livingston, that during the
Crusades Bireh, which was controlled by the Knights Templar and
called La Grande Mahomerie, was both a main fortress and a place
of pilgrimage. He writes: "It seems significant that the
Crusaders chose this spot to defend rather than Beitin. It is *the*
place on the Jerusalem-Nablus road to effect a roadblock. The
Israelis made good use of this fact in the Six-Day War when they
captured this spot early in the fighting. Jeroboam may also have

made good use of it in putting a temple there" (Livingston 42).
Hence Rainey's statement that Bethel would not have been situated
on the border does not seem necessarily correct.

We should note, furthermore, that the ridge which Rainey
believes was the border between Israel and Judah is the same as
that which Livingston believes was the border, and that Bireh
lies precisely on this ridge (cf. Livingston 42; Rainey 184).
Since Rainey seems to accept that this border was the same as
that between Ephraim and Benjamin (183), and since Bethel is
definitely stated to have been situated on the Ephraim-Benjamin
border (Jos 16: 1-2; 18: 12-13), this seems to support rather
than weaken the identification of Bireh with Bethel.

Livingston's other topographical arguments concern the shape
of the land around Bethel and Ai in the biblical references to
their situation, their relationship to other places, and the lack
of correspondences between the biblical information and actuality
if Bethel = Beitin and Ai = et-Tell. We have already noted these
among Livingston's objections to the Ai = et-Tell equation, and
need not discuss them further, since Rainey does not offer any
reply to them. He merely points out that "allusions to a hill or
a valley are not so crucial without other indications" (by which
he means the matters of the border and the highways), and says
it is not hard to take the biblical passages describing the
relationship between Bethel and Ai "and to find similar
topographical situations at various places in the same general
region" (180). He offers no real reply to Livingston's point
that with Bethel situated at Beitin and Ai at et-Tell, the
topographical situation is *not* that described in the Bible.

The final point concerns patristic evidence for the location
of Bethel. According to Eusebius and Jerome, Bethel lay twelve
miles north of Jerusalem, on the right of the road to Neapolis.
Livingston examines the relevant passages and points out that
Eusebius and Jerome are speaking of mile-*markers*, not simply
miles (Livingston 34). The latest mile-markers between Jerusalem
and Beitin are those of Marcus Aurelius (162 AD). The fifth of
these has been found more than a mile southwest of er-Ram (the
Rama of Eusebius and Jerome), which means that the sixth must have
been located near to er-Ram, just a short way to the south of the
place. Eusebius and Jerome imply that this was the case (cf.
ibid: 35). Livingston argues that since Rama is slightly more than
half way from Jerusalem to Bireh and a little beyond the sixth
mile-marker, the twelfth mile-marker must have been in or near

Bireh, depending on the exact route taken, which is not known
(36). The Eusebius-Jerome statement concerning the twelfth
marker from Jerusalem, if taken as a measurement of distance from
the Damascus Gate, brings one to an indefinite point *between* Bireh
and Beitin. However, Livingston cites authorities who have
argued that the O-milestone stood not at the Damascus Gate, as is
commonly supposed, but well within Jerusalem (36, 37 with n.62),
pointing out that this suggests a location for the twelfth
mile-marker near or in modern Bireh (37). "The point is, whether
you measure by distance or milestones, neither measurement brings
you to Beitin. We feel justified in concluding that the last
evidence remaining for identifying Beitin with Bethel (that of
Eusebius-Jerome), actually identifies Bethel with another site"
(ibid) - that site being Bireh.

Rainey argues that Eusebius always gives for towns north of
Jerusalem "the approximate point along the Jerusalem-Neapolis
road where one would find the *turn off* to each city" (Rainey 185).
Therefore when Eusebius says Bethel is in the vicinity of the
twelfth milestone, he means that this is where the turn off to
the town lies (ibid: 186). Thus "Mr. Livingston's attempt to
move the twelfth milestone back to *el-Bireh* is superfluous" (187),
because the turn off for Bethel angled off from the main road in a
northeasterly direction, i.e. leading to Beitin.

But Rainey produces no evidence at all to support this last
statement concerning the position and direction of the turn off,
and one suspects it is an *ad hoc* assumption. It certainly makes
sense of the statements in Eusebius and Jerome and at the same
time allows Bethel to be located at Beitin, but it does not
support a location of Bethel at Beitin in preference to Bireh.

Rainey's claim that if the twelfth marker had been exactly
at Bireh this would prove that Bethel is *not* to be located there,
because Eusebius only says that Bethel (or the turn off to it,
in Rainey's interpretation) was *in the vicinity* of the marker, is
an unnecessarily pedantic quibble. Livingston does not *insist*
that the marker was exactly in modern Bireh (though he clearly
thinks it may well have been), and in any case the Bethel of
Eusebius's day may not have been exactly in the centre of modern
Bireh.

In short, while Rainey effectively provides an alternative
understanding of the patristic evidence, permitting the
identification of Bethel with Beitin to be maintained, he does

not prove Livingston's interpretation to be wrong, nor does he show his own interpretation to be preferable to Livingston's.

In conclusion, while Rainey's article should make us cautious about adopting Livingston's theory without more positive evidence being adduced in its favour, it does not manage to disprove the theory. Livingston's reasons for rejecting the identification of Bethel with Beitin may not seem so strong in the light of Rainey's arguments, but the evidence in favour of the traditional identification still seems no stronger than that which Livingston produces for locating Bethel at Bireh.

The only thing which can decide the issue is an archaeological survey of the region around Bireh. Excavation of the small tell which Livingston suggests may be Ai would be an important part of such a survey. As Wiseman has remarked, in an article which is basically favourable to Livingston's suggestion, the latter "must remain an unproven theory until checked by archaeological soundings at both places, for the evidence for the identification and location of Bethel and Ai is interrelated" (Wiseman 1971: 5).

The important point to note is that if Livingston's theory is held to be at all possible, then a further possibility is opened up, namely that Ai may cease to be the anomaly which it is at present. In the context of the theory put forward in the present work, the problem of Ai would be resolved if the alternative site showed evidence of occupation and destruction at the end of the MBA. However, Bireh would also have to yield similar evidence before it could be accepted as the site of Bethel - unless the present fashion were to be reversed, so that Jos 8 became accepted as historical, while Jdg 1: 22-25 became the aetiological legend!

If on the other hand Livingston's theory turns out to be mistaken, Ai will remain an anomaly, but at least a neutral anomaly from the point of view of dating the Exodus, since et-Tell provides evidence for neither the 15th century nor the 13th century date. (Nor does it provide evidence for a later date, as we have seen previously.) Et-Tell is in this sense as impartial (or ambiguous) a guide as Beitin, which was destroyed at the close of the MBA and in the 13th century, and can therefore be interpreted to support either date, as we have seen in earlier sections where it has been (for convenience) assumed that Bethel = Beitin.

7.4   *The Problem of Shechem*

The archaeology of Shechem has shown that "there was no destruction between *c.* 1300-1150, and probably not between the early fourteenth century and the early eleventh" (Albright 1963: 30).   In connection with the view which places the Conquest in the 13th century BC, this has been seen as in keeping with the biblical tradition, which omits any reference to an attack on Shechem during the conquest of the land (cf. ibid: 31-2).   It has also been suggested that Shechem became a Hebrew centre as early as patriarchal times, when the city was attacked and plundered by Jacob's sons or by Jacob himself (cf. Gen 34 and 48: 22).   Thus it has been supposed that there was no necessity to attack Shechem during the Conquest, because it was already in Hebrew hands.   Jack, for example, suggests that "the covenant made at Mount Ebal (Deut 27; Josh 8) represents the entry of these Shechem Israelites into the Joshua community and the recognition of their worship by the latter body" (1925: 151-2; cf. Albright 1963: 32; also Wright 1962a: 77).

At the end of the MBA, however, Shechem was destroyed twice, and after the second destruction remained unoccupied for some time (Wright 1965a: 73-6) /8/.   Wright suggests that the first of these destructions was the work of Amosis, between 1550 and 1545 BC, and that the second was the work of his son (and successor) Amenhotep I, who reigned *c.* 1545-1525 BC on the chronology followed by Wright (cf. ibid: 75).   How are these findings to be reconciled with the view put forward in the present thesis?

It must first be noted that the dates offered by Wright for the two destructions mentioned above are not firm.   If the end of the MBA is brought down by about a century, as proposed in the present work, these two destructions may also be brought down by that amount, though they could in theory be brought down by a lesser amount.   The first could be attributed to Amenhotep I, to whom Wright attributes the second, and the second could be attributed to either Thutmosis I or Thusmosis III /9/.   It is interesting in this connection that Thutmosis III's lists of subjected cities include references to a Jacob-el and a Joseph-el (cf. Jack 1925: 36-7; Pritchard 1955: 242-3), and W. Harrelson has suggested that these two names (either or both) may "refer to Shechem, since we know from the Old Testament that both Jacob and Joseph were closely associated with the city" (1957: 4).   Shechem appears to have been a continuous problem for Egypt.   It seems to feature as a centre of opposition to Egypt during the Middle

Kingdom /10/, and it appears as such again in the Amarna period.
If it persistently caused problems for Thutmosis III, it is
possible that he resorted to the expedient of destroying it,
though this was not normal Egyptian practice, as will be seen
subsequently.

Whatever the truth concerning the exact agents of destruction,
I would suggest that Shechem had already been destroyed before the
arrival of the Israelites, and was an abandoned ruin at the time
of the Conquest. This seems to me to offer a more satisfactory
picture than that offered along with the 13th century date for
the Exodus. For if Shechem was a thriving "Israelite" centre when
Joshua and his people entered the land, and if the covenant in
Jos 24 was a covenant which took the Shechemites into Joshua's
community, why is there no clearer indication of this in any of
the traditions?

Furthermore, the references to Shechem's so-called "conquest"
in Jacob's day only provide evidence that it was attacked and
plundered, not that "the city was actually captured" as Wright
assumes (1965a: 20). The first part of the story in Gen 34 may
well, as Wright suggests (ibid), represent a treaty or covenant
between Jacob's people and the Shechemites, allowing intermarriage
between the two groups; but his suggestion that the rest of the
story means that the city was conquered and taken over by the
Hebrew tribes is quite unwarranted (cf. Soggin 1972: 16).

Concerning Gen 48: 22, which Wright assumes is a further
reference to an early conquest of Shechem (ibid), we should note
that not all translators agree that Shechem is referred to here;
$\check{s}e\underline{k}em$ may simply mean "mountain-slope" in this verse (and is so
rendered in RSV; cf. NEB "ridge of land"). Further, whereas in
Gen 34 the attack on Shechem was accomplished by Jacob's sons,
the deed referred to here was apparently accomplished by Jacob
himself. As von Rad comments, "How could he promise to one of
his sons what his sons had conquered?" (1972: 419). Also, the
deed of Gen 34 caused Jacob distress, but the deed of 48: 22 is
one in which he glories. And while Amorites are Jacob's
opponents in 48: 22, the "prince of the land" is a Hivite in
34: 2. For these reasons it is unlikely that the reference in
Gen 48 is to a capture of Shechem by Jacob or his sons.

In short there is nothing in the biblical narrative to
suggest that Shechem became a permanent Hebrew centre before the
sojourn in Egypt. The silence of the narrative concerning a

conquest of Shechem after the Exodus is explained best by the view that it was already destroyed and abandoned before the Israelites arrived in Canaan, rather than by the theory that it was somehow already "Israelite".

I suggest therefore that the theory associated with the 13th century date for the Exodus provides a less satisfactory picture than the one offered here, because in the late date framework Shechem was an occupied site when the Israelites arrived; there is no reason to believe that Shechem itself was already "Israelite", and yet there are no mentions of any hostilities against the city. This problematical situation is resolved if the site was an unoccupied ruin at the time of the Conquest, so that the Israelites were able to move unhindered into the area. There they buried the bones of Joseph, in land bought by Jacob from the Shechemites, and Joshua led the people in a covenant-making ceremony.

CHAPTER 8:
SUMMARY AND CONCLUSION

Chapter 8:   Summary and Conclusion

The time has now come to take a broader look at the evidence and to assess the strength of support for the theory put forward in this work.

A point which must be stressed first is that the shift of the end of the MBA proposed above should not be viewed as a desperate expedient to provide archaeological evidence for an early Exodus. Rather, the early dating of the Exodus proposed in the first part of this work and the late dating of the MBA destructions proposed in the second, should be viewed as two sides of the same coin, two complementary propositions which seem to make good sense of both the biblical traditions and the archaeological record of Palestine.

We have seen that several of the Conquest traditions remain problematical in the context of a late date for the Exodus. We have also seen that there is no logical reason to attribute the wave of destructions which mark the end of the MBA to Egyptian armies or marauding Hyksos. On the one hand, we have a collection of traditions concerning the Israelite destruction of several cities, but in many instances we have no cities for the Israelites to destroy. On the other hand we have clear archaeological evidence for the fall of almost all the cities involved in these traditions at the end of the MBA, but no attackers to whom we can logically attribute their destruction. I have tried to show that the Conquest and the end of the MBA cities can both be dated in such a way that they are seen to be the same event. Their identity is not normally recognized because, through a series of unfortunate scholarly "accidents", the Exodus has been dated too late and the end of the MBA has been dated too early.

A large part of the argument has been directed to showing the complete lack of support for the conventional chronology of the end of the MBA. The evidence in favour of the proposed alternative consists of the fact that it "works" in a remarkable way. That is, the biblical traditions and the archaeological evidence relate with striking accuracy.

This can be demonstrated as follows in relation to the 13th century dating of the Exodus and Conquest. Below is a list of all the cities which are unequivocally stated in the biblical narratives to have been destroyed by Israelite groups, and which are also identified with at least a fair degree of certainty. For the purposes of this list, the identification of Bethel with Beitin and of Ai with et-Tell will be retained. Alongside this list, in two columns, are signs to indicate the degree of correspondence between the biblical traditions and the archaeological record, (A) in terms of the scheme proposed here, and (B) in terms of a 13th century date. A positive sign indicates complete correspondence, a query indicates questionable or only partial correspondence, and a negative sign indicates a total lack of correspondence.

	A	B
Jericho	+	-
Ai	-	-
Bethel	+	?
Hazor	+	?
Debir	+	+
Lachish	+	?
Hebron	+	-
Hormah	+	-
Dan	+	-

It will be noted that in the left hand column we have a positive mark in every case except that of Ai. In the right hand column we have only *one* positive mark. Bethel and Lachish are allotted queries because their destructions cannot be dated with confidence to the appropriate time (Bethel may well have fallen *early* in the 13th century, and Lachish may well have fallen in the 12th century); Hazor is allotted a query because it is impossible to account for its reappearance in Jdg 4 in terms of the conventional view.

Gibeon and Arad are omitted from the list because they are not said to have been destroyed, but they also provide points in favour of the scheme proposed here, since suitable MBA cities are evidenced for both of these sites, but no city appears to have existed at either site in the LBA. In other words, *no less than six cities* which figure in the Conquest narratives *did not even exist* (so far as present evidence indicates) in the period to which the Conquest is most commonly dated. Putting it another way, *over half* of the cities just mentioned (the list of nine, plus Gibeon and Arad) would be absent from maps of 13th century BC Palestine. In striking contrast, the correspondence provided by the scheme offered here is almost complete. Ai alone remains problematical.

We may also remind ourselves of ways in which the archaeological evidence from individual cities is seen to relate closely to the biblical traditions in the scheme outlined above. Thus in the case of Jericho we have archaeological evidence for plague, earthquake, and the deliberate destruction of the city by fire, each of which is attested in the narrative. At Ḥazor we have not only the burning of the city attested by both the narrative and the archaeological evidence, but also the resurgence of the city and its subsequent collapse in the 13th century. In other words, in cases where the narrative supplies details other than the simple fact that the Israelites destroyed the city, those additional details are also found to be corroborated by the archaeological record /1/.

There is a further way in which the archaeological evidence corresponds with the biblical traditions when the Conquest is placed at the end of the MBA. Judges 1 contains a list of cities where the Israelites were not successful in their attempts to dislodge the Canaanites (1: 27-33). Many of these places are either not identified or not excavated, but in the case of major cities where excavations have been carried out, such as Megiddo, Taanach, Beth-shan and Gezer, in each instance there is seen to be *no break in occupation* at the point of transition from MBA to LB I /2/. This is in striking contrast to the case of the other MBA cities we have discussed previously, where we have clear evidence of destructions followed by a gap in occupation which sometimes lasted for the whole of the LBA /3/.

The archaeological findings from the Negeb provide particularly strong support for the case I have put forward. To emphasize this, I can do no better than to quote a remarkable passage from a recent article by Aharoni subtitled "Re-writing Israel's Conquest". This article discusses a survey of five sites in the Negeb, including Tel Malhata (Arad) and Tel Masos (Hormah). Aharoni assumes that the Exodus and Conquest occurred in the 13th century BC, and that the MBA ended in the 16th century BC. After discussing the lack of Late Bronze Age remains from the Negeb, Aharoni says this (1976: 73, my emphasis):

> "We therefore arrive at a most startling conclusion: the biblical traditions associated with the Negeb battles cannot represent historical sources from the days of Moses and Joshua, since nowhere in the Negeb are there any remains of the Late Bronze Age. However, the reality described in the Bible *corresponds exactly to the situation during the Middle Bronze Age,* when two tels, and two tels only, defended the eastern Negeb against the desert marauders, and the evidence points towards the identification of these tels with the ancient cities of Arad and Hormah. Thus the biblical tradition *preserves a faithful description* of the geographical-historical situation as it was some three hundred years or more prior to the Israelite conquest."

He is led to the following deduction: "Only one of two alternatives is possible: either the biblical tradition concerning the wars in the Negeb is lacking even an historical kernel, in spite of its accuracy regarding the early settlements (which would have been difficult to conjecture in the later periods), or the conquest narratives are composed of several traditions emanating from different tribes who roamed for several centuries on the borders of Eretz-Israel and its environs" (ibid). His conclusion is that narratives dealing with the Conquest and settlement should be viewed as "a collection of traditions covering a long period and different groups, whose chronological position cannot be established according to their literary sequence in the Bible, but only on the basis of external criteria, particularly the archaeological evidence" (ibid: 74).

An unquestioning acceptance of the assumptions on which current views are founded prevents Aharoni from seeing an obvious third alternative, even though he approaches it so closely. That third alternative seems to me far more satisfactory than Aharoni's conclusion; namely, that the Conquest occurred at the end of the MBA.

Mention must finally be made of some of the implications of redating the end of the MBA as proposed above. One is that the MB II B-C cities are no longer seen as "Hyksos", but simply as Canaanite. Another is that it is these cities and not those of the LBA which appear in the lists of Thutmosis III. The present theory may be thought to meet with difficulties here, since it is often supposed that Thutmosis III destroyed the cities which he lists, whereas the MBA cities were not destroyed until the end of that pharaoh's reign or later in the theory I am proposing, and therefore show no signs of destruction *during* his reign. But in fact neither do the LBA counterparts of the MBA cities in the conventional chronology, and the lists of Thutmosis III do not actually require us to understand that the cities mentioned were destroyed.

Thutmosis III's campaigns into Palestine were often merely parades of strength or tours of inspection, during which tribute was collected, and the listed cities are simply those which dutifully made payment (cf. Pritchard 1955: 238; Drower 1973: 452). In some cases, of course, hostilities may have occurred in which a rebel city was besieged and perhaps sometimes destroyed, as we have already suggested happened at Shechem, but this was probably a very rare event. We have seen that even in the case of Megiddo, there is no mention in the Egyptian records of the city being destroyed after its disloyalty, and the archaeological evidence (as conventionally understood), indicates no destruction during Thutmosis III's reign /4/. We may note in this connection a statement by Aharoni concerning what seems to have been the usual Egyptian attitude to Canaanite cities: "The Egyptians were not interested in the destruction of the cities which they exploited so profitably, they had to punish them in cases of mutiny, but they did not destroy them" (1957: 145).

This incidentally underlines how unwarranted would be the belief that the Egyptians destroyed the Canaanite cities at the end of the MBA now that those cities are seen to have had no connection with the detested Hyksos. In the case of the MBA cities, the destructions (usually by burning) were deliberate and total, and often resulted in the abandonment of the site for centuries. This does not square with normal Egyptian practice at all, but certainly illustrates the Israelite attitude to conquered cities as exemplified in Jos 6: 21-26.

A further implication of our theory is that the Israelite settlement in Canaan dates from the beginning of the LBA, not from

the beginning of the Iron Age as is required by the conventional
view. Are there any cultural changes at the start of LB I which
could attest the arrival of Israelite groups?

Unfortunately the answer to this question is, no. I do not
consider that this in any way weakens the theory offered here in
comparison with the conventional view, for we have seen that the
late date theory is similarly unable to draw support from the
appearance of any cultural trait which can be described (except
hypothetically) as Israelite. The main support from archaeology
which has been claimed for the late date view consists of the
destruction of certain cities, and a general deterioration in
culture which has been interpreted as evidence for the arrival of
nomadic groups. Much the same can be said for the view offered
here, and with far more justification in the matter of the
destroyed cities.

The deterioration in material culture which has been observed
at the end of the LBA has been traced back by some writers to
LB II. Kenyon speaks of "a marked deterioration" with the
transition from LB I to LB II (1970: 209), and Weippert sees the
state of affairs which existed at the start of Iron I as part of
a continuing decline which began during the LBA (1971: 133).
B.K. Waltke has constructed a cogent argument for placing the
arrival of the Israelites at the beginning of LB II, taking his
lead from remarks made by Kenyon. Kenyon has stated that for
LB II A, "The archaeological remains are undistinguished and the
objects found suggest a low level of artistic ability" (1970: 209)
She considers that "Such a situation would well reflect the state
of affairs during the acclimatisation to settled life of wanderers
such as the Ḫabiru bands of the Amarna Letters and the Israelites
of the Old Testament" (ibid). Waltke quotes these, and other
sentences from Kenyon, with approval, and concludes: "In a word,
the material culture suggests the date 1400 B.C. as the most likel
time for the Israelite occupation [of the hill country]" (1972:
36-7). This constitutes part of Waltke's argument in favour of a
date of c. 1440 BC for the Exodus.

However, while it is certainly true that the state of affairs
observable during Iron I had its origins in the LBA, it now
appears that Kenyon may have over-emphasised the poverty of LB II A
In a recent assessment of this period by M.W. Several, we find the
following statements: "Structural remains from excavations point t
the LB II A as a stable, peaceful, and generally wealthy period".

"Of the three centuries of the Late Bronze Age (1500-1200 B.C.),
the fourteenth century in Palestine, on balance, probably had the
richest material culture. It was definitely superior to the
preceding LB I ..." (1972: 128). Thus Several depicts LB II A
as a time of material improvement after a comparatively poor LB I.
It was during LB II A that some of the cities destroyed at the
end of the MBA, such as Tell Beit Mirsim and Beitin, were rebuilt
/5/. It is possible, therefore, that the remarks made by Kenyon
and Waltke concerning LB II A apply more properly to LB I.

It is not difficult to see reasons why we have no direct
material evidence for the settlement of the Israelites after the
destructions of the MBA cities. Waltke makes the following
pertinent comment: "... Migratory groups such as the Israelites
had been would not be expected to carry large equipment or durable
material objects. Their containers may well have been made mainly
of skin, and their place of worship was portable and temporary,
a tent" (1972: 36). Kenyon writes concerning migratory groups:
"History and archaeology show again and again how such bands,
coming amongst a settled population, tend to adopt the material
culture (which alone is reflected archaeologically) of that
population" (1970: 209).

The biblical record itself provides evidence that the
Israelites adopted the culture (including the religious practices)
of the peoples among whom they settled. The history of subsequent
periods, including the monarchic period, is punctuated by the
complaints of its writers and editors against the Israelite
tendency towards syncretism and compromise. According to Jdg 2:
11-23, the process of assimilation set in during the immediate
post-Conquest period, and there is no reason to assume that the
truth was otherwise. G.E. Gowan has written: "One need only read
the books of Judges, Samuel and Kings to be convinced that
Israelite worship from the Conquest on was thoroughly mingled
with aspects of the Canaanite fertility religion, and that this
was not, for the majority of Israelites, considered apostasy, but
was the commonly accepted thing" (1968: 96-7).

It is not difficult, therefore, to imagine many of the
Israelites mingling with the Canaanite population and adopting
both their material culture and their religious practices only a
short time after the Conquest. The cities built afresh during
LB II A were probably the work of a mixed Israelite and Canaanite
population, and their temples as much "Israelite" as Canaanite.
In other words, many of the LBA cities which have hitherto been

regarded as Canaanite cities destroyed by the Israelites, were probably half-Israelite.

Viewed in the light of the biblical record, the archaeological evidence for the periods following the end of the MBA is very much what one would expect. The Bible records the successful conquest and destruction of numerous cities, but a subsequent failure to displace the majority of Canaanites and a period of settlement during which the Israelites "dwelt among the Canaanites" (cf. Jdg 1: 30-33), sometimes in their major cities (e.g. Jdg 1: 29, where the Ephraimites are said to have dwelt in Gezer alongside the Canaanites). The archaeological record shows the destruction of many major cities, but no substantial change in material culture. Thus in my opinion the archaeological evidence is once again found to be in accord with the biblical record.

The main conclusions of the present work can be summarised as follows:·

Evidence normally offered in support of a 13th century date for the Exodus is insubstantial. It therefore provides no reasons for dismissing the prima facie evidence of the biblical information, which indicates a date in the first half of the 15th century BC.

The Conquest should be dated to the second half of the 15th century BC; it is to be identified with the fall of Palestine's fortress-cities at the end of the MBA.

Such widespread destruction of fortified cities could only have been achieved through the concerted efforts of a large body of people. It is therefore likely that the situation sketched in the biblical traditions - a large and fairly unified group of people migrating from Egypt to Canaan - should be given credence.

The attribution of LBA culture to the Canaanites needs to be modified; it was in fact Canaanite-Israelite, and, as such, its material remains elucidate the syncretism which characterised the time of the judges and which set the scene for the monarchic period.

A great deal more research can be done to test these conclusions and to explore their implications. A thorough re-examination of traditional assumptions throughout the field of ceramic chronology would probably yield many useful results. A re-assessment of earlier periods of Hebrew history with the present theory in mind also promises to be fruitful, as I have indicated elsewhere /6/.

APPENDICES

Appendix 1   *THE AMARNA LETTERS AND THE ḪABIRU*

This appendix is by no means intended as a full discussion of the Amarna period, still less of the complex Ḫabiru question. Its aim is simply to give a brief answer to the question: What place do the events in Palestine during the Amarna period have in the reconstruction offered in the present work? I hope to deal with this question at greater length elsewhere. Here I only intend to give an outline of what seems the most satisfactory approach.

As we saw in the Introduction, during roughly the first half of this century several writers assumed that the Ḫabiru mentioned in the Amarna letters should be identified with the biblical Hebrews invading Canaan under the leadership of Joshua. The identification was suggested initially by H. Zimmern immediately after the publication of the letters written by the king of Jerusalem. It was taken up widely and enthusiastically as providing support for a 15th century dating of the Exodus.

The equation coloured the interpretation of the letters from the outset, so that the Ḫabiru were viewed as invaders from outside Canaan (e.g. Jack 1925: 19, 44, 129), though some writers, such as Eerdmans and Dhorme, made early protests against this interpretation. The equation weakened when Ḫabiru began to occur in many more texts from widely-separated times and places. In addition, further study of the Amarna correspondence itself has shown that it does not attest an invasion at all, but rather internal rebellion; Ḫabiru did not appear from outside Canaan, rather groups and cities within Canaan *became* Ḫabiru (cf. Campbell 1960; Mendenhall 1973: 122-41).

The term Ḫabiru is now popularly seen as designating a certain stratum in society (cf. Greenberg 1955: 87-8; Bright 1972:

93-4), and many have followed Mendenhall's view that it particularly indicates those who have opted out of the accepted structure of society and forfeited their citizenship (cf. Mendenhall 1962: 66-87; 1973: 122ff).

This does not mean, however, that moves to link the Ḥabiru and the biblical Hebrews have now been abandoned. Although it is clear that a simple equation of the two groups is out of the question, most writers argue that some kind of link should be maintained.

In 1939, F.H. Hallock (in Mercer 1939: II, 843) asserted that there probably was some association between the Hebrews of the Old Testament and the Habiru of other texts, though admitting that we cannot be certain just what that association was. He felt the best thing to say was that "all Israelites were Hebrews (Ḥabiru), but not all Hebrews (Ḥabiru) were Israelites...". Such a view is by no means cautious enough, as has been well demonstrated by Weippert 1971: 63-102), who argues, among other things, that even a straightforward equating of the terms "Hebrew" and "Israelite" is not admissible. It is commonly held today, however, that the biblical Hebrews (ʿIḇrîm) were "not so much an ethnic group as a sociological phenomenon" (Cazelles 1973: 23), and that they should be viewed as belonging to the class of Ḥabiru (cf. Campbell 1960: 11; Mendenhall 1962: 66-87; 1973: 135-40). Even this strikes some as an oversimplification of the issues involved. This is not the place for even a summary of those issues; the reader is referred to the thorough discussion by Weippert (1971: 63-102), which includes criticisms of the currently popular Mendenhall view. Weippert feels that the Ḥabiru = ʿIḇrîm equation has been sustained "primarily on linguistic or even emotive grounds" (ibid: 63-4), and underlines the many uncertainties which complicate the problem. In a recent refining of the equation, Rowton has argued that the biblical and extra-biblical terms denote "approximately - but not quite - the same thing", for while the latter denotes "the uprooted, the social outcast", the biblical term "is confined to the uprooted from tribal society, and therein only to the detribalized from one people, Israel" (1976: 19).

It has, however, been asserted by at least one writer that the terms should not be equated in any sense at all. This is the view outlined in a series of articles by M.G. Kline (1956 and 1957). In particular, the third of these (1957: 46-70) gives a critical examination of supposed Ḥabiru-Hebrew links and parallels. On the linguistic side, Kline discusses the phonetic relation of

Ḫa-BI-ru to *'Iḇrî* (ibid: 54-61) and stresses obstacles to the
theory of a common derivation. According to Cazelles, however
(1973: 5-6), certain of these difficulties have been eased since
Kline's articles appeared. In his examination of the use of the
term *'Iḇrîm* in the Old Testament, Kline argues that there it "has
uniformly an ethnic meaning..." (1957: 53). We must note,
however, that some of the passages he discusses are taken by
others to indicate that the term had a sociological significance
(Mendenhall 1973: 136; Rowton 1976: 19-20). A writer's
conclusions in this area seem to depend very much on his own prior
suppositions.

The present writer would prefer to leave open the question
of whether the biblical term *'Iḇrî* has any connection with the
extra-biblical *ḫab/piru*. Since forms of the latter occur from
various parts of the Ancient Near East from the third milennium
onwards, a common origin for the terms is not impossible (cf.
Cazelles 1973). The question which concerns us here is whether
the Ḫabiru of the Amarna letters are to be connected in any way
with the activities of the biblical Hebrews in the Conquest or
post-Conquest period.

Study of the Amarna correspondence itself shows that the
role of the Ḫabiru in the Amarna period does not resemble the
activities of the invading Hebrews during the Conquest as
presented in the biblical traditions.

Briefly, the situation of the Amarna period can be
summarised as follows. At this time city-states in Canaan were
ruled by Canaanite vassals of Egypt. We read of only a few
political centres in the hill country, each of which must have
ruled a fairly extensive area (cf. Aharoni 1967: 159ff). We
learn nothing at all of Gilead, south Transjordan and cities in
the Negeb. Although the Canaanite princes of the various cities
were under Egyptian administration, this did not prevent some of
them being referred to as "king" on occasions (Akkadian *šarru*,
Canaanite *milku*; cf. Albright 1966: 8). Certain of the
Canaanite princes were endeavouring to obtain independence from
Egypt and to increase their territory at the expense of their
neighbours, employing troops of mercenaries to this end. In
letters written by princes loyal to Egypt, these bands of
mercenaries appear as Ḫabiru or SA.GAZ.

The precise meaning of the term Ḫabiru (if it *had* a precise
meaning) is uncertain, but it seems to have meant stateless,

landless folk who lacked permanent status, whatever their exact
origins or activities (for discussions of the meaning see
Greenberg 1955: 87ff; Mendenhall 1962: 66-87; 1973: 122ff;
Cazelles 1973). There is no hint whatever in the letters that
the Ḫabiru mentioned there were from outside Canaan. Hence
Harrison writes: "The situation appears to have been one of
internecine strife rather than invasion by a powerful united
enemy". "... It appears difficult to reconcile the situation
relating to the Ḫabiru of the Tell el-Amarna tablets with the
conquering activities of the Biblical Hebrews under the leadership
of Joshua..." (1970: 319, 321).

The two situations can in fact only be reconciled if the
biblical picture of a fairly concerted invasion is abandoned, as
in Mendenhall's view (see Introduction). It is one of the major
arguments of the present work that the biblical picture should
not be abandoned.

There is a further way in which the present work divorces
the Hebrew Conquest from the Amarna disturbances; it places the
Conquest considerably earlier in time than the Amarna troubles.
While the Amarna letters derive from the first half of the 14th
century BC, I have suggested dating the Conquest to the second
half of the previous century, in the decades around 1430 BC.
This still leaves open the possibility, of course, that the
Ḫabiru of the letters may have consisted, at least in part, of
groups of recently arrived Hebrews. We will return to this
later. It is worth pausing here to note how readily a combination
of biblical traditions and archaeological material supports a
placement of the Conquest before the Amarna period.

The fact that various Canaanite cities important in other
periods do not feature in the Amarna correspondence is adequately
accounted for by the fact that the incoming Israelites had
destroyed them just a few decades before. Cities which do not
feature include Gibeon, Jericho, Hebron and Bethel. We have
already noted at length the sparseness of LBA material from the
first two of these sites; Hebron has yielded no LBA remains at
all, and we have noted that Bethel (Beitin) seems to have taken
some while to recover as a city after the onslaught at the end of
the MBA. The important political centres of the Amarna
correspondence are Jerusalem, which the Israelites apparently
failed to take (Jdg 1: 21; see above, chapter 7.2, on the
traditions concerning Jerusalem; on Jdg 1: 8, cf. de Vaux 1971:
502-3), Megiddo, which they failed to take (Jdg 1: 27), Gezer,

which they failed to take (Jdg 1: 29), Hazor, which revived
fairly soon after Joshua's destruction of the MBA city (above,
chapter 6.6), Lachish, which seems from the archaeological
evidence to have revived quite quickly after its MBA destruction
(cf. Kenyon 1971: 25), and Shechem, which I have suggested was
abandoned at the time of the Conquest, the LBA city being built
soon afterwards.

Concerning Ḥazor, we may note that the description of this
city in Josh 11: 10 as "formerly the head of all those kingdoms"
(i.e. the northern territories listed in 11: 1-3) does not fit
at all well the LBA city of the Amarna period or later (hence
Millard 1973: 42 has to say that Hazor "seems to have enjoyed some
pretence to be 'head of all those kingdoms'..."). On the other
hand it seems to be an excellent description of the MBA city, as
Malamat (1960) noted. Yadin's suggestion that "formerly" in
Josh 11: 10 referred to the time of the MBA city rather than to
just before the LBA city's destruction is unnecessary in the
scheme offered here: the Hazor which flourished up to the Conquest
was the MBA city.

The role of the Israelites in the Amarna period was probably
mixed. After the Conquest, while many Israelites were attempting
to settle in areas away from the Canaanites which they had
failed to dislodge, others were settling among those Canaanites,
as we gather from Jdg 1: 29, 32 and 33. Similarly, while some
Israelite groups probably preferred non-involvement in the
disturbances of the Amarna period, others, especially those who
had begun to merge into Canaanite society, could well have been
involved as members of the Ḥabiru bands.

Writing of the Ḥabiru, Aharoni notes that "their presence is
alluded to mainly with reference to the hill country" (1967: 164).
His suggestion concerning a possible connection between these
Ḥabiru and the Israelites is that "The groups of ʿapiru which
penetrated into the hill regions during that period must have been
absorbed into the Israelite tribes when they arrived about a
century later" (ibid). In the scheme offered here, the Israelites
had entered the hill country before the first mention of Ḥabiru in
this region. But the fact that Israelite settlement in the hill
country seems to have been comparatively strong from an early
period (cf. Josh 11: 16-23; Jdg 1) perhaps strengthens the
possibility that some Israelites were subsequently involved in the
Ḥabiru activities of the Amarna period.

It might be argued that it is further strengthened by the
fact that in the Amarna correspondence Labayu, king of Shechem,
is charged with being in league with the Ḫabiru (*EA* 254), while
Israelite links with Shechem are attested for a later period in
Jdg 9. On the other hand, the king of Hazor is also charged in
the letters with aiding the Ḫabiru (*EA* 148), but Hazor is a
centre of *opposition* to Israel in Jdg 4-5. Clearly, one cannot
hope to reconstruct a neat picture equating Ḫabiru with
Israelites from this sort of evidence. One can only say that
some Israelites *may* have become Ḫabiru after the Conquest. One
could suggest in the case of Hazor that the city's involvement
with Ḫabiru in the Amarna period is reflected in the following
century by its employment of mercenary troops led by Sisera
(Jdg 4-5). Since Sisera's troops *oppress* Israel, this is
virtually to suggest that some Ḫabiru groups, far from being
associated with the Israelites, were sometimes their enemies.

Kline (1957: 61ff) actually develops an argument in which
the oppression of Israel by Cushan-rishathaim (Jdg 3: 8-10) is
linked with the activities of the Ḫabiru in the Amarna letters.
Such specific hypothetical identifications are best avoided, but
one could readily agree that the Amarna disturbances belong within
the Judges period, and that sometimes the Israelites may have
suffered at the hands of Ḫabiru-type groups. In that period one
meets with racially mixed (cf. Jdg 3: 13; 6: 3), drifting groups
of uncertain status, whose activities are not unlike those of the
Ḫabiru of the letters. In addition to the possible example of
Sisera's troops acting in the role of mercenaries on behalf of
Jabin of Hazor, groups of Ammonites and Amalekites apparently act
as mercenaries against Israel for Eglon of Moab in Jdg 3: 13.

I argued in chapter 2 of this work that the Book of Judges
should by no means be taken as a complete record of the period
with which it deals. Rather, it is a commentary on that period,
making its points by recording selected incidents. We should
therefore not necessarily expect specific events of the Amarna
period to be reflected in the Book of Judges. Also, the Amarna
correspondence itself gives a very incomplete picture of the
decades from which it derives (cf. Aharoni 1967: 159), so we
should not be surprised that it does not reflect specific biblical
events of the Judges period.

I have tried to avoid speculation here concerning possible
points of contact between the biblical record and the testimony of
the letters. I have tried chiefly to show that there is no real

difficulty in placing the Conquest prior to the Amarna period.
Having explored tentatively the possibility of a connection
between the Ḫabiru of the letters and the Israelites, we have
seen that no firm conclusions can be drawn in this area.   We
should certainly not affirm some connection simply on the basis
of a possible link between the names Hebrew and Ḫabiru.   While
some Israelite groups *may* have joined or become Ḫabiru bands in
this period, others may not, and some may actually have suffered
hostilities from such bands.

Since the situation contains too many unknowns for profitable
speculation, I prefer not to go beyond these few remarks here.   I
would certainly not wish to use the appearance of the Ḫabiru in
the Amarna letters to support the early date for the Exodus and
Conquest; rather I would simply assert that nothing in our
knowledge of the Amarna period tells against the view that it
belongs after, rather than before, the Conquest.

Appendix 2: *THE EXODUS IN EGYPTIAN HISTORY*

Within the framework of the conventional chronology for Egypt, the date of the Exodus proposed here places the event in the reign of Thutmosis III. As was noted in the Introduction, the more traditional early dating places it in the reign of that pharaoh's successor, Amenhotep (or Amenophis) II. The idea that Thutmosis III was the pharaoh of the Exodus requires a brief demonstration of its feasibility.

In Ex 5 we find the Israelites labouring to make bricks for pharaoh. That brick-making should have been a task of the enslaved people during Thutmosis III's reign is in keeping with the fact that Thutmosis is known to have carried out building operations at Memphis and apparently also at Heliopolis (cf. Rea 1960: 65, contrary to Rowley's claim, 1950: 24, that no known building operations of this pharaoh took place in the Delta region /1/).

It is a requirement of the narrative that the pharaoh's residence was not far from the area where the Israelites worked, since Moses travels with ease between the work site and the pharaoh. The capital of Thutmosis III was at Memphis, at the southern tip of the Delta, several days' sail from the area of Goshen/Rameses, which may seem to pose a problem for our theory. However, while the main Israelite settlement was clearly still at Goshen/Rameses at the time of the Exodus (cf. Ex 8: 22; 9: 26; 12: 37), it is quite feasible to suggest that many Israelites were employed on a work camp quite close to Memphis at this time. As noted above, Thutmosis III carried out building operations at Memphis and at nearby Heliopolis; and a tradition that the Israelites built at Heliopolis is added to Ex 1: 11 in the LXX. (I have suggested above that the reference to Pithom and Raamses in Ex 1: 11 relates to the *start* of the Oppression, not its end;

but it is possible that a memory of work at Heliopolis preserved
in an independent tradition from the later period would have been
incorporated here simply to put the three place-names together.)
It may be,therefore, that Moses' journeys to the pharaoh were not
from Goshen but from somewhere in the Heliopolis-Memphis area /2/.

The reign of Thutmosis III has been variously dated.   The
dating adopted in the revised *CAH* is 1504-1450 BC.   The
Borchardt-Egerton chronology, followed by Albright, Wright,
Pritchard and others, dates his reign to 1490-1436 BC.   From his
second year of reign, for about twenty years, Thutmosis shared
his rule with his aunt/step-mother/mother-in-law Hatshepsut,
assuming sole rule around 1483 BC by the earliest dating *c*. 1470
by the latest.   The dating of the Exodus proposed here therefore
places the event at or near the beginning of the period when
Thutmosis reigned alone.   If we date the Exodus to *c*. 1470 BC and
allow Moses a considerable time away from Egypt before the
Exodus (cf. the 40 years implied by Ex 7: 7 when taken with the
tradition in Acts 7: 23), we may identify the pharaoh from whom
he fled as Thutmosis II.   This is perfectly possible, since
nothing in either Ex 2: 23 or 4: 19 implies that Moses' return to
Egypt came immediately after the death of the pharaoh who sought
his life; we may therefore place his return well into the reign
of Thutmosis III.

During the first twenty years of his independent reign,
Thutmosis III led at least sixteen campaigns into Syria and
Palestine (though some of these were merely parades of strength
and did not involve any fighting; cf. Pritchard 1955: 234).   The
entry into Palestine of the migrating Israelites would not have
taken place until after this period, and probably not until after
the two campaigns of his successor Amenhotep II /3/.

Thutmosis III was a strong pharaoh, and this may seem to
militate against his being the pharaoh during whose reign the
Israelites made their escape.   However, we should remember that
the biblical account depicts a man of strong character, whose
resolve and control was shaken only by events which are presented
as miraculous.   In this sense, Thutmosis III fits well as the
pharaoh of the Exodus.   As to the events which temporarily
undermined his control of the situation, we can only guess at
their precise nature.   Volcanic and seismic activity of the kind
envisaged by J.B.E. Garstang, affecting Egypt and Palestine
together, should not be ruled out /4/.

Finally, something must be said concerning the Oppression and the Hyksos Period. There is no reason to assume that this period brought a relaxation of the Oppression for the Israelites. It is quite illogical to assume that because both Hyksos and Israelites were of Semitic stock there would be feelings of identity and friendship between them. The politics of the Near (or Middle) East in both ancient and modern times underline the fallacy of such an assumption. Egyptian traditions concerning the Hyksos refer to them as treating with great brutality all whom they found in Egypt, taking many into slavery (e.g. in Manetho, as quoted by Josephus, *Against Apion* I, 14). There is nothing inherently improbable in the notion that the Hyksos continued the Oppression of the Hebrews whom they found in Egypt /5/.

It is likely, however, that under the XVIIIth Dynasty pharaohs, conditions for the enslaved Asiatics became even harsher. After the expulsion of the Hyksos overlords from Avaris, Egyptian rulers were determined to avoid any repetition of the Hyksos domination. Egyptian suspicion of Asiatics, attested in very early times, was intensified into hatred by the Hyksos episode.

If the reported decree of the pharaoh that all male Israelite babies should be killed (Ex 1: 22) has any historical basis, it is probably to be placed at the beginning of the XVIIIth Dynasty, where it may be seen as marking the start of a phase of increased Egyptian hostility towards Asiatics. It is an interesting fact (though it may be no more than that) that if the expulsion of the Hyksos occurred at about 1550 BC, then the interval between the pharaoh's decree and our suggested date for the Exodus, *c.* 1470 BC, would be about 80 years, which is the interval indicated in Ex 7: 7.

NOTES

NOTES

Chapter 1

/1/   I hope to publish separately other material from my
doctoral thesis not included in the present work. This
material supports the biblical tradition of a sojourn in
Egypt of about 400 years, and hence a date for an entry into
Egypt around 1870 BC; this is the date arrived at by adding
400 years to the date for the Exodus offered later in the
present work. This date for the entry requires that
Sesostris III (1878-1843 BC) be identified as the pharaoh of
Joseph, an identification which can be supported in numerous
ways from correspondences between the events of the Joseph
Story and events reflected in contemporary Egyptian material.
I also offer detailed criticisms of the view of the Joseph
Story presented by D.B. Redford (Redford 1970a) in which it
is seen simply as a literary concoction of a very late period.
     With the initial migration into Egypt placed in the reign
of Sesostris III, the beginning of the period of enslavement
is logically to be placed at the end of the XIIth Dynasty.
This can be supported by extra-biblical material pertaining
to a decline in the status of Asiatics in Egypt. At this
same time, a new city in the region of Khataᶜna-Qantir was
being expanded as an administrative and trading centre
(cf. Van Seters 1966: 92-96), and it is the involvement of
Hebrew slaves in this project which is referred to in Ex 1: 11.

/2/   The notion that Bethel fell earlier than Debir and
Lachish depends on the superior quality of its pottery.
Kitchen points out that the overall culture of LBA Bethel was
superior to that at Debir and Lachish, and says: "Thus, the
Bethelites may simply have maintained a higher over-all
cultural standard than did less important Debir, or Lachish
subject to greater foreign (Egyptian) exploitation, and the
chronological time-lag may be illusory" (1966: 66). Kitchen
cites Ugarit as an example of a site with a high degree of
culture not destroyed until *c.* 1200 BC (ibid: n.35). While
this argument makes it *possible* that LBA Bethel's destruction
should be dated in line with the fall of Debir and Lachish, it
by no means *proves* that it should be so dated, and one wonders
if such a move would ever have been suggested but for a desire
to connect these LBA destructions with the Israelite Conquest.

/3/   Yadin says Aharoni is "correct in seeing in these
Galilee settlements the earliest efforts of the nomadic
Israelite tribes to settle in a more permanent way" (1972:
131). But Yadin and Aharoni differ over the chronological
relationship between the settlement of these sites and the
destruction of Late Bronze Age Hazor, which they both
attribute to the Israelites. Aharoni believes the settlement
of the Galilee sites should be viewed as part of a peaceful
infiltration by the Israelites which preceded the destruction
of Hazor by a generation or so (1967: 200-01, 207-8). Yadin,
on the other hand, asserts that the archaeological evidence
cannot be interpreted in this way, and that the Galilee
settlements date from "*after* the fall of the Canaanite cities"
(1972: 131).

NOTES

Chapter 2

/1/   J. Van Seters has argued that the accounts of the
conquest of the kingdoms of Sihon and Og in Numbers are
secondary, being dependent upon the accounts in Deut 2: 26-37
and 3: 3-10 (1972: 182-97). He thus wishes to make the Num
traditions very late, and says they "must be regarded with
grave suspicion" on the historical level (ibid: 197). He
considers that the "highly ideological character" of the
deuteronomistic references (including Jdg 11: 19-26) makes
them "historically untrustworthy" (ibid). It is doubtful
whether such arguments warrant this degree of scepticism.
Van Seters' arguments against the generally accepted literary
analysis (cf. Moore 1895: 283, 290ff; also Driver 1902:
xiv-xix) are not convincing, and even if they were, the
origin of the deuteronomistic narratives would still have
to be accounted for.

/2/   On Merneptah's Stele, the name *Israel* is given the
hieroglyphic determinative of a people, not a territory.
This has been taken to indicate that Israel had not become
a settled nation at the time of Merneptah's encounter, and
hence that the initial entry of Israel into Canaan preceded
that encounter by only a short interval (cf. Wright 1962a: 71;
Yeivin 1971: 30, 85). Wilson describes this argument as
"good, but not conclusive, because of the notorious
carelessness of Late-Egyptian scribes and several blunders
of writing in this stela" (Wilson in Pritchard 1955: 378,
n.18; cf. also Harrison 1970: 323; Hyatt 1971: 40). However,
other scribal errors on the Stele are very minor compared
with the one necessary to give Israel the wrong determinative,
so this possibility does not commend itself very strongly.
Even so, there is no reason to take the inscription as
evidence that Israel was not a settled people in Merneptah's
time. We should remember that the term Israel was primarily
the name of a people, and not of that people's territory.
Israel was a nation named and existing independently of its
territory. Buccellati has discussed this subject at length,
classifying Israel as what he calls a national state, in
contrast to a territorial state in which the name of the
population is borrowed from the name of the territory
(Buccellati 1967: 75-135). If the term Israel anciently

referred only to a people, and not to a territory or to a city-state, is this not sufficient to explain why the "people" determinative is used for Israel in Merneptah's inscription instead of the "land" determinative? Israel was simply *not* the name of a land. I see no reason, therefore, why the "people" determinative could not be used of the loosely united *sedentary* tribal groups of which, in my view, Israel probably consisted in the 13th century BC.

/3/ Evidence that Judges is an incomplete record of events affecting Israel is perhaps to be found in I Sam 12: 11, where an otherwise unknown Judge called Bedan is mentioned along with Gideon (Jerubbaal), Jephthah and Samson. The emendation to "Barak" (e.g. in the RSV) is far from certainly correct (Fohrer 1970: 212).

/4/ According to Josh 13: 15, the Transjordanian territory north of the Arnon was settled by the tribe of Reuben. It has often been noted that this tribe soon drops into obscurity, apparently losing its territory at an early date (cf. Noth 1960: 64-5; Weippert 1971: 43-4; Bright 1972: 157).

/5/ I do not consider that Rameses II's failure to mention Israel at all in connection with the Moab campaign, although he may have reached Moab by passing through the centre of western Palestine, is a problem for the view that Israel was settled in this latter region at the time. There is no reason why Rameses should have mentioned Israelite groups if he was not specifically campaigning against them and if he did not clash with them in any way.

NOTES

Chapter 3

/1/   It may be through a totalling of the given periods, with the addition of certain estimates, or figures from extra-biblical traditions, that Josephus arrives at a total of 612 years between the Exodus and the building of the first temple (*Ant* XX, x, l; *Against Apion* II, 2). Elsewhere Josephus gives this period as 592 years. (*Ant* X, viii, 5; cf. VII, iii, 2).

/2/   Van Seters (1972: 182-197) has argued that the accounts of the Israelite victories over Sihon and Og in Numbers are late, being dependent on the accounts in Deut 2: 26-37 and 3: 3-10. He considers these accounts, and the reference to the victory over Sihon in Jdg 11 (which is also deuteronomistic), to be "historically untrustworthy" (ibid: 197). For a brief comment on Van Seters' view, see note /1/ to chapter 2, above.

/3/   The 5 years given for the settlement of the land in the first table in Sauer's article (1968: 10) are deduced from Jos 14: 7, 10. However, since subsequent to Caleb's statement of his age we have an account of the taking of Hebron and Debir (Jos 14: 13-15; 15: 13-19), it is not safe to assume that the Conquest was complete by Caleb's 85th year. (This assumption is apparently made by Josephus in *Ant* V, i, 19). Sauer's second table gives the period of Joshua as 25 years, but this, as has already been noted, is based on an extraordinary misreading of Jos 14: 10. Josephus gives a period of 20 years between the end of the war of conquest and the death of Joshua, *Ant* V, i, 28.

/4/   Anthropoid clay coffins found at Beth-shan, Tell el-Farah (South) and Lachish have been linked with the Philistines by some archaeologists, and their archaeological contexts have led to the suggestion that Philistine settlement in Canaan began before 1200 BC (cf. Dothan 1957: 154-64; Wright 1959: 66; 1966: 74; Barnett 1969: 10). However, Oren has shown that the arguments linking these coffins with the Philistines are extremely weak (Oren 1973: 131-140). Among other points, he notes that a coffin lid ornamented with

zigzag lines and vertical fluting, claimed to depict a form
of head-dress seen in Rameses III's reliefs of the Sea-peoples
at Medinet Habu, "does not exist in reality and is a mere
sketch combining the pattern of two different coffin lids"
(ibid: 135). This sketch has been incorrectly produced by
several writers (e.g. Wright 1959: 55, fig. 2:3) as
depicting an actual find from Beth-shan. Yadin has
multiplied the number of such coffin lids by using the same
sketch to illustrate lids supposedly found at Lachish and
Tell el-Farah (Yadin 1963: 345).

/5/   Old Testament verses which assume that Philistines
were settled in Canaan *before* the Exodus and Conquest
(Gen 21: 22-34; 26: 1-16; Jos 13: 2-3) are commonly treated
as anachronistic (as also are the terms "land of the
Philistines" and "sea of the Philistines" in Ex 13: 17 and
23: 31 respectively). For suggested alternative
understandings of the references to Philistines in the
patriarchal narratives, cf. Kitchen 1966: 80-81; Harrison
1970: 312.

/6/   Kitchen (1973b: 63) has argued that "the main clash"
between Israel and the Philistines "came not in the twelfth
century B.C. but from *c.* 1100 B.C. onwards". He relates this
main clash with the events of Jdg 13-16 (describing Jdg 3: 31
as an "isolated incident" and making no reference to 10: 7),
thus forcing all the events of Jdg 3-12 into only about 100
years. This seems an unlikely degree of compression, and
is, of course, flatly contradicted by Jdg 11: 26.

/7/   Multiplying 25 years by 19 produces 475 years. Adding
this to 970 BC (as a round figure for the start of Solomon's
reign) takes us to 1445 BC; an additional generation of 25
years, which may well be required in view of David's long
reign, takes us to *c.* 1470 BC.

/8/   These writers note that Saul was anointed as a *bahur*
(I Sam 9: 2), which term they take to indicate that he was
a "young man" (cf. Kitchen and Mitchell 1962: 217; Kitchen
1966: 75-6; Harrison 1970: 713). However, the term need not
be limited to this meaning; it can indicate someone in the
prime of manhood, and B.E. Shafer (1968: 649) has argued that
bahur was a specialised collective term denoting "men who
perform military or work-corps service for the king"; used of
Saul, it may simply mean that he was of military age. Hence

we may agree with H.P. Smith (1899: 59), who writes
concerning I Sam 9: 2 that there is "no necessary
contradiction between the language used here and the later
account, according to which Saul had a son already grown".

/9/   Other information is in keeping with the ages and
relative dating adopted here for Eli, Samuel, Saul, David
and Solomon. In I Sam 14: 3, we find that Ahijah, son of
Ichabod's brother Ahitub, is a priest under Saul. Ahitub
must have been born before the end of Eli's judgeship,
because his mother dies very soon after Eli's death, while
giving birth to Ichabod (I Sam 4: 19-22). If, in keeping
with what has been worked out above, we place Eli's death
c. 1080 BC (i.e. roughly 40 years after 1120), we may
provisionally place Ahitub's birth a few years earlier,
c. 1085 BC. Ahitub's son Ahijah, who is priest under Saul
in I Sam 14: 3, could therefore have been born between 1065
and 1060 BC, and Saul's reign would have fallen between the
4th and 6th decades of his life. Ahitub's other son
Ahimelech (cf. I. Sam 21: 1; 22: 11-12) could have been born
between 1060 and 1055 BC. Ahimelech's son Abiathar, who
joins David in I Sam 22: 20, could therefore have been born
about 1035 BC. Abiathar was clearly only a young man at
the beginning of David's reign, since he is still alive in
the reign of Solomon (I Kgs 4: 4), and by our present
reckonings he would be about 30 at the start of David's
reign, if David's reign began in the last decade of the 11th
century, as suggested above. This means that if David reigned
a full 40 years, Abiathar would be in his 70's at the
beginning of Solomon's reign, when he was dismissed from
priestly office (I Kgs 2: 26-27). He is not heard of
again after this, except for a reference to him in I Kgs 4: 4.

/10/   Albright also assumes here that the reference to Shamgar
in the Song of Deborah (5: 6) shows that Shamgar antedates
the events described in the Song (and hence argues that
since Shamgar routed the Philistines, the Philistine invasion
had already occurred before the battle of Deborah and Barak).
But we have already noted that the Shamgar of the Song may
not be the same as the Shamgar of Jdg 3: 31 (compare the two
names in the LXX). In any case we should note the argument
of Mayes (1974: 84-94) that the verses of the Song of
Deborah which refer to Shamgar belong to a secondary
extension to the Song.

/11/   It is therefore misleading of Boling to write of "the massive destruction debris of the early twelfth-century city, which can only be correlated with the Abimelech story" (Boling 1975: 184).

NOTES

Chapter 4

/1/   In spite of Kenyon's objection to Albright's terminology
on the ground that what the latter calls MB I "has even less
to do with the rest of the Middle Bronze Age than with the
Early Bronze Age" (1966b: 8), there do seem to be good
reasons for classifying it with the rest of the MBA rather
than considering it totally distinct or grouping it with the
EBA. The assertion that there are no ceramic links between
Albright's MB I and MB II (cf. Dever 1970b: 144) is incorrect
(cf. Thompson 1974: 163-5). It is true that ceramic links
also exist between MB I and the end of the EBA (cf. ibid:
162-3), but other factors seem to distinguish MB I from the
EBA while linking it, albeit lightly, with the rest of the
MBA. The EBA is separated from MB I by a number of
destructions at important sites, and by the arrival of new
population groups which some consider to have been the
destroyers of the EBA cities; the end of MB I, on the other
hand, shows "no indication of major destruction", and the
incoming MB II A populous is assumed to have been similar in
ethnic background to the MB I groups, and is assumed to have
absorbed them (cf. Heusman 1975: 7; also works by Wright and
Amiran cited there). This is not to deny that the designation
MB I is far from ideal; but since the various terminologies
suggested for this period number no less than eleven (cf.
Dever 1973: 38), for my present purposes I adhere to
Albright's, since it is the one used in a good many of the
works I shall be quoting.

/2/   Kenyon simply says (1957: 263): "Any difficulties of
reconciling this date with evidence from elsewhere may well
be accounted for by the small scale of this actual invasion
led by Joshua, and the gradual spread of Israelite influence".
When we recall that archaeology does not indicate the fall
of other cities mentioned in the Bible until roughly a century
after Kenyon's date for the fall of Jericho, this seems an
improbable scheme of events. It also requires a drastic
departure from the biblical tradition of consecutive attacks
on several cities within a short period.

/3/   Note that Kenyon in 1971: 21 seems prepared to place
the Mycenaean vessels from Tomb 13 in the 13th century BC,
but nearer to 1300 BC than Kitchen's argument requires; she
says there is "nothing suggestive of the later thirteenth
century".

/4/   While Kenyon originally dated LBA reoccupation of
Jericho to c. 1400 BC, she has more recently stated that
the site was reoccupied "perhaps as early as the second
half of the fifteenth century" (1971: 21), though asserting
that the reoccupation can only have been on a very small
scale at that period.

/5/   I am indebted to Mr. E. Schorr for the suggestion that
the plague evidenced by the archaeological discoveries
should be identified with the one related in the biblical
tradition.

/6/   Other types of pottery absent from Jericho are Cypriote
Black Lustrous Wheel-made and Monochrome vessels (cf. Kenyon
1971: 5, 21). The argument offered here concerning bichrome
ware naturally applies to other contemporary types of
Cypriote pottery also.

NOTES

Chapter 5

/1/   Albright reports the finding of "a secondary scarab of
the first known Semitic Hyksos ruler, Ya'qub" in Stratum E2
at Tell Beit Mirsim (cf. conveniently 1967: 213).

/2/   It is also important to note that the relative dating
of the introduction of bichrome ware affects other important
considerations. In Ehrich (ed) (1965) we have an interesting
contradiction which illustrates this. On p.23, H.J. Kantor
cites bichrome vessels found in Egypt and ascribed to the
Hyksos Period as evidence that LB I in Palestine began before
the Hyksos Period had ended. But on p.56 we have the
assertion by Albright that bichrome ware appeared "along
the coast and in the low hill country before the end of
MB II C...". Albright's statement undermines Kantor's
deduction completely. In actual fact, however, bichrome
ware samples from Egypt probably date from the XVIIIth
Dynasty, as will be argued subsequently.

/3/   Kenyon does mention the discovery of a bichrome bowl at
Tell Abu Hawam, but makes the comment that it "may antedate
the first buildings" (1971: 20), a suggestion which sounds
somewhat arbitrary.

/4/   Kenyon herself accepts a date "early in the fourteenth
century" for the founding of Tell Abu Hawam (1971: 20), which
is in fact the date suggested originally by Hamilton - "soon
after 1400 B.C." (see text above).

/5/   This statement is actually incorrect; as we have seen,
there is no real evidence for a destruction at Megiddo at
the end of the MBA.

/6/   Kenyon has also recently adopted the view that Egyptian
expeditions into Palestine probably could not have occurred
until late in the reign of Amosis, for whose reign she now
accepts dates of 1570-1546 BC (1971: 3). However, Kenyon
apparently wishes to retain as early a date as possible for
the fall of the MBA cities. This seems to be why she
suggests that the MBA cities were destroyed by Hyksos groups

after the fall of Sharuhen, which she suggests took place early in Amosis' reign (ibid). The logic behind this is difficult to see.

/7/   In 1965 Albright offered the following dating for the MBA:

    MB I   before 2000 to before 1800 BC
    MB II A   about 18th century
    MB II B   about 17th and early 16th centuries
    MB II C   about 1575-1500 BC
    (in Ehrich 1965: 57).

/8/   That the chronology of Cypriote pottery during the period when bichrome ware was in use cannot be fixed independently of Palestine is very clear in Åström's attempt to date the end of Middle Cypriote III and the beginning of Late Cypriote I (1957: 271-3). Åström's date for the transition, 1600/1580 BC, is arrived at from dates assigned to strata in which bichrome ware, White Slip and Base-ring wares occur at Alalakh, from the dating of bichrome ware finds at Ras Shamra, Tell el-ʿAjjul and in Egypt, and from other pottery finds in Egypt which are dated typologically rather than stratigraphically. It is important to note in the context of our present discussion that the dates assigned to the earliest examples of bichrome ware are used to date the beginning of Late Cypriote I, not vice versa. The difficulty of establishing a date for bichrome ware finds from Egypt has already been noted. Åström's other criteria are also invalid; the relevant strata at Alalakh, Ras Shamra and Tell el-ʿAjjul can all be dated later than is done at present, and it will be argued below that later dates should be adopted. In other words, the Palestinian and Syrian strata which Åström uses to fix the ceramic chronology of Cyprus are not fixed themselves.

/9/   This information was conveyed to me by Mr. E. Schorr. I am not aware that Artzy's findings have as yet been published.

/10/   Lowering the date for the *end* of this level need not of course upset the fact that the city of this time was ruled for a while by Yarim-Lim I, a king known to have been a contemporary of Hammurabi of Babylon. However, Hammurabi's dates themselves are rather a moot point, his reign being dated as early as 1792-1750 BC and as late as 1704-1662 BC (cf. Campbell 1961: 217-18; Harrison 1970: 165-6 for refs.).

/11/ Woolley's rejection of the low chronology for Alalakh does not in fact stand even in the context of the conventional framework. This has been shown by Åström (1957: 271-2), who supports the late dating and answers Woolley's objections point by point in a short but interesting discussion.

/12/ Stewart's use of Cypriote pottery chronology to support the early dating of bichrome ware at ʿAjjul (1974: 62-3) is entirely unconvincing in view of the fact that this chronology is itself without anchorage apart from its relation to the chronology of Palestine. Note that the chronology for Cyprus which Stewart uses is basically that worked out by Åström (Åström 1957: 257-73), using various criteria derived from Palestine, including Stewart's proposed chronology for bichrome ware at ʿAjjul! (cf. ibid: 273).

/13/ In the same footnote, Kempinski asserts: "Pottery groups associated with the bichrome ware start around 1600 B.C.". But the only reference he gives in connection with this statement is to Kantor 1965: 23. Here Kantor is citing examples of bichrome ware from Egypt and assigning them to the Second Intermediate Period. We have already seen that there is no firm evidence for ascribing bichrome ware from Egypt to pre-XVIIIth Dynasty dates.

/14/ Stewart also suggests that the end of occupation at the southern Tell el-Farʿah should be redated along with ʿAjjul I and Tell Beit Mirsim D to a point before the end of the Hyksos Period. He points out that if this is correct, Tell el-Farʿah cannot have been Sharuhen (the city to which the Hyksos retreated after the fall of Avaris), as is normally supposed (1974: 63). Stewart (ibid) and Kempinski (1974: 149-51) both suggest that Tell el-ʿAjjul, rather than Tell el-Farʿah, should be identified with Sharuhen. This does not seem particularly convincing to the present writer. The only reason offered by Stewart for abandoning the identification of Tell el-Farʿah with Sharuhen is the one just mentioned, and this clearly does not stand if Stewart's dating of the end of ʿAjjul I, Tell Beit Mirsim D and Tell el-Farʿah is rejected. Kempinski's argument for this move depends partly on the absence of bichrome ware at Tell el-Far'ah; he objects that one would expect to find quantities of this ware at the site of the most important Hyksos city of southern Palestine. But this reasoning begs an important question, since it hinges on the assumption that bichrome ware was common during the last part of the Hyksos period. This cannot be proven, except by Kempinski's redating of the strata at 'Ajjul, which is difficult to accept.

The location of Sharuhen remains uncertain, though from the point of view of ceramic chronology the commonly accepted site of Tell el-Far'ah remains a plausible candidate. There appears to be no evidence against dating the end of MBA occupation here before the end of the MB II C period throughout Palestine, which is a necessary prerequisite for the site of Sharuhen in the framework of the revision I am proposing. After the Hyksos had retreated to Sharuhen, the city was besieged by Egyptian armies for three years. If its final collapse occurred during the second half of the 16th century BC, it occurred roughly a century before the date I am suggesting for the destruction of Palestine's MB II C cities. In terms of archaeological periods, therefore, the fall of Sharuhen took place *during* MB II C, rather than at the end of that period.

/15/ The archaeological periods of Cyprus have been viewed as paralleling the archaeological periods of Crete and the Greek mainland. Thus the end of Middle Minoan III and Middle Helladic III has been placed to coincide with the end of Middle Cypriote III and with the end of the MBA in Palestine (cf. Schaeffer 1948: 350; Åström 1957: 263, n.3). This parallelism is, however, somewhat artificial, and in any case does not interfere with the revision of dates for Cyprus and Palestine which I have proposed here. The Minoan and Helladic-Mycenaean dates are arrived at ultimately through finds of datable Egyptian objects, which again only provide *termini post quem* until the Amarna period. The middle Minoan and Middle Helladic periods are commonly dated as ending at the same time as the MBA, and hence their end is often dated c. 1550 BC, but there is no reason why it should not be dated somewhat later. There is a great deal of flexibility in the chronology of the following periods (Late Minoan I and Mycenaean I-II A). Thus while Schachermeyr (1964) dates the end of Late Minoan I as early as 1470 BC, Pendlebury (1939), Matz (1962) and others date

it as late as 1400 BC, and there is much uncertainty over
whether or not the Late Minoan I pottery styles overlap with
the Late Minoan II "Palace Style".

/16/   It would be a dubious enterprise to date the tomb
involved in this argument independently by means of its
contents; as Epstein points out (1966: 121-127), many of
the Ras Shamra graves were used over very long periods and
show a piling up of grave-goods around the periphery which
makes the association of vessels with other goods extremely
difficult. Epstein does not actually discuss the tomb to
which Åström refers (No. LVII), but since she gives bichrome
ware a *terminus post quem* of *c.* 1575 BC, she clearly disagrees
with Åström's dating of the bichrome ware in this tomb to
before 1580 BC (Åström 1957: 273).

NOTES

Chapter 6

/1/   It is odd that Kenyon should express such an opinion in view of her dating of bichrome ware and the importance which she elsewhere attaches to its presence or absence at various sites. Yet Kenyon has recently affirmed at least three times that there was a much reduced population at Hazor, and perhaps even a gap, for the latter part of the 16th century and much of the 15th (1966a: 25; 1970: 341; 1971: 12). Yadin has opposed this view, 1972: 45, n.2.

/2/   Rowton had earlier (1953) argued a two-phase Exodus theory, which has been discussed in the Introduction to the present work. (pp.26ff).

NOTES

Chapter 7

/1/   Compare the view of Montet (1940: 188, 212), that
Num 13: 22 refers to the founding of Israelite Hebron seven
years before Tanis was founded on the ruins of Avaris and
Pi-Ra'messe, which event he dated *c.* 1110 BC.

/2/   Since the above was written, a report of the third
(1975) season of excavations at Tel Masos has been published
(Kempinski 1976: 52ff). Beneath the earliest Iron Age
stratum, which this report dates as "post-1180 B.C.", an
earlier phase has been uncovered, which has been labelled
Stratum 3b. "Pottery forms typical of it were cooking-pots,
bowls and deep bowls in the tradition of the Late Bronze
Age." This phase is dated to the late 13th century.
However, the stratum "consisted only of loose beaten earth
floors and ash pits and indicates the first settlement of
the site". These finds therefore do not alter the picture
presented above; the earliest buildings date from the early
Iron Age stratum (3a).

/3/   It has been suggested (Negev 1972: 19) that discoveries
at Arad and Dibon support the view that the Israelite
attack on Ai was directed against et-Tell's Iron Age I
village. It is pointed out that Arad and Dibon show no
occupation between the end of the EBA and Iron I, and the
assumption is therefore made that the settlements referred
to in the Conquest narratives must have been Iron Age I
villages. This argument is unwarranted in the case of Arad
once it is allowed that the Canaanite city was situated at
Tel Malhata. As for Dibon, this is mentioned only as a
locality (Num 21: 30; 32: 3, 34; Jos 13: 9, 17), not as a
city with a king as in the case of Arad. So the absence of
a city at this site between the EBA and Iron I does not
require that we doubt the historicity of the narratives, or
that we place the Conquest in Iron I.

/4/   In 1966: 145 Biran states that "a thick layer of ash
indicates the destruction of Stratum VII"; it is apparent
in all subsequent reports, however, that this statement was
incorrect; there is evidence of burning at the end of
Stratum *V,* but none at the end of Stratum VII, as Biran makes

quite clear in the 1974 article. The burnt layer at the
end of Stratum V is dated to the middle of the 11th century.
This destruction can obviously not be identified (within the
conventional framework) as that wrought by the Danites if
Strata VI and V are identified as Israelite. It could be
identified as such, however, within a framework which placed
the Conquest in the 12th century and which did not identify
Israelite occupation with Iron I strata at Hazor and
elsewhere. But such a hypothesis is unnecessary. The
burning of Stratum V can be adequately explained as a
destruction of Israelite Dan which Jdg 18: 31 has been taken
to imply occurred roughly at the time Shiloh was destroyed;
this is in fact the suggestion offered by Biran in 1974:
37-9.

/5/   H.J. Franken has recently noted the irony of the fact
that the lack of archaeological evidence from et-Tell to
support the view that Ai played a historical role at the time
of the Conquest has led to the situation in which "the
identification made by the biblical writer himself is
refuted, instead of our identification of Ai with et-Tell"
(1976: 6) - referring to the view of Albright and others
that the biblical writer mistakenly wrote of Ai instead of
Bethel.

/6/   There is no need to discuss the location of Beth-aven
here. But note that Grintz's argument for locating it at
et-Tell depends in part on the assumption that Beitin =
Bethel, which is questioned below.

/7/   It is worth noting the possibility, pointed out by
Livingston (41, n.83), that the name Bireh is related to Luz,
which is stated in Jdg 1: 23 to have been the original name
of Bethel: *bireh*, described in Brown, Driver and Briggs 1952:
108 as a "late word" means "castle or fortified place,
palace", while Luz, according to Albright, means "hiding
place, fastness, stronghold" (Albright 1963: 29).

Since completing this chapter, the writer has obtained
a copy of Livingston's own reply to Rainey (Livingston 1971:
39-50). This argues along similar lines to the present
discussion, but at greater length, adding interesting detail
to some areas of the debate, especially concerning the
patristic evidence.

/8/   Kenyon (1971: 17-19) has proposed dating Shechem's East
         Gate into the first part of the LBA, thereby altering the
         interpretation of the archaeological evidence offered by
         Wright. But J.D. Seger has since examined the evidence in
         detail and has shown that there is nothing to support
         Kenyon's view; the excavators correctly dated the East Gate
         to MB II C (Seger 1974: 117-30).

/9/   Wright's statement (1965a: 75) concerning the final MBA
         destruction, that to suggest it was the work of Thutmosis I
         or Thutmosis II "is too late for the pottery chronology", is
         no objection to what I am proposing here, since my
         suggestion must be understood in the context of a revision
         of the pottery chronology itself.

/10/   Sesostris III led a campaign into Palestine in order
         to overthrow troublesome Asiatics at Shechem; cf. Breasted
         1906a: I 304; Gardiner 1961: 132; Hayes 1961: 47; Posener
         1965: 9, 14, 26. In execration texts from subsequent
         reigns, Shechem is mentioned again; cf. Hayes 1961: 47-8.

NOTES

Chapter 8

/1/   A word should be said about the burning of cities as an
Israelite practice. On the basis of Jos 11: 13 Tufnell
assumes that the burning of defeated cities was not normal
Israelite policy. This assumption constitutes one of her
arguments against attributing the destruction of LBA Tell
ed-Duweir (Lachish) to the Israelites; because that city *was*
destroyed by burning, Tufnell argues that the Israelites
cannot have been its destroyers (1967: 302). If this
understanding of Jos 11: 13 is correct, it would obviously
constitute an argument against identifying the burning of
certain MB II C cities as the work of the Israelites.
However, I think it is fairly clear that the verse is not a
statement of general Israelite policy. Jos 11: 10-14 is
concerned with the destruction of the northern towns whose
rulers had formed a coalition against Joshua (11: 1-3).
Understood in its context (cf. especially verse 12), the verse
obviously means that *of those northern towns* only Hazor was
razed to the ground. It gives no indication of the general
practice. It would seem from the instances of Jericho, Ai,
Hazor and Dan that the burning of conquered cities was
fairly common. We should not assume that a conquered city
was not burned simply because the narrative does not
specifically record the fact.

/2/   The Beth-shemesh of Jdg 1: 33 is not the same as the
Beth-shemesh of Jos 15: 10, I Chr 6: 59 etc. (cf. Gold 1962:
403), which is identified with Tell er-Rumeileh. Also the
Aphik of Jdg 1: 31 is not the same as the town in Jos 12: 18,
I Sam 4: 1 etc. (cf. Morton 1962: 156), which is generally
identified with Tell Ras el-Ain. The Beth-shemesh and
Aphik of the Jdg 1 list have not yet been located.

On continuous occupation from MBA-LBA at Megiddo, cf.
Epstein 1966: 172; on Beth-shan, cf. Kenyon 1971: 15-17;
Negev 1972: 51; James 1975: 212. At Taanach there is some
evidence of a destruction of the final MBA phase, but it was
only partial, and there was no break in occupation; the city
quickly recovered and continued to enjoy "one of its most
flourishing eras" (Lapp 1967: 8; also Kenyon 1971: 11). The
same appears to be true of Achzib (Jdg 1: 31), though here

the destruction seems to have occurred during LB I (cf.
Prausnitz 1963: 337; 1975: 28). Gezer shows no break at
all in the transition from MBA to LBA. There is evidence
of a later destruction, during LB I, but even here there
was immediate reoccupation and recovery (Wright 1965b:
252-3; Dever 1966: 277-8; 1972a: 158-60; 1976: 438).
Dever's suggestion (1972a: 159; 1976: 438) that this
destruction of Gezer must be attributed to Thutmosis III
must, of course, be considered incorrect in the context
of the theory offered here; if the MBA-LBA transition is
dated c. 1430 BC, this destruction must be dated later
than that (i.e. after the reign of Thutmosis III) if it
occurred during LB I. However, Thutmosis IV (c. 1410-1402
BC) makes brief reference, in an inscription in his
mortuary temple at Thebes, to captives from Gezer (cf.
Dever 1976: 429), and the alternative suggestion made
elsewhere by Dever (1966: 277; 1970a: 226) and also by
Wright (1965b: 253), that this later pharaoh was responsible
for the destruction mentioned above, is quite plausible in
the context of a lowered ceramic chronology.

/3/   To bring together the evidence pertaining to this
point: we have seen that at Jericho, Hebron, Gibeon,
Hormah and Arad, the gap in occupation seems to have lasted
from the end of the MBA down to the start of the Iron Age;
at Tell Beit Mirsim and Beitin, too, a gap in occupation
followed the destruction of the MBA cities (cf. Albright
1967: 214; 1968a: 28 47), though at these sites it was not
of such great duration. At Lachish the situation is not
quite so clear, but in Kenyon's opinion, "On the evidence
so far available it would seem quite possible that there
was a gap in occupation at Tell ed-Duweir after the end
of the Middle Bronze Age" (1971: 25). Kenyon also suggests
that Hazor suffered at least a drastic reduction in
population for the period immediately following the
destruction of the MBA city (1966a: 25; 1971: 12).

/4/   It is sometimes said that Thutmosis III's annals
record the destruction of Gezer (e.g. Dever 1972a: 159;
1976: 438; Yamauchi 1974: 713). Actually all that is
attested is the acquiring of captives from Gezer (a scene
on the walls of the Temple of Amon at Karnak), not the
destruction of the city. Hence even though a destruction
of Gezer occurred during LB I (see above, note 2), some
writers are content to date this later than Thutmosis III,

and some are content to place it earlier (Wright 1965b: 253;
Seger 1973: 250), leaving no archaeological evidence for a
destruction of this city during Thutmosis III's reign.

Drower (1973: 475) says that "Several sites in
Palestine show signs of destruction which may be attributable
to the passage of the armies of Thutmosis I, Thutmosis III
and Amenophis II", but the works cited in connection with
this statement merely contain suggestions relating to
Lachish, Shechem, 'Ajjul and Megiddo IX. Since the
last-mentioned should really be excluded, this hardly
constitutes a list of "several sites" destroyed by these
pharaohs' campaigns.

In the records of Thutmosis III's campaigns in north
Syria there are occasional references to the destruction
of a town, e.g. Kadesh in the sixth campaign, and Irqata in
the final campaign (cf. Pritchard 1955: 239, 241), but even
here the towns may not have been completely destroyed;
Wilson remarks, in connection with Thutmosis' claim to have
"destroyed" Kadesh, that the term "is not to be taken
literally; Thut-mose may have done no more than destroy its
food supplies" (ibid: 239). It is only in the records of
Thutmosis III's eighth campaign, when he crossed the bend
of the Euphrates to deal with "that enemy of the wretched
Naharin", that we find unequivocal reference to the
destruction of towns by burning (ibid: 240).

/5/   Several incorrectly includes Taanach, Gezer, Megiddo
and Jericho in his list of towns reoccupied after being
"long abandoned"; there is no evidence whatever for a break
in occupation at any of the first three towns during LB I
(see above, note 2), and at Jericho the period of
abandonment probably lasted to the Iron Age, as has already
been suggested, with only temporary settlements in the
interim.

/6/   See Chapter 1, note /1/.

NOTES

Appendix Two

/1/   However, the statement made by both Rea and Wood that
Thutmosis titles himself "Lord of Heliopolis" on two red
granite obelisks erected in that city appears to be incorrect.
Wood (1970: 81) cites Hayes in this connection (Hayes 1959:
II, 118), but from the relevant passage by Hayes it would
appear that the title on the obelisks relates to the god Atum,
not to the pharaoh himself.

/2/   It might be objected that the archaeological finds in
the Goshen/Rameses area do not support the view that this
region was still inhabited at the date for the Exodus
proposed here, c. 1470 BC. The excavations at Tell ed-Dabᶜa,
in this area, are said to indicate that occupation there
terminated at the very beginning of the XVIIIth Dynasty, i.e.
almost 100 years earlier than the date I have suggested for
the Exodus (cf. Leclant 1969; Bietak 1975a: 30-31; for the
full report on the excavations, see Bietak 1975b). However,
viewed in terms of the revised ceramic chronology proposed in
this book, the date for the start of the occupation gap at
Tell ed-Dabᶜa needs to be significantly lowered. Occupation
there clearly lasted until the introduction of bichrome ware,
since this pottery has been found in Level D (cf. Leclant
1969: 250). In terms of the revised ceramic chronology,
according to which bichrome ware did not appear in Palestine
until c. 1450 BC, occupation must have lasted until shortly
after the Exodus.

/3/   This would certainly be the case with the higher dates
for Amenhotep II's reign, c. 1450-1425 BC, since the campaigns
took place in his 7th and 9th years according to the Memphis
stele, which would place them both before 1440 BC. Actually
the dates on the Memphis stele may be reckoned from the
beginning of a co-regency between Amenhotep II and Thutmosis
III which may have lasted several years (cf. J.A. Wilson in
Pritchard 1955: 245, n.1).

/4/   The theory put forward by Galanopoulos and Bacon (1969),
linking the plagues of Egypt and the event at the "Reed Sea"
with the eruption of the volcanic island of Santorini (Thera),
north of Crete, has received little attention, presumably

because it requires a 15th century date for the Exodus, which most scholarship has rejected. However, though the theory is an ingenious one, it is not likely to be correct if, as some researchers now suspect, the eruption was not nearly so powerful as was first thought.

/5/   It will be clear from this statement that I do not favour the view (e.g. Van Seters 1966) that the Hyksos ascendancy which ended the XIIIth Dynasty's control of Egypt was an escalation of the Asiatic presence already existing in Egypt prior to that time; for a recent example of an alternative view, involving a veritable Hyksos invasion, cf. Redford 1970b.

BIBLIOGRAPHY

Bibliography

The aim of this bibliography is simply to provide details of all the works referred to in parentheses. No attempt has been made to separate articles, monographs and Festschriften; all works are listed together according to authors' surnames arranged in alphabetical order.

A note on abbreviations

Most of the abbreviations used are standard, and can be found in Eissfeldt 1965b, Index III (with some minor variations). Those not to be found there are as follows:

AJBA   *The Australian Journal of Biblical Archaeology.*

AOTS   *Archaeology and Old Testament Study,* ed.
                D. Winton Thomas, Oxford, 1967.

BANE   *The Bible and the Ancient Near East,* ed.
                G.E. Wright, London, 1961.

CAH   *The Cambridge Ancient History.*

EAEHL   *Encyclopedia of Archaeological Excavations in
                the Holy Land,* ed. M. Avi-Yonah; vol. I, 1975,
                vol. II, 1976 (London).

HDB   *A Dictionary of the Bible,* ed. J. Hastings, 5
                vols., 1898-1904.

IBD   *The Interpreter's Dictionary of the Bible,* ed.
                G.A. Buttrick, 4 vols., New York-Nashville, 1962.

NBD   *The New Bible Dictionary,* ed. J.D. Douglas,
                London, 1962.

POTT   *Peoples of Old Testament Times*, ed. D.J. Wisema
                     Oxford, 1973.

Ackroyd P.R.
       1971   *The First Book of Samuel*,   Cambridge.

Aharoni Y.
       1957   "Problems of the Israelite Conquest in the Ligh
                     of Archaeological Discoveries", *Antiquity and
                     Survival*, 2, pp. 131-50.

       1967   *The Land of the Bible*,   London.

       1968   "Arad: Its Inscriptions and Temple", *BA*, 31, i,
                     pp. 2-32.

       1970   "New Aspects of the Israelite Occupation in the
                     North", in J.A. Sanders (ed.) *Near Eastern
                     Archaeology in the Twentieth Century*   (Glueck
                     Festschrift), New York, pp. 254-67.

       1972   "The Stratification of Israelite Megiddo",
                     JNES 31, pp. 302-11.

       1976   "Nothing Early and Nothing Late", *BA*, 39, ii,
                     pp. 55-76.

Aharoni Y. and Amiran R.
       1964   "Excavations at Arad: Preliminary Report on the
                     First Season, 1962", *IEJ*, 14, pp. 131-47.

       1975   "Arad", in M. Avi-Yonah (ed.) *EAEHL*, vol. I,
                     pp. 74-89.

Aharoni Y. and Avi-Yonah M.
       1968   *Macmillan Bible Atlas*,   London.

Aharoni Y., Fritz V. and Kempinski A.
       1972   "Tel Masos (Khirbet el-Meshash)", *IEJ*, 22,
                     p. 243.

       1973   "Vorbericht über die Ausgrabungen auf der
                     Ḥirbet el-Mšaš (Tel Masos) 1st Kampaign 1972",
                     ZDPV, 89, pp. 197-210.

Albright W.F.
       1918   "Historical and Mythical Elements in the Joseph
                     Story", *JBL*, 37, pp. 111-43.

       1921   "A Revision of Early Hebrew Chronology", *JPOS*, 1
                     pp. 49-79.

Albright (Cont'd.)

1922 "Palestine in the Earliest Historical Period", *JPOS*, 2, pp. 110-38.

1922/3 "Ai and Beth-Aven", *AASOR*, 4, pp. 141-9.

1924 "Researches of the School in Western Judaea", *BASOR*, 15, pp. 2-11.

1926 "The Jordan Valley in the Bronze Age", *AASOR*, 6, pp. 56-62.

1932 *The Excavations of Tell Beit Mirsim, I. The Pottery of the First Three Campaigns* (= *AASOR* 12).

1933 *The Archaeology of Palestine and the Bible* (second edn.).

1934 "The Kyle Memorial Excavation at Bethel", *BASOR*, 56, pp. 2-15.

1935a "Observations on the Bethel Report", *BASOR*, 57, pp. 27-30.

1935b "Archaeology and the Date of the Hebrew Conquest of Palestine", *BASOR*, 58, pp. 10-18.

1936 "The Song of Deborah in the Light of Archaeology", *BASOR*, 62, pp. 26-31.

1937 "Further Light on the History of Israel from Lachish and Megiddo", *BASOR*, 68, pp. 22-6.

1938a "The Present State of Syro-Palestinian Archaeology", in E. Grant (ed.) *The Haverford Symposium on Archaeology and the Bible*.

1938b *The Excavation of Tell Beit Mirsim. II. The Bronze Age* (= *AASOR* 17).

1938c "The Chronology of a South Palestinian City, Tell el-ʿAjjûl", *AJSL*, 55, pp. 337-59.

1939 "The Israelite Conquest of Canaan in the Light of Archaeology", *BASOR*, 74, pp. 11-23.

1940a "New Light on the History of Western Asia in the Second Millennium B.C.", *BASOR*, 77, pp. 20-32.

1940b An untitled note appended to Engberg 1940, *BASOR*, 78, pp. 7-9.

Albright (Cont'd.)

1941   "The Land of Damascus between 1850 and 1750 B.C.", *BASOR*, 83, pp. 30-6.

1943   "Note to article of N. Glueck; Three Israelite Towns in the Jordan Valley", *BASOR*, 90, pp. 17-18).

1944   "The Oracles of Balaam", *JBL*, 63, pp. 207-33.

1945   "The Chronology of the Divided Monarchy of Israel", *BASOR*, 100, pp. 16-22.

1948   "Exploring in Sinai with the University of California African Expedition", *BASOR*, 109, pp. 5-20.

1949   *The Archaeology of Palestine* (1st edn.).

1951   "The Old Testament and the Archaeology of Palestine", in H.H. Rowley (ed.), *The Old Testament and Modern Study*, Oxford, pp. 1-26.

1954   "Northwest-Semitic Names in a list of Egyptian Slaves from the Eighteenth Century B.C.", *JAOS*, 74, pp. 222-33.

1955   *The Biblical Period from Abraham to Ezra* (second edn.), New York.

1956   "Stratigraphic Confirmation of the Low Mesopotamian Chronology", *BASOR*, 144, pp. 26-30.

1957a   *From the Stone Age to Christianity* (3rd edn.), New York.

1957b   "Further Observations on the Chronology of Alalakh", *BASOR*, 146, pp. 26-34.

1960   *The Archaeology of Palestine* (4th edn.), Harmondsworth.

1961   "Abram the Hebrew: A New Archaeological Interpretation", *BASOR*, 163, pp. 36-54.

1962   "The Chronology of Middle Bronze I (Early Bronze - Middle Bronze)", *BASOR*, 168, pp. 36-42.

1963   *The Biblical Period From Abraham to Ezra* (4th edn.), New York.

Albright (Cont'd.)
  1965 "Some Remarks on the Archaeological Chronology of Palestine before about 1500 B.C.", in R.W. Ehrich (ed), *Chronologies in Old World Archaeology*, Chicago, pp. 47-60.

  1966 "The Amarna Letters from Palestine", revd. *CAH* (vol. II, ch. XX), fasc. 51.

  1967 "Debir", in D. Winton Thomas (ed.), *AOTS*, Oxford, pp. 207-20.

  1968a in J.L. Kelso, Albright, et. al., *The Excavation of Bethel* (1934-1960) (=*AASOR* 39).

  1968b *Yahweh and the Gods of Canaan*, London.

  1973a "From the Patriarchs to Moses" *BA*, 36, pp. 5-33, 48-76.

  1973b "The Historical Framework of Palestinian Archaeology Between 2100 and 1600 B.C.", *BASOR*, 209, pp. 12-18.

  1975 "Beit Mirsim, Tell", in M. Avi-Yonah (ed.), *EAEHL*, vol. I, pp. 171-8.

Alt A.
  1966 "The Settlement of the Israelites in Palestine", in *Essays on Old Testament History and Religion*, Oxford; trans. by R.A. Wilson from *Die Landnahme der Israeliten in Palästina* 1925.

Amiran R.
  1970 *Ancient Pottery of the Holy Land*, New Brunswick.

Amiran R. and Eitan A.
  1963 "Tel Nagila", *IEJ*, 13, pp. 143-4, 333-4.

  1964 "A Krater of Bichrome Ware from Tel Nagila", *IEJ*, 14, pp. 219-31.

  1965 "A Canaanite-Hyksos City at Tel Nagila", *Archaeology*, 18, pp. 113-23.

Amiran R. and Worrell J.E.
  1976 "Hesi, Tel", in M. Avi-Yonah (ed.), *EAEHL*, vol. II, pp. 514-20.

Anderson G.W.
    1966   *The History and Religion of Israel,* Oxford.

Artzy M.
    1973   "The Late Bronze 'Palestinian' Bichrome Ware in
                its Cypriote Context", in H.A. Hoffner Jr. (ed.),
                Orient and Occident, essays presented to Cyrus H.
                Gordon... *Alter Orient und Altes Testament,* 22,
                pp. 9-16.

Artzy M., Asaro F. and Perlman I.
    1973   "The Origin of the 'Palestinian' Bichrome Ware",
                JAOS, 93, pp. 446-61.

Åström P.
    1957   *The Middle Cypriote Bronze Age,* Lund.

Avi-Yonah M.
    1968   See Aharoni and Avi-Yonah 1968.

    1975-6   (ed.) *EAEHL,* vol. I (1975), vol. II (1976).

Avi-Yonah M. and Ephan Y.
    1975   "Ashkelon", in Avi-Yonah (ed.), *EAEHL,* vol. I,
                pp. 121-30.

Barnett R.D.
    1969   "The Sea Peoples", revd. *CAH,* fasc. 68.

Bartlett J.R.
    1965   "The Edomite King-list of Gen. 36: 31-9 and
                I Chron. 1: 43-50", *JTS,* 16, pp. 301-14.

    1969a   "The Land of Seir and the Brotherhood of Edom",
                JTS, 20, pp. 1-20.

    1969b   "The Historical Reference of Numbers 21: 27-30",
                PEQ, 101, pp. 94-100.

    1970   "Sihon and Og, Kings of the Amorites", *VT* 20,
                pp. 257-77.

    1972   "The Rise and Fall of the Kingdom of Edom",
                PEQ, 104, pp. 26-37.

    1973   "The Moabites and Edomites" in *POTT,* Oxford,
                pp. 229-58.

Beagle D.M.
1971   Review of Glueck 1970, *CBQ,* 33, p. 580.

van Beek G.W.
1962   "Megiddo", in *IDB,* vol. III, pp. 335-42.

Bell B.
1971   "The Dark Ages in Ancient History: I.   The First
            Dark Age in Egypt", *AJA,* 75, pp. 1-26.

1975   "Climate and the History of Egypt: The Middle
            Kingdom", *AJA,* 79, pp. 223-69.

Bierbrier M.L.
1975   *The Late New Kingdom in Egypt,* Warminster.

Bietak M.
1975a   "Die Haupstadt der Hyksos und die Ramsesstadt",
            Antike Welt 1975, pp. 28-43.

1975b   *Tell el-Dabʿa II,* Vienna.

Biran A.
1966   "Tel Dan", *IEJ,* 16, pp. 144-5.

1969   "Tel Dan", *IEJ,* 19, pp. 121-23.

1974   "Tel Dan", *BA,* 37, pp. 26-51.

Blenkinsopp J.
1972   *Gibeon and Israel,* Cambridge.

Bliss F.J.
1874   *A Mound of Many Cities: Tell el-Hesy Excavated.*

Bliss F.J. and Macalister R.A.S.
1902   *Excavations in Palestine 1898-1900.*

Boling R.G.
1975   *Judges,* New York.

Breasted J.H.
1906a   *Ancient Records of Egypt,* vols. I-III.

1906b   *A History of Egypt.*

1924   "The Decline and Fall of the Egyptian Empire",
            ch. 8 of *CAH*[1] vol. II, pp. 164-95.

Bright J.
    1972   *A History of Israel,* 2nd edn., London.

Brown F., Driver S.R. and Briggs C.A.
    1952   *A Hebrew and English Lexicon of the Old Testament,* corrected impression, Oxford.

Bruce F.F.
    1962   "Deborah" in *NBD,* p.303.

    1963   *Israel and the Nations,* Exeter.

Brugsch E.
    1872   "Beiträge zu den Untersuchungen über Tanis", *ZÄS,* 10, pp. 16-20.

    1875   *L'Exode et les monuments Égyptiens.*

Buccellati G.
    1967   *Cities and Nations of Ancient Syria.*

Bull R.J.
    1960   "A Re-examination of the Shechem Temple", *BA,* 23, pp. 110-19.

Burney C.F.
    1903   *Notes on the Hebrew Text of the Books of Kings.*

    1919a   *Israel's Settlement in Canaan: The Biblical Tradition and its Historical Background.*

    1919b   *The Book of Judges, with Introduction and Notes,* 2nd edn..

Burrows M.
    1941   *What Mean These Stones?*

Callaway J.A.
    1965   "The 1964 ʿAi (Et-Tell) Excavations", *BASOR,* 178, pp. 13-40.

    1968   "New Evidence on the Conquest of Ai", *JBL,* 87, pp. 312-320.

    1969   "The 1966 ʿAi (Et-Tell) Excavations", *BASOR,* 196, pp. 2-16.

Callaway (Cont'd.)
　　　1970　　　"The 1968-1969 'Ai (Et-Tell) Excavations",
　　　　　　　　　BASOR, 198, pp. 7-31.

Callaway J.A. and Nicol M.B.
　　　1966　　　"A Sounding at Khirbet Ḥaiyân", *BASOR*, 183,
　　　　　　　　　12-19.

Campbell E.F. Jr.
　　　1960　　　"The Amarna Letters and the Amarna Period",
　　　　　　　　　BA, 23, pp. 2-22.

　　　1961　　　"The Chronology of Israel and the Ancient Near
　　　　　　　　　East: (B) The Ancient Near East: Chronological
　　　　　　　　　Bibliography and Charts", in Wright (ed.), *BANE*,
　　　　　　　　　pp. 214-228.

　　　1965　　　"Archaeological News: Hebron", *BA*, 28, pp. 30-32.

　　　1975　　　"Moses and the Foundations of Israel",
　　　　　　　　　Interpretation, 29, pp. 141-54.

Campbell E.F. Jr. and Ross J.F.
　　　1963　　　"The Excavation of Shechem and the Biblical
　　　　　　　　　Tradition", *BA*, 26, pp. 2-27.

Campbell E.F. Jr. and Wright G.E.
　　　1969　　　"Tribal League Shrines in Amman and Shechem"
　　　　　　　　　BA, 32, pp. 104-116.

Cazelles H.
　　　1973　　　"The Hebrews", in Wiseman (ed.), *POTT*,
　　　　　　　　　Oxford, pp. 1-28.

Chabas F.J.
　　　1873　　　*Recherches pour servir à l'histoire de la XIX
　　　　　　　　　dynastie et spécialement à celle des temps de
　　　　　　　　　l'Exode.*

Childs B.S.
　　　1974　　　*Exodus, a Commentary,*　London.

Courville D.A.
　　　1971　　　*The Exodus Problem and its Ramifications,*
　　　　　　　　　Loma Linda, California, 2 vols.

Craft C.F.
    1962   "Shamgar", in *IDB,* vol. IV, pp. 306-7.

Crown A.D.
    1973   Review of Yadin 1972, in *AJBA,* 2, pp. 113-14.

Cundall A.E.
    1968   *Judges,* London.

Curtis E.L.
    1898   "The Chronology of the Old Testament", in
                HDB, vol. I, pp. 397-403.

Dever W.G.
    1966   "Gezer", *IEJ,* 16, pp. 277-8.

    1970a   "Tel Gezer", *IEJ,* 20, pp. 226-7.

    1970b   "The 'Middle Bronze I' Period in Syria and
                Palestine", in J.A. Sanders (ed.), *Near Eastern
                Archaeology in the Twentieth Century,* (Glueck
                Festschrift) New York, pp. 132-63.

    1972a   "Tel Gezer", *IEJ,* 22, pp. 158-60.

    1972b   "Shechem", *IEJ,* 22, pp. 239-40.

    1973   "The EB IV - MB I Horizon in Transjordan and
                Southern Palestine", *BASOR,* 210, pp. 37-63.

    1976   "Gezer" in Avi-Yonah (ed.), *EAEHL,* vol. II,
                pp. 428-443.

Dorrell S.
    1965   "The Preservation of Organic Materials in the
                Tombs at Jericho", Appendix L of *Excavations at
                Jericho,* vol. II, ed. Kenyon, London; pp. 704-17.

Dothan M.
    1973   "The Foundation of Tel Mor and of Ashdod",
                IEJ, 23, pp. 1-17.

Dothan T.
    1957   "Archaeological Reflections on the Philistine
                Problem", *Antiquity and Survival,* 2, pp. 151-64.

Drioton E.
    1950   *Cahiers d'histoire égyptienne,* III.

Drioton (Cont'd.)
1955　　　"La date de l'Exode", in *La Bible et l'Orient,
= Cahier No. 1 de la Revue d'Histoire et de
Philosophie Religieuses.*

Driver S.R.
1899　　　"Joseph" in *HDB*, vol. II, 767-775.

1902　　　*A Critical and Exegetical Commentary on
Deuteronomy*, 3rd. edn. *(ICC).*

1911a　　*The Book of Genesis*, revd. edn.

1911b　　*The Book of Exodus.*

1913a　　*Notes on the Hebrew Text and the Topography
of the Books of Samuel*, 2nd. edn.

1913b　　*An Introduction to the Literature of the Old
Testament*,　　9th. edn.

Drower M.S.
1973　　　"Syria *c.* 1550-1400 B.C.", ch. 10, revised *CAH*,
vol. II, part I, pp. 417-525.

Ehrich R.W.
1954　　　(ed.) *Relative Chronologies in Old World
Archaeology*, Chicago.

1965　　　(ed.) *Chronologies in Old World Archaeology*
(a revised edition of the above), Chicago.

Eissfeldt O.
1965a　　"Palestine in the Time of the Nineteenth Dynasty,
(a) The Exodus and Wanderings", revd.*CAH*
(vol. II, ch. 26a), fasc. 31.

1965b　　*The Old Testament: An Introduction*, trans. by
P.R. Ackroyd from 3rd. German edn., Oxford.

Engberg R.M.
1938　　　see Guy and Engberg

1939　　　*The Hyksos Reconsidered*, Chicago.

1940　　　"Historical Analysis of Archaeological Evidence:
Megiddo and the Song of Deborah",
BASOR,78, pp. 4-7.

Englebach R.
    1924   "The Egyptian Name of Joseph", *JEA*, 10, pp.
                204-06.

Epstein C.M.
    1966   *Palestinian Bichrome Ware*, Leiden.

Finegan J.
    1946   *Light From the Ancient Past*, London.

    1963   *Let My People Go*, New York.

Fisher C.S.
    1923   "Bethshean", *Museum Journal of the University
                of Pennsylvania*, 14, pp. 227-48.

    1929   *The Excavation of Armageddon*, OIC no.4,
                Chicago

Fitzgerald G.M.
    1967   "Beth-shean", in D.W. Thomas (ed.), *AOTS*,
                Oxford, pp. 185-96.

Fohrer G.
    1970   *Introduction to the Old Testament*, trans.
                D. Green from 10th German edn., London.

Franken H.J.
    1968   "Palestine in the Time of the Nineteenth
                Dynasty, (b) Archaeological Evidence", revd.
                CAH (vol. II, ch. 26b), fasc. 67.

    1969   *Excavations at Tell Deir ʿAlla I: A
                Stratigraphical and Analytical Study of the Early
                Iron Age Pottery*, Leiden.

    1976   "The Problem of Identification in Biblical
                Archaeology", *PEQ*, 108, pp. 3-11.

Franken H.J. and Power W.J.A.
    1971   "Glueck's 'Explorations in Eastern Palestine'
                in the light of recent evidence", *VT*, 21,
                pp. 118-23.

Freedman D.N.   "The Chronology of Israel and the Ancient Near
                East: (A) Old Testament Chronology", in Wright
                (ed.), *BANE*, pp. 203-14.

Freedman (Cont'd.)
    1965   "The Biblical Languages", in J.P. Hyatt (ed.),
              The Bible in Modern Scholarship, Nashville,
              pp. 294-312.

Fritz V.
    1973   "Das Ende der spätbronzezeitlichen Stadt Hazor
              Stratum XIII und die biblische Überlieferung
              in Josua 11 und Richter 4", *Ugarit Forschungen,* 5,
              pp. 123-39.

Galanopoulos A.G. and Bacon E.
    1969   *Atlantis: The Truth Behind the Legend,* London.

Gampert A.
    1917   "Les '480 ans' de I Rois vi, I", *Revue de*
              théologie et de philosophie, 5, pp. 241-7.

Gardiner A.H.
    1918   "The Delta Residence of the Ramessides",
              JEA, 5, pp. 127-38, 179-200, 242-71.

    1920   "The Ancient Military Road between Egypt and
              Palestine", *JEA,* 6, pp. 99-116.

    1922   "The Geography of the Exodus", in *Recueil*
              d'Études égyptologiques dédiées à la mémoire de
              J.F. Champollion.

    1924   "The Geography of the Exodus: An Answer to
              Professor Naville and Others", *JEA,* 10, pp. 87-96.

    1933   "Tanis and Pi-Ramesse: A Retraction", *JEA,* 19,
              pp. 122-8.

    1947   *Ancient Egyptian Onomastica,* vols. I and II,
              London.

    1958   "Only One King Siptah and Twosre not his Wife",
              JEA, 44, pp. 12-22.

    1961   *Egypt of the Pharaohs,* Oxford.

Garstang J.
    1930   "Jericho", *PEFQS,* pp. 123-32.

    1931   *The Foundations of Bible History: Joshua-*
              Judges, London.

    1940   (with J.B.E. Garstang) *The Story of Jericho.*

Glueck N.

1935 *Explorations in Eastern Palestine II* (= *AASOR* 15).

1939 *Explorations in Eastern Palestine III* (= *AASOR* 18-19).

1940 *The Other Side of the Jordan,* 1st edn.

1955 "The Age of Abraham in the Negeb", *BA,* 18, pp. 2-9.

1959 *Rivers in the Desert,* London.

1967 "Transjordan", in D.W. Thomas (ed.), *AOTS,* pp. 428-52.

1970 *The Other Side of the Jordan,* 2nd edn., Cambridge, Mass.

Gold V.R.

1962 "Beth-shemesh", in *IDB,* vol. I, pp. 401-3; "Makkedah", in *IDB,* vol. III, p. 228.

Good E.M.

1962 "Joshua, Book of", in *IDB,* vol. II, pp. 988-95.

Gowan G.E.

1968 "The Syncretistic Cult in Israel", in J. Coert Rylaarsdam (ed.),*Transitions in Biblical Scholarship,* Chicago, pp. 96ff.

Gray J.

1962 *Archaeology and the Old Testament World,* London.

1966 "Hazor", *VT,* 16, pp. 26-52.

1970 *I and II Kings,* second edn.

Greenberg M.

1955 *The Ḫab/piru,* New Haven, Connecticut.

1965 "Response to Roland de Vaux's 'Method in the Study of Early Hebrew History'", in J.P. Hyatt (ed.), *The Bible in Modern Scholarship,* Nashville, pp. 37-43.

Griffiths J.S.

1923 *The Exodus in the Light of Archaeology.*

Grintz J.M.
    1961   "Ai which is beside Beth-aven", *Biblica,* 42,
                pp. 201-16.

Grollenberg L.H.
    1956   *Atlas of the Bible,* trans. and ed. by J.M.H.
                Reid and H.H. Rowley, London.

Guy L.P.O. and Engberg R.M.
    1938   *Megiddo Tombs.*

Habachi L.
    1954   "Khata'na-Qantir", in *Annales du Service
                des Antiquités de l'Égypte,* 52, pp. 443-559.

Hall H.R.
    1920   *The Ancient History of the Near East,*
                5th edn.

    1923   "The Middle Kingdom and the Hyksos Conquest",
                ch. 8 of CAH^1 vol. I, pp. 299-325.

Hamilton R.W.
    1935   "Excavations at Tell Abu Hawam", *Quarterly of
                the Department of Antiquities in Palestine,*
                vol. 4, pp. 1-69.

Hammond P.C.
    1965   "Hebron", *RB,* 72, pp. 267-70.

    1966   "Hebron", *RB,* 73, pp. 566-69.

    1968   "Hebron", *RB,* 75, pp. 253-58.

Hamza M.
    1930   "Excavations of the Department of Antiquities
                at Qantir (Faqûs District)", *Annales du
                Service des Antiquités de l'Égypte,* 30, pp.
                31-68.

Haran M.
    1971   "The Exodus Routes in the Pentateuchal Sources",
                Tarbiz, 40, pp. 113-143.

Harding G.L.
    1958   "Recent Discoveries in Jordan", *PEQ,* 90, pp. 7-18.

Harding (Cont'd.)
    1959   *The Antiquities of Jordan*, London.

Harrelson W.
    1957   "Shechem in Extra-biblical References", *BA*, 20, pp. 2-10.

Harris J.R. and Chapman A.T.
    1898   "Exodus and Journey to Canaan", in *HDB*, vol. I, pp. 802-06.

Harrison R.K.
    1970   *Introduction to the Old Testament*, London.

Hayes W.C.
    1937   *Glazed Tiles from a Palace of Ramesses II at Kantir*, Metropolitan Mus. of Art Papers, no. 3, pp. 5-8.

    1959   *The Sceptre of Egypt*, 2 vols., New York.

    1961   "The Middle Kingdom in Egypt", revd. *CAH* (vol. I, ch. 20), fasc. 3.

Helck W.
    1965   "Tkw und die Ramses-Stadt", *VT*, 15, pp. 35-48.

Hennessy J.B.
    1963   *Stephania. A Middle and Late Bronze-Age Cemetary in Cyprus*, London.

    1966   "Excavation of a Late Bronze Age Temple at Amman", *PEQ*, 98, pp. 155-162.

Herbert A.S.
    1962   *Genesis 12-50: Introduction and Commentary*, London.

Herrmann S.
    1973   *Israel in Egypt*, Eng. trans., London.

    1975   *A History of Israel in Old Testament Times*, Eng. trans., London.

Hertzberg H.W.
    1964   *I and II Samuel*, trans. by J.S. Bowden from the 2nd German edn., London.

Heurtley W.A.
 1939   "A Palestinian Vase Painter of the Sixteenth
               Century B.C.", *Quarterly of the Department of
               Antiquities in Palestine,* 8, pp. 21-34.

Heusman J.E.
 1975   "Archaeology and Early Israel: The Scene Today",
               CBQ, 37, pp. 1-16.

Hoehner H.W.
 1969   "The Duration of the Egyptian Bondage",
               Bibliotheca Sacra, 126, pp. 306-16.

Hooke S.H.
 1947   *In The Beginning,* Oxford.

 1962   "Genesis" *in Peake's Commentary on the Bible,*
               ed. M. Black and H.H. Rowley, London, pp.
               175-207.

Hyatt J.P.
 1970   "Were There an Ancient Historical Credo in
               Israel and an Independent Sinai Tradition?", in
               H.T. Frank and W.L. Reed (eds.), *Translating and
               Understanding the Old Testament,* Essays in
               honour of H.G. May, Nashville, pp. 152-70.

 1971   *Commentary on Exodus,* London.

Jack J.W.
 1924   "The Israel Stele of Merneptah", *The Expository
               Times,* 36, pp. 40-44.

 1925   *The Date of the Exodus in the Light of
               External Evidence.*

James F.
 1975   "Beth-shean", in M. Avi-Yonah (ed.),
               vol. I, pp. 207-12.

James T.G.H.
 1965   "Egypt: From the Expulsion of the Hyksos to
               Amenophis I", revd. *CAH* (vol. II, ch. 8),
               fasc. 34.

Kantor H.J.
    1965   "The Relative Chronology of Egypt and Its
Foreign Correlations before the Late Bronze Age",
in R.W. Ehrich (ed.), *Chronologies in Old World
Archaeology*, Chicago, pp. 1-46.

Kempinski A.
    1974   "Tell el-ʿAjjûl - Beth-Aglayim or Sharuhen?"
IEJ, 24, pp. 145-52.

    1976   (with V. Fritz) "Tel Masos", *IEJ*, 26, pp. 52-4.

Kenyon K.M.
    1951   "Some Notes on the History of Jericho in the
Second Millennium B.C.", *PEQ*, 83, pp. 101-38.

    1956   "The Jericho of Abraham's Time", *The Illustrated
London News*, May 19th 1956, pp. 552-5.

    1957   *Digging Up Jericho*, London.

    1964   "Megiddo, Hazor, Samaria and Chronology",
*Bulletin no. 4 of the University of London
Institute of Archaeology*, pp. 143-56.

    1966a   "Palestine in the Middle Bronze Age", revd.
CAH (vol. II, ch. 3), fasc. 48.

    1966b   *Amorites and Canaanites*, London.

    1967   "Jericho" in D.W. Thomas (ed.), *AOTS*, pp. 264-75.

    1969   "The Middle and Late Bronze Age Strata at
Megiddo", *Levant* 1, pp. 25-60.

    1970   *Archaeology in the Holy Land*, 3rd. edn.,London.

    1971   "Palestine in the Time of the Eighteenth
Dynasty", revd. *CAH* (vol. II, ch. 11), fasc. 69.

    1976   "Jerusalem: History of the Excavations", in
Avi-Yonah (ed.), *EAEHL*, vol. II, pp. 591-7.

Kirkbride D.
    1965   "Scarabs", Appendix E of *Excavations at
Jericho*, vol. II, ed. Kenyon, London, pp.
580-655.

Kitchen K.A.
    1956/7   "A Recently Published Egyptian Papyrus and its bearing on the Joseph Story", *Tyndale House Bulletin*, no. 2, pp. 1-2.

    1961   Review of Vergote 1959, in *JEA*, 47, pp. 158-64.

    1962   The following articles in the *NBD*:
"Asenath", p. 94;
"Camel", pp. 181-3;
"Egypt", pp. 337-53;
"Exodus", pp. 402-4;
"Jericho", pp. 611-13;
"Joseph: (i) In the Old Testament", pp. 656-60;
"Magic and Sorcery: (ii) Egyptian and Assyro-Babylonian", pp. 768-71;
"Moses", pp. 843-50;
"Potiphar", p. 1012;
"Potipherah", p. 1012;
"Prison: (i) In the Old Testament", p. 1035;
"Slave, Slavery: (i) In the Old Testament", pp. 1195-1198;

    1964   "Some New Light on the Asiatic Wars of Ramesses II", *JEA*, 50, pp. 47-70.

    1966   *Ancient Orient and Old Testament*, London.

    1973a   *The Third Intermediate Period in Egypt*, Warminster

    1973b   "The Philistines", in D.J. Wiseman (ed.), *POTT*, pp. 53-78.

    1973c   Review of Redford 1970a, in the *Theological Students' Fellowship Bulletin*, 67, pp. 24-6.

Kitchen K.A. and Mitchell T.C.
    1962   "Chronology of the Old Testament", in *NBD*, pp. 212-23.

Kline M.G.
    1956   "The Ḫa-BI-ru - Kin or Foe of Israel?", pts. I and II, *WTJ*, 19, pp. 1-24, 170-84.

    1957   "The Ḫa-BI-ru - Kin or Foe of Israel?", pt. III, *WTJ*, 20, pp. 46-70.

Kochavi M.
　　1967　　　"Tel Malḥata", *IEJ*, 17, pp. 272-3.

　　1968　　　"Tel Malḥata", *RB*, 75, pp. 392-5.

　　1974　　　"Khirbet Rabûd = Debir", *Tel Aviv*, 1, pp. 2-33.

Landes G.M.
　　1962　　　"Amalek", in *IDB*, vol. I, pp. 101-02.

Lapp P.W.
　　1967　　　"Taanach by the Waters of Megiddo", *BA*, 30,
　　　　　　　pp. 2-27.

　　1969　　　"The 1968 Excavations at Tell Taʿannek", *BASOR*
　　　　　　　195, pp. 2-49.

Leclant J.
　　1969　　　"Tell ed-Dabʿa", *Orientalia*, 38, pp. 248-251.

Lepsius C.R.
　　1949　　　*Letters from Egypt, Ethiopia, and the Peninsula
　　　　　　　of Sinai ... With extracts from the chronology
　　　　　　　of the Egyptians, with reference to the Exodus
　　　　　　　of the Israelites*, trans. L. and J.B. Horner,
　　　　　　　published in *Bohn's Antiquarian Library*.

Lilley J.P.U.
　　1962　　　"Eglon", in *NBD*, p. 337;
　　　　　　　"Makkedah", in *NBD*, p. 773.

Livingston D.
　　1970　　　"The Location of Biblical Bethel and Ai
　　　　　　　Reconsidered", *WTJ*, 33, pp. 20-44.

　　1971　　　"Traditional Site of Bethel Questioned", *WTJ*,
　　　　　　　34, pp. 39-50.

Loud G.
　　1948　　　*Megiddo II: Seasons 1935-1939*, OIP, vol. 52.

Lucas A.
　　1938　　　*The Route of the Exodus*.

Macalister R.A.S.
　　1913　　　*The Philistines*, reprinted 1965, Chicago.

Mahler E.
    1901   "The Exodus", *Journal of the Royal Asiatic Society*, pp. 33-67.

Malamat A.
    1954   "Cushan Rishathaim and the Decline of the Near East around 1200 B.C.", *JNES*, 13, pp. 231-42.

    1960   "Hazor 'the head of all those kingdoms'", *JBL*, 79, pp. 12-19.

Mallon A.
    1921   *Les Hébreux en Égypte*.

Marquet-Krause J.
    1935   "La Deuxième Campagne de fouilles à Ay (1934)", *Syria*, 16, pp. 325-345.

Marston C.
    1934   *The Bible is True*.

    1937   *The Bible Comes Alive*.

Maspero G.
    1877   Report on Inscriptions from Tell el-Maskhouta, *Revue archéologique*, 34, pp. 320ff.

Matz F.
    1962   "Minoan Civilisation: Maturity and Zenith", revd. *CAH*, fasc. 12.

Mauchline J.
    1971   *I and II Samuel*, London

May, H.G.
    1935   *Material Remains of the Megiddo Cult*, OIP, vol. 26.

Mayani Z.
    1965   *Les Hyksos et le monde de la Bible*, Paris.

Mayes A.D.H.
    1969   "The Historical Context of the Battle Against Sisera", *VT*, 19, pp. 353-60.

    1974   *Israel in the Period of the Judges*, London.

Mazar B.

1951   (as Maisler) "The Stratification of Tell Abu
            Huwam on the Bay of Acre", *BASOR*, 124, pp. 21-25.

1952/3   (as Maisler) "Beth-She'arim, Gaba, and
            Harosheth of the Peoples", *HUCA*, pp. 75-84.

1968   "The Middle Bronze Age in Palestine", *IEJ*,
            18, pp. 65-97.

1969   "The Historical Background of the Book of
            Genesis", *JNES*, 28, pp. 73-83.

1975   "Jerusalem in the Biblical Period", in
            Jerusalem Revealed, produced by the Israel
            Exploration Society, Jerusalem, pp. 1-8.

Meek T.J.
1936   *Hebrew Origins*.

Mendenhall G.E.
1962   "The Hebrew Conquest of Palestine", *BA*, 25,
            pp. 66-87.

1965   "Response to Roland de Vaux's 'Method in the
            Study of Early Hebrew History'", in Hyatt (ed.),
            The Bible in Modern Scholarship, Nashville,
            pp. 30-36.

1973   *The Tenth Generation: The Origins of the
            Biblical Tradition*, Baltimore.

Mercer S.A.B.
1922/3   "Merneptah's Stele and the Exodus", *Anglican
            Theological Review*, 5. pp. 96-107.

1939   *The Tell El-Amarna Tablets*, 2 vols.

Merrillees R.S.
1970   "Evidence for the Bichrome Wheel-made Ware in
            Egypt", *AJBA*, 1, no. 3, pp. 3-27.

1971   "The Early History of Late Cypriote I", *Levant*,
            3, pp. 56-79.

Millard A.
1973   "The Canaanites", in Wiseman (ed.), *POTT*,
            Oxford.

Mitchell T.C.
 1962 "Chariot", in *NBD,* pp. 204-6.

Mittmann S.
 1970 "Beitrage zur Siedlungs- und Territorial-
     geschichte des Nordlichen Ostjordanlandes",
     Abhandlungen des Deutschen Palastina-Vereins.

Montet P.
 1930 "Tanis, Avaris, et Pi-Ramses", *RB,* 39, pp. 1-28.

 1933 *Les Nouvelles Fouilles des Tanis* (1929-32).

 1940 *Le Drame d'Avaris.*

 1957 *Œographie de l'Egypt ancienne,* I.

 1959 *L'Egypt et la Bible.*

Montgomery J.A. and Gehman H.S.
 1951 *A Critical and Exegetical Commentary on the
     Books of Kings,* Edinburgh *(ICC).*

Moore G.F.
 1895 *A Critical and Exegetical Commentary on Judges
     (ICC).*

Morton W.H.
 1962 "Aphek", in *IDB,* vol. I, p. 156.

Muller W.M.
 1901 "Egypt", in T.K. Cheyne and J. Sutherland Black
     (eds.), *Encyclopaedia Biblica,* vol. II, cols.
     1241ff.

McKenzie J.L.
 1967 *The World of the Judges,* London.

McNeile A.H.
 1908 *The Book of Exodus.*

Naville E.
 1885/1888 *The Store-City of Pithom and the Route of
     the Exodus,* 1st edn./3rd edn.

 1891 *Bubastis.*

 1893 "Exodus", in W. Smith (ed.), *Dictionary of the
     Bible,* vol. I, pt. II, pp. 1023ff.

 1924 "The Geography of the Exodus", *JEA,* 10,
     pp. 18-39.

308

Naville (Cont'd.)
1926   "The Egyptian Name of Joseph", *JEA*, 12, pp. 16-18.

Negev A.
1972   (ed.) *Archaeological Encyclopedia of the Holy Land*, Jerusalem.

Nicholson E.W.
1973   *Exodus and Sinai in History and Theology*, Oxford.

Nöldeke T.
1869   "Die Chronologie der Richterzeit", in *Untersuchungen zur Kritik des Alten Testaments*, pp. 173-98.

North R.
1967a   *Archaeobiblical Egypt*, Rome.
1967b   *Les Fouilles dans la Région de Jéricho*, Rome.

Noth M.
1948   *Überlieferungsgeschichte des Pentateuch*.
1953   *Das Buch Josua*, 2nd edn., Tübingen
1960   *The History of Israel*, 2nd edn., London.
1962   *Exodus*, London.

Oren E.D.
1969   "Cypriot Imports in Late Bronze I Context of Palestine", *Opuscula Atheniensia*, 9, pp. 127-38.
1973   *The Northern Cemetery of Beth Shan*, Leiden

Orr J.
1909   *The Problem of the Old Testament*.

Ovadiah A.
1976   "Gaza", in Avi-Yonah (ed.), *EAEHL*, vol. II, pp. 408-17.

Peet T.E.
1922   *Egypt and the Old Testament*.

Pendlebury J.D.S.
    1939   *The Archaeology of Crete.*

Perkins A.
    1950   Review of Schaeffer 1948, in *JAOS*, 70, pp. 51-4.

Petrie W.M.F.
    1890   *Illahun, Kahun, and Gurob.*

    1906   *Hyksos and Israelite Cities.*

    1911   *Egypt and Israel.*

    1932   *Ancient Gaza II.*

Pfeiffer C.F.
    1966   (ed.) *The Biblical World: A Dictionary of Biblical Archaeology,* Grand Rapids, Mich.

Poole R.S.
    1893   "Chronology", in W. Smith (ed.), *Dictionary of the Bible,* vol. I, pt. I, pp. 590ff.

Posener G.
    1957   "Les Asiatiques en Égypte sous les XIIe et XIIIe dynasties", *Syria,* 34, pp. 145-63.

    1965   "Relations with Egypt", in "Syria and Palestine *c.* 2160-1780 B.C.", by G. Posener, J. Bottero and K.M. Kenyon, revd. *CAH* (vol. I, ch. 21), fasc. 29, pp. 3-29.

Prausnitz M.
    1963   "Achzib", *IEJ,* 13, pp. 337-8.

    1975   "Achzib", in Avi-Yonah (ed.), *EAEHL,* vol. I, pp. 26-30.

Pritchard J.B.
    1955   (ed.) *Ancient Near Eastern Texts Relating to the Old Testament,* 2nd edn., Princeton, N.J.

    1960   "Gibeon's History in the Light of Excavation", *VT* Supplement 7, pp. 1-12.

    1962   *Gibeon Where the Sun Stood Still,* Princeton, N.J.

310

Pritchard (Cont'd.)
      1965   "Culture and History", in Hyatt (ed.), *The Bible in Modern Scholarship*, Nashville, pp. 313-24.

von Rad G.
      1938 ET   "The Form-Critical Problem of the Hexateuch",
      1966   in *The Problem of the Hexateuch and Other Essays*, London, pp. 1-78.

      1972   *Genesis*, 3rd edn., based on 9th German edn., London.

Rainey A.F.
      1971   "Bethel is still Beitin", *WTJ*, 33, pp. 175-88.

Rea J.
      1960   "The Time of the Oppression and the Exodus", *Bulletin of the Evangelical Theology Society*, 3, pp. 58-69.

      1961   "New Light on the Wilderness Journey and the Conquest", *Grace Journal*, vol. 2, no. 2, pp. 5-13.

Redford D.B.
      1963   "Exodus I.11", *VT*, 13, pp. 401-18.

      1967   *The History and Chronology of the Eighteenth Dynasty of Egypt*,   Toronto.

      1970a   *A Study of the Biblical Story of Joseph (Genesis 37-50)* (= *VT* Supplement 20), Leiden.

      1970b   "The Hyksos Invasion in History and Tradition", *Orientalia*, 39, pp. 1-51.

Reed W.L.
      1967   "Gibeon", in D.W. Thomas (ed.), *AOTS*, pp. 231-43.

Richter W.
      1964   *Die Bearbeitungen des 'Retterbuches' in der deuteronomischen Epoche*.

Robinson E.
    1856   *Biblical Researches in Palestine, Mount Sinai,*
                and Arabia Petraea, vols. I-III, 2nd edn.,
                London.

Robinson T.H.
    1932   *A History of Israel,* vol. I.

Rost L.
    1965   *Das kleine Credo und andere Studien zum Alten*
                Testament.

Rowley H.H.
    1950   *From Joseph to Joshua,* London.

Rowton M.B.
    1953   "The Problem of the Exodus",*PEQ,* 85, pp. 46-60.

    1962   "Western Asia", in "Chronology: Egypt, Western
                Asia and the Aegean Bronze Age", by W.C. Hayes,
                M.B. Rowton and R.H. Stubbings, revd. *CAH* (vol. I,
                ch. 6), fasc. 4, pp. 23-69.

    1976   "Dimorphic Structure and the Problem of the
                ʿApirû-ʿIbrîm", *JNES,*35, pp. 13-20.

Sapin J.
    1974   "25 ans d'Archéologie en Syrie-Palestine
                (1946-1971)", *Études théologiques et religieuses,*
                pp. 558-65.

Sauer G.
    1968   "Die chronologischen Angaben in den Büchern
                Deut. bis 2. Kön.", *TZ,* 24, pp. 1-14.

Säve-Söderbergh T.
    1951   "The Hyksos Rule in Egypt", *JEA,* 37, pp. 53-71.

Sayce A.H.
    1897   *The Early History of the Hebrews.*

    1900   "Pithom", in *HDB,* vol. III, pp. 886-7.

Schachermeyr F.
    1964   *Die minoische Kultur des Alten Kreta,*
                Stuttgart.

312

Schaeffer C.F.A.
1948 *Stratigraphie comparée et chronologie de l'Asie occidentale (IIIe et IIe Millénaires),* London.

Schofield J.N.
1967 "Megiddo", in D.W. Thomas (ed.), *AOTS,* pp. 309-28.

Seger J.D.
1973 "Tel Gezer", *IEJ,* 23, pp. 247-51.
1974 "The MB II C Date of the East Gate at Shechem", *Levant,* 6, pp. 117-30.

Several M.W.
1972 "Reconsidering the Egyptian Empire in Palestine During the Amarna Period", *PEQ,* 104, pp. 123-33.

Shafer B.E.
1968 "A Theological Study of the Root *bḥr*...", *HTR,* 61, pp. 649-50.

Simons J.J.
1942 "Caesurae in the History of Megiddo", *Oudtestamentische Studiën,* 1, pp. 17-54.

Sjöqvist E.
1940 *Problems of the Late Cypriote Bronze Age,* Stockholm.

Smith G.A.
1931 *The Historical Geography of the Holy Land,* 25th edn.

Smith H.P.
1899 *A Critical and Exegetical Commentary on the Books of Samuel (ICC).*

Smith S.
1940 *Alalakh and Chronology,* London.

Soggin J.A.
1972 *Joshua,* London.

Stewart J.R.
1974   *Tell el-ʿAjjul: The Middle Bronze Age
            Remains,*   Studies in Mediterranean Archaeology,
            vol. 38, Göteborg.

Stinespring W.F.
1962   "Ekron", in *IDB,* vol. II, p. 69.

TAUIA
1974   *Excavations in the Negev: Beer-Sheba and
            Tel Masos,* Tel Aviv University Institute of
            Archaeology.

Thiele E.R.
1944   "The Chronology of the Kings of Judah and
            Israel", *JNES,* 3, pp. 137-86.

1965   *The Mysterious Numbers of the Hebrew Kings,*
            2nd edn., Grand Rapids, Michigan.

Thompson T.L.
1974   *The Historicity of the Patriarchal Narratives*
            (= *BZAW* 133), Berlin.

Toombs L.E. and Wright G.E.
1961   "The Third Campaign at Balatah (Shechem)",
            BASOR, 161, pp. 11-54.

Tufnell O.
1967   "Lachish", in D.W. Thomas (ed.), *AOTS,*
            pp. 296-308.

1975   "El-ʿAjjul, Tell", in Avi-Yonah (ed.),
            EAEHL, vol. I, pp. 52-61.

Tufnell O. et al.
1940   *Lachish II (Tell ed-Duweir). The Fosse Temple,*
            London.

1953   *Lachish III (Tell ed-Duweir). The Iron Age,*
            London.

1958   *Lachish IV (Tell ed-Duweir). The Bronze Age,*
            London.

Tushingham A.D.
1953   "Excavations at Old Testament Jericho",
            BA, 16, pp. 46-67.

314

Tushingham (Cont'd.)
  1954   "Excavation at Old Testament Jericho",
              BA, 17, pp. 98-104.

Unger M.F.
  1957   *Israel and the Aramaeans of Damascus*,
              Michigan.

Uphill E.P.
  1968   "Pithom and Raamses: their location and
              significance", part I, *JNES*, 27, pp. 291-316.

  1969   "Pithom and Raamses: their location and
              significance", part II, *JNES*, 28, pp. 15-39.

Van Seters J.
  1966   *The Hyksos, a new investigation*,   New Haven.

  1972   "The Conquest of Sihon's Kingdom: A Literary
              Examination", *JBL*, 91, pp. 182-97.

  1975   *Abraham in History and Tradition*, New Haven.

de Vaux R.
  1938   "La Palestine et la Transjordanie au IIe
              millénaire et les origines israélites",
              ZAW, 15, pp. 225-38.

  1965   "Method in the Study of Early Hebrew History",
              in J.P. Hyatt (ed.), *The Bible in Modern
              Scholarship*, Nashville, pp. 15-29.

  1970   "On Right and Wrong Uses of Archaeology", in
              J.A. Sanders (ed.), *Near Eastern Archaeology in
              the Twentieth Century*" (Glueck Festschrift),
              New York, pp. 64-80.

  1971   *Histoire Ancienne d'Israël*, Paris.

Vincent L.H.
  1930   "La Chronologie des ruines de Jéricho",
              RB, 39, pp. 403-33.

  1932   "Céramique et Chronologie", *RB*, 41, pp. 264-84.

  1935   "Jéricho et sa chronologie", *RB*, 44, pp. 583-605.

  1937   "Les Fouilles d'Et-Tell", *RB*, 46, pp. 231-66.

Vincent (Cont'd.)
1939   "Les Fouilles de Tell ed-Duweir = Lachis',
            RB, 48, pp. 406-33, 563-82.

Waddell W.G.
1940   Loeb Classical Library volume on *Manetho,*
            London.

Wainwright G.A.
1936   "The Coming of Iron", *Antiquity,* 10, pp. 5-24.

Waltke B.K.
1972   "Palestinian Artifactual Evidence
            Supporting the Early Date for the Exodus",
            Bibliotheca Sacra, 129, pp. 33-47.

Weiner H.M.
1923   *Ancient Egypt.*

Weippert M.
1971   *The Settlement of the Israelite Tribes in
            Palestine,* trans. J.D. Martin from the
            German edn. of 1967. London.

Weiser A.
1961   *Introduction to the Old Testament,* trans.
            D.M. Barton from the 4th German edn., 1957.
            London.

Wellhausen J.
1885   *Prolegomena to the History of Israel.*

1889   *Die Composition des Hexateuchs und der
            historischen Bücher des Alten Testaments,*
            3rd edn.

Wenham J.W.
1967   "Large Numbers in the Old Testament",
            Tyndale Bulletin, 18, pp. 19-53.

Winnett F.V.
1937   "The Founding of Hebron", *Bulletin of the
            Canadian Society of Biblical Studies,* 3,
            pp. 21-9.

Wiseman D.J.
    1967   "Alalakh", in D.W. Thomas (ed.), *AOTS*,
              pp. 119-35.

    1971   "Ai in Ruins", *Buried History*, 7, pp. 4-6.

de Wit C.
    1960   *The Date and Route of the Exodus*,   London.

Wolf C.U.
    1966   "The Location of Gilgal", *Biblical Research*,
              9, pp. 42-51.

Wood L.T.
    1970   "The Date of the Exodus", in J. Barton Payne
              (ed.), *New Perspectives on the Old Testament*,
              Waco, Texas, pp. 67-86.

Woolley C.L.
    1955   *Alalakh: an account of the Excavations at
              Tell Atchana in the Hatay*, 1937-49, Oxford.

Wright G.E.
    1941   "Archaeological Observations on the Period
              of the Judges and the Early Monarchy",
              JBL, 60, pp. 27-42.

    1942   "Two Misunderstood Items in the Exodus-Conquest
              Cycle", *BASOR*, 86, pp. 32-35.

    1945   *Westminster Historical Atlas to the Bible*,
              chs. 2-7, 10 and 18 (other chs. by F.V. Filson),
              Philadelphia.

    1953   "Archaeological Notes and News", *BA*, 16, pp.
              67-8.

    1959   "Philistine Coffins and Mercenaries", *BA*, 22,
              pp. 54-66.

    1961   "The Archaeology of Palestine", in *BANE*,
              pp. 73-112.

    1962a   *Biblical Archaeology*, 2nd edn., London.

    1962b   "Exodus, Book of", in *IDB*, vol. II, pp. 188-97.

    1965a   *Shechem: the biography of a biblical city*,
              London.

317

Wright (Cont'd.)
1965b   "Gezer", *IEJ,* 15, pp. 252-3.

1966   "Fresh Evidence for the Philistine Story", *BA,* 29, pp. 70-86.

1971   "A Problem of Ancient Topography: Lachish and Eglon", *BA,* 34, pp. 76-86.

Yadin Y.
1957   "Further Light on Biblical Hazor", *BA,* 20, pp. 34-47.

1958   "The Third Season of Excavation at Hazor, 1957", *BA,* 21, pp. 30-47.

1959a   "Excavations at Hazor, 1958", *IEJ,* 9, pp. 74-88.

1959b   "The Fourth Season of Excavations at Hazor", *BA,* 22, pp. 2-20.

1960a   "New Light on Solomon's Megiddo", *BA,* 23, pp. 62-8.

1960b   (ed.) *Hazor II: An account of the Second Season of Excavations,* Jerusalem.

1963   *The Art of Warfare in Biblical Lands in the Light of Archaeological Discovery,* London.

1967   "Hazor", in D.W. Thomas (ed.), *AOTS,* pp. 245-63.

1968   "'And Dan, why did he remain in ships?' (Judges V, 17)", *AJBA,* 1, pp. 9-23.

1969   "The Fifth Season of Excavations at Hazor, 1968-1969", *BA,* 32, pp. 50-71.

1972   *Hazor: the head of all those kingdoms,* London.

1973   "A Note on Aharoni's 'The Stratification of Israelite Megiddo'", *JNES,*32, p. 330. (A reply to Aharoni 1972.)

1975   *Hazor,* London.

Yamauchi E.M.
1973   *The Stones and the Scriptures,* London.

1974   "A Decade and a Half of Archaeology in Israel and in Jordan", *Journal of the American Academy of Religion,* 42, pp. 710-26.

318

Yeivin S.
1960   *A Decade of Archaeology in Israel*, 1948-58, Istanbul

1963   "The Age of the Patriarchs", *Revista degli Studi Orientali*, Rome, pp. 277-302.

1971   *The Israelite Conquest of Canaan*, Istanbul.

Zeuner F.E.
1955   "Notes on the Bronze Age Tombs of Jericho", *PEQ*, 87, pp. 118-28.

MAPS &
CHARTS

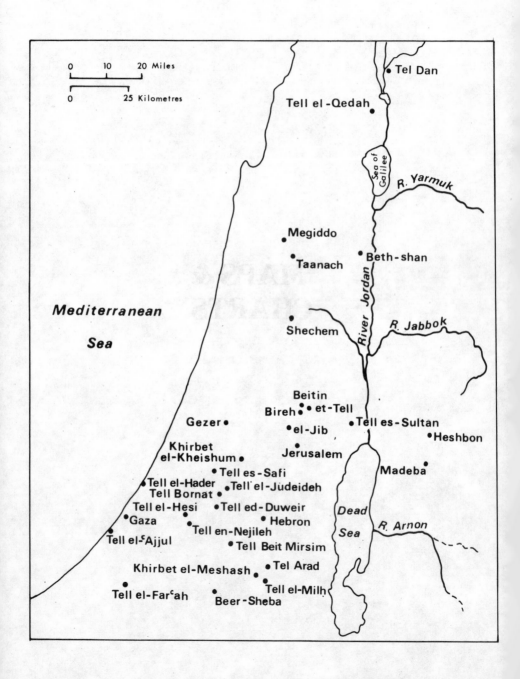

Scale:
0   10   20 Miles
0   25 Kilometres

Mediterranean
Sea

Tel Dan

Tell el-Qedah

Sea of Galilee

R. Yarmuk

Megiddo

Taanach

Beth-shan

River Jordan

R. Jabbok

Shechem

Beitin
Bireh et-Tell

Gezer

el-Jib

Tell es-Sultan

Heshbon

Khirbet
el-Kheishum

Jerusalem

Madeba

Tell es-Safi

Tell el-Hader
Tell Bornat

Tell el-Judeideh

Dead

Tell el-Hesi

Tell ed-Duweir

Sea

R. Arnon

Gaza

Hebron

Tell el-ᶜAjjul

Tell en-Nejileh

Tell Beit Mirsim

Khirbet el-Meshash

Tel Arad

Tell el-Farᶜah

Tell el-Milḥ

Beer-Sheba

Table of Identification

Tel Dan	=	Dan
Tell el-Qedah	=	Hazor
Beitin	=	Bethel?
Bireh	=	Bethel?
et-Tell	=	Ai?
Tell es-Sultan	=	Jericho
El-Jib	=	Gibeon
Khirbet el-Kheishum	=	Makkedah?
Tell es-Safi	=	Makkedah? or Libnah?
Tell el-Judeideh	=	Libnah?
Tell Bornat	=	Libnah?
Tell el-Hader	=	Ashkelon
Tell ed-Duweir	=	Lachish
Tell el-Hesi	=	Eglon?
Tell en-Nejileh	=	Eglon?
Tell Beit Mirsim	=	Debir
Tel Arad	=	Arad (Iron Age)
Tell el-Milh	=	Arad (M.B. Age)
Khirbet el-Meshash	=	Hormah
Tell el-Far^cah	=	Sharuhen

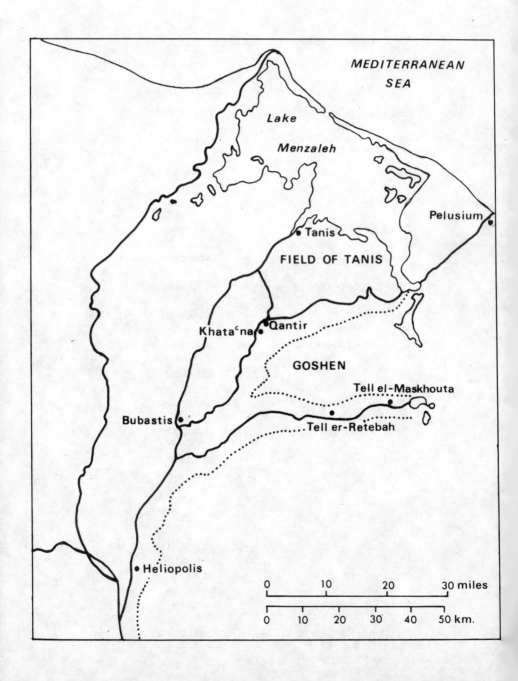

MEDITERRANEAN
SEA

Lake

Menzaleh

Pelusium

• Tanis

FIELD OF TANIS

Khataᶜna •Qantir

GOSHEN

Tell el-Maskhouta

Bubastis •

Tell er-Retebah

• Heliopolis

0   10   20   30 miles

0   10   20   30   40   50 km.

CHRONOLOGICAL TABLE

Dates BC	Archaeological periods in Palestine	Events of biblical narrative	Egyptian dynasties
1900			
1850		Hebrew tribes enter Egypt (c. 1870 BC)	XIIth Dynasty
1800			
1750			(c. 1780 BC)
1700			XIIIth Dynasty
1650	MIDDLE BRONZE	Bondage in Egypt	
1600	II		HYKSOS
1550			PERIOD
1500			
1450		Exodus (c. 1470 BC)	
c.1430	(Fall of MBA cities)	Wilderness wanderings	XVIIIth Dynasty
1400	LATE BRONZE I	Conquest of Canaan	
1350			
1300	LATE		
1250	BRONZE II	Period of the	
1200		Judges	XIXth Dynasty
1150	IRON AGE		(c. 1180 BC)
			XXth Dynasty

SUGGESTED CHRONOLOGY OF THE JUDGES PERIOD

Oppression by Cushan-rishathaim and judgeship of Othniel	Early 14th century ?
Oppression by Eglon and judgeship of Ehud	14th-13th centuries?
Oppression by Jabin and victory of Deborah and Barak	13th century
Midianite oppression and judgeship of Gideon	13th century
Burning of Shechem by Abimelech	c. 1190 BC
Judgeship of Tola	c. 1190-1170 BC
Judgeship of Jair	c. 1170-1150 BC
Ammonite oppression	c. 1150-1130 BC
Judgeship of Jephthah	c. 1130-1124 BC
Judgeship of Eli (including periods of minor judges Ibzan, Elon and Abdon totalling 25 years)	c. 1120-1080 BC (c. 1120-1095 BC)
Judgeship of Samuel (from death of Eli until accession of Saul)	c. 1080-1030 BC
Period of Philistine oppression c. 1095-1055 BC (including 20 years' judgeship of Samson)	
Reign of Saul	c. 1030-1010 BC
Reign of David	c. 1010-970 BC

INDICES

Index of Names and Subjects

(References to major treatments are italicised).

Index of Biblical Passages

(References to major treatments are italicised).

338

Index of Authors